UNDERSTANDING KINGDOM PRAYER

LEARNING TO PRAY THE WORD BACK TO GOD

UNDERSTANDING KINGDOM PRAYER

ALEXYS V. WOLF

Understanding Kingdom Prayer

Copyright © 2020, 2015 by Alexys V. Wolf. All rights reserved.

No part of this publication may be reproduced, stored in a retrieval system or transmitted in any way by any means, electronic, mechanical, photocopy, recording or otherwise without the prior permission of the author except as provided by USA copyright law.

Scripture quotations marked "" are taken from the New American Standard Bible ®, Copyright © 1960, 1962, 1963, 1968, 1971, 1972, 1973, 1975, 1977, 1995 by The Lockman Foundation. Used by permission. All rights reserved.

Cover design by Rebecacovers of Fiverr

Interior design by Aalishaa of Fiverr

Editors Pamela Scholtes, Major General (Ret) & Author Richard Scholtes, Helen T. Melcher

The opinions expressed by the author are those of The Fiery Sword Ministries.

Published by The Fiery Sword Publications
Published in the United States of America

ISBN: 978-1-952668-08-1

1. Nonfiction > Religion > Christian Life > Prayer
2. Nonfiction > Religion > Faith

Table of Contents

Section One: Kingdom Insights 1
    Chapter One: Introduction to Kingdom Prayer 2
    Chapter Two: Why Learn a New Way to Pray? 7
    Chapter Three: Come Boldly Before the
                        Throne Room of Grace...............................11

Section Two: Prayers..20
    One: Abandoned..21
    Two: Accepting God's Hand..24
    Three: Accepting Others As They Are..27
    Four: Armor of God..32
    Five: Attitude of "Want To" 35
    Six: Attitude of Praise 38
    Seven: Binding Spirits...41
    Eight: Blame Game..48
    Nine: Blessing God..51
    Ten: Blessing Enemies..54
    Eleven: Body of Christ 57
    Twelve: Breaking Curses 61

Thirteen: Breaking Evil Soul-Ties 65
Fourteen: Children: The Righteous Seed of Abraham 69
Fifteen: Children: Righting Wrongs 72
Sixteen: Character of God 75
Seventeen: Circumcise My Heart 78
Eighteen: Confession 81
Nineteen: Conformed Unto God 85
Twenty: Consume Me 88
Twenty-One: Daily Prayer 91
Twenty-Two: Discernment 94
Twenty-Three: Embodiment of Jesus 97

Fear Scriptures and Commentary 100
Twenty-Four: Fear to Love 106
Twenty-Five: Fear No More 109
Twenty-Six: Financial Trouble 112
Twenty-Seven: Focus on God 115

Forgiveness Scriptures and Commentary 118
Twenty-Eight: Forgiveness of Others 124
Twenty-Nine: Forgiveness of Self 127
Thirty: Forgiveness of Anger, Hatred, and Malice 130
Thirty-One: Forgiveness of Bitterness and Resentment ... 133
Thirty-Two: Forgiveness of Greed and Jealousy 136

Freedom Scriptures and Commentary 139
Thirty-Three: Freedom 144
Thirty-Four: Freedom from Religious Bondage 147
Thirty-Five: Freedom from Rejection 150
Thirty-Six: Freedom from Shame and Condemnation 153
Thirty-Seven: Governing Authorities 156
Thirty-Eight: Grief 164

  Thirty-Nine: God's Will Above All 167
  Forty: Holiness 170

Holy Spirit Scriptures and Commentary 172
  Forty-One: Holy Spirit: Fan the Flame 182
  Forty-Two: Holy Spirit Leading 185
  Forty-Three: Holy Spirit: Weighing According
    to the Spirit 188

Humility and Pride Scriptures and Commentary 191
  Forty-Four: Humility 204
  Forty-Five: Pride 207

Identity Scripture and Commentary 209
  Forty-Six: Identifying with God 219
  Forty-Seven: Identity in Christ 222
  Forty-Eight: Life without Lack 225
  Forty-Nine: Love 228

Marriage Scriptures and Commentary 231
  Fifty: Marriage: Surrender 237
  Fifty-One: Marriage: Loving with God's Love 239
  Fifty-Two: Marriage: Taking Dominion 242
  Fifty-Three: Marriage: Husband's Prayer 245
  Fifty-Four: Marriage: Wife's Prayer 248

Mindset Scriptures and Commentary 251
  Fifty-Five: Mindset: New and Improved 258
  Fifty-Six: Mind Set on Heaven 260
  Fifty-Seven: Mindset: Taking Every Thought Captive 262
  Fifty-Eight: Mindset: Natural to Supernatural 265
  Fifty-Nine: Mindset: PTSD 268
  Sixty: Navigating the Word 272

Sixty-One: Nightly 275
Sixty-Two: No Longer an "Old Dirty Sinner" 278
Sixty-Three: Obedience..281
Sixty-Four: Outside the City Gate 284
Sixty-Five: Overcoming Evil with Good..............................287
Sixty-Six: Parenting..295
Sixty-Seven: Patience 301
Sixty-Eight: Peace and Joy 304
Sixty-Nine: Pretense Removal 307
Seventy: Quickened Spirit...310
Seventy-One: Racism..313
Seventy-Two: Release and Let Go...317

Repentance Scriptures and Commentary..320
Seventy-Three: Repentance of Sin-Nature.........................328
Seventy-Four: Repentance of Adultery 331
Seventy-Five: Repentance of Anxiety and Fear 334
Seventy-Six: Repentance of Idolatry....................................337
Seventy-Seven: Restoration of Health.................................340
Seventy-Eight: Restoration General.....................................343
Seventy-Nine: Sacrifice of Obedience 346
Eighty: Seeing God's Hand 349
Eighty-One: Self-Control 352
Eighty-Two: Set Apart Unto God..355

Sexual Purity Scripture and Commentary 358
Eighty-Three: Sexual Purity: Adultery and Fornication.....372
Eighty-Four: Sexual Purity: Homosexuality.......................374
Eighty-Five: Sexual Purity: Masturbation..........................377
Eighty-Six: Sexual Purity: Singlehood.................................379
Eighty-Seven: Shield of Faith 381

Eighty-Eight: Sleep Disturbances 384
Eighty-Nine: Slow to Speak 389

Sowing and Reaping Scripture and Commentary 392
Ninety: Sowing and Reaping: Finishing a Bad Harvest 402
Ninety-One: Sowing Good Seed 404
Ninety-Two: Spirit and Truth 407
Ninety-Three: Splitting Soul from Spirit 410
Ninety-Four: Storms of Life 425
Ninety-Five: Submission 428
Ninety-Six: Surgery 431
Ninety-Seven: Teach Me Your Ways 434
Ninety-Eight: Temptation 437
Ninety-Nine: Thankfulness 444
One-Hundred: Transformation 447
One-Hundred-One: Trauma 450
One-Hundred-Two: Unbelief 453
One-Hundred-Three: Understanding Personal
    Application 456
One-Hundred-Four: Understanding the Mysteries of
    Christ 459
One-Hundred-Five: Unity 462
One-Hundred-Six: Victory Over Darkness 465
One-Hundred-Seven: Victory Over Your Enemy: 468
One-Hundred-Eight: Washed with the Water 471
One-Hundred-Nine: Wisdom 474
One-Hundred-Ten: Words of My Mouth 477

Introduction to Christ 483
Author Catalog 492

SECTION ONE

Kingdom Insights

CHAPTER ONE

Introduction to Kingdom Prayer

What exactly is Kingdom prayer? First, we need to establish that "praying without ceasing" means constant communion with God. It does not mean constantly praying ad nauseam the same ol' thing over and over until your dead! Furthermore, "Kingdom prayers," specifically, are a matter of moving the heart of God out of a spiritually mature perspective stemming from a life lived unto God alone. Kingdom prayers are not about words alone, but a heart set on God; a heart willing to put aside anything of the fleshly man and reconcile themselves unto the ways of God's holy Kingdom. Heaven is a holy Kingdom, a government. On the flipside, hell is a kingdom, an unholy government. There is a war between the two opposing governments. In order to defeat the unholy government, we must know how to unify with the holy government. We are instructed by God—the reigning King—to study to show ourselves approved of Him. That means study the constitution of His government—the Holy Bible. We cannot float along only listening to other peoples' Kingdom insight and expect that to be sufficient. We must be proactive in every area having a heart set on—but not limited to:

1. Pleasing the King.
2. Studying the King's instructions.
3. Learning the past biblical experiences of God's people to know what to and not to do.
4. Living a life separated unto God.
5. Learn the Word and its meaning to become equipped in the evil day.
6. Knowing the tactics of the enemy to be prepared in and out of season.
7. Recognizing our loyalties need to be on the Kingdom of God, not the things of Earth.
8. Learning how to pray with efficacy, not prayers only during crisis mode.

Over the last twenty years, I have composed a catalog of prayers for people from all walks of life. They are spread throughout my various teachings and writings. Countless people have requested these prayers to be compiled and placed in one book. This book is filled with specific prayers for issues common to mankind. Some prayers many people know to pray, and others may not be as familiar. Prayer alone is not enough in so much as, God expects us to be proactive. For example, if we're praying for self-discipline, it won't just fall upon our heads. We must purpose in our hearts and minds to be self-disciplined. We must make better choices. Prayers must coincide with action.

Understanding Kingdom Prayer includes 100+ template prayers to serve as a guide for practical application. You will, of course, want to pray according to the leading of Holy Spirit, but this is a template of how to properly apply the Scriptures. With any of God's promises, the idea is to proclaim, declare, and decree those promises over situations instead of asking for God to do this or that. If He's already promised, asking is not required. Rather, we are to apply and stand in faith in His provision and resolve.

Praising and thanking God is first and foremost in prayer. We ought never to be a people always asking or using His Kingdom power and authority without first thanking Him for being who and how He is—loving, merciful, gracious, kind, patient, sovereign, omniscient, omnipresent, and omnipotent. Although I didn't write words of praise at the beginning of each prayer, praising must come first according to Matthew 6:9. After praising the Lord, the succeeding prayer should follow. Never neglect thanksgiving of God's grace and mercy. This must come solely from your authentic heart of contrition.

For too long, I knew to pray, but I had no clue I could take God's promises straight from the Bible and offer them as a prayer unto God. What I have learned over the last twenty years is that knowing how to apply and pray the Scriptures is vital to healthy communication with the Lord and an open door to see prayers answered. Numerous times, I have gotten together with my prayer intercessory group and felt like I had nothing to pray, nothing to bring to the table. I often felt blah. When that happens, one can never go wrong by beginning prayer with praising God with His truth and promises. I have discovered that, when Holy Spirit doesn't seem to be moving, once I begin to thank Him and pray His Word back to Him, His Spirit begins to flow. This needs to be common knowledge and practice among the body of Christ and it isn't, at least it isn't among believers I've experienced these last fifty-two years on Earth. I have spent years scouring the Word to become acquainted with His. From that, I have composed correlating prayers.

Pleading the blood of Jesus is vital as you and I have no access to God except through Christ's shed blood. Unfortunately, many who say, "*I plead the blood of Jesus*" either don't understand the magnitude of the name and blood of Jesus, or they think the words are magic. Both are errant. Jesus' blood is the key that unlocks all God's promises of provision. We know this through such verses as Luke 22:44, *"And being in agony He was praying very fervently; and His sweat became like drops of blood, falling down upon the ground,"* and John 19:33-34, *"but coming to Jesus, when they saw that He was already dead, they did not break His legs. But one of the soldiers pierced His side with a spear, and immediately blood and water came out."*

To effectively plead the blood of Jesus, one must believe in the power of the blood and that it is the blood of Christ behind the words that lends its power. Hebrews 1:3 states, *"And He is the radiance of His glory and the exact representation of His nature, and upholds all things by the word of His power…"* It does not read, *"The power of His words"* but instead, *"The word of His power."* This is vital if we want to pray with efficacy. When we utter anything in prayer, the words are not, in and of themselves, powerful. No. The power is God since God is power. When He speaks, His words express the power that He is. In like fashion, since we have died and Christ has become our life, our words are powerful. Life and death are in the power of the tongue. Why?

If we—those in or out of Christ—speak negatively outside the will of God, soul-power—that which Adam used in the Garden of Eden pre-Fall—*we* are the source of the power. The words aren't power by themselves, but, because they are an expression of soul-power, they become empowered. When, adversely, we speak the Word of God into any situation, we who are driven by the God of all creation through His Son residing within us, our words become sanctioned by God. Now that's power! Our words are merely a vocalization of He who is within us. This information should make us watch what we say, for certain! When I pray, *"I plead the blood of Jesus,"* the words aren't magical, they are so much more. The words are the power of God coming through my lips. The words, then, are miraculous.

For more information about prayer and how to properly utilize the Word of God, I suggest *Wielding the Sword of the Spirit*.

Journaling

CHAPTER TWO

Why Learn a New Way to Pray?

"For as the rain and the snow come down from Heaven, and do not return there without watering the Earth and making it bear and sprout, and furnishing seed to the sower and bread to the eater; so will My Word be which goes forth from My mouth; it will not return to Me empty, without accomplishing what I desire, and without succeeding in the matter for which I sent it (Isaiah 55:10-11)."

As little children, even many who did not regularly attend church, we are taught to pray. Pray for what you want and need, pray for things that bother, upset, or otherwise cause us anxiety and fear. Pray, pray, pray! This is advisable given the fact we're instructed to pray without ceasing. However, when a person of any age is not taught *how* to pray with power through the authority of Jesus within us, or how to pray in a way so that our requests actually reach the third Heaven and touch the heart of the King, we will soon give up praying altogether except, perhaps, in times of desperation. There is a better way!

Prayer is open and continual communion with God. Prayer is one source of properly utilizing the Sword of the Spirit, which is the Word of God. Unfortunately, prayer, as a general rule, has become so dumbed-down that people don't see any power in it. As a result, people cease praying as they have lost hope in its efficiency. The problem, as I see it, is that the body of Christ has not learned to pray according to the Spirit and, understandably, their prayers become of little productivity. There is power in prayers stemming from the heart of God, in those where His people are speaking God's holy Word back to Him. His promise is that His Word will not return to Him void (Isaiah 55:11). When we learn His Word, we will begin to pray to open Heaven and enact transformative change in everyday life.

In the beginning of any relationship with YHWH, any prayer is good as one is learning how to open a dialog with God. However, just as we do not continue to speak as we did as a toddler, we must sharpen our prayers in accordance to that which moves the heart of God. I spoke better at eighteen than I did at eight and, at eight, I spoke better than when I was five. In my fifties, I'm still learning how to speak and write better, properly, in a way which moves people to listen. I have better diction, grammar, and grace the longer I live. I've always taught my daughters the old adage, *"A person well spoken is a person well respected."* The better we can convey something, the better results we will receive. So it is with our heavenly communication with our Creator. He told us how to pray and, in so doing, it must be the better way than whatever we may feel at any given moment. The more we learn the tools of how to pray to get God's attention, the more we'll see answered prayers.

People are often offended when I speak of this and rebut with, *"I pray in my own way. God knows my heart."* The problem is that they don't usually have *God's heart* in mind because they do not know God's heart. For the mature believer, they must seek the heart, face, and purpose of God if they want to see God move in more specific areas of life. Prayer is warfare! Proper, or rather, properly executed prayers move Heaven and Earth. It's time God's people begin to equip themselves with the Word of God and start praying according to His instruction instead of their own selfish gain or fluid emotions. Since God promised that His Word will not return to Him empty, we need to send His Word back to Him in faith He will reply.

Journaling

CHAPTER THREE

Come Boldly Before the Throne Room of Grace

"For we wrestle not against flesh and blood, but against the rulers, against the principalities, against the powers, against the rulers of the darkness of this world, against the spiritual forces of wickedness in the heavenly places (Ephesians 6:12 KJV)."

Daniel 10:12-13 reads, *"Then he said to me, 'Do not be afraid, Daniel, for from the first day that you set your heart on understanding this and on humbling yourself before your God, your words were heard, and I have come in response to your words. But the prince of the kingdom of Persia was withstanding me for twenty-one days; then behold, Michael, one of the chief princes, came to help me, for I had been left there with the kings of Persia."* God heard Daniel's words immediately. The *prayers* did not have to travel through the three Heavens so that God could receive them. There was no fight between moving from Earth to get to the third Heaven where the Lord is. Contrarily, the *answers* to our prayers *do* have to travel down from the third Heaven—throne room of God—through the second Heaven—powers and principalities—through the first Heaven—skies—to materialize on Earth. Satan's kingdom and his principalities fight to keep those answers from arriving safely. Daniel prayed. God heard immediately. God responded immediately. It took twenty-one days to arrive in the Earth because of the battle between evil forces and God's forces.

The "king of Tyre" is mentioned in Ezekiel 28. Both the king of Tyre and Satan are described in detail. This allows us to recognize that demonic forces, aka powers and principalities, are working against God's people through mankind. The king of Tyre was a man of flesh and blood who, though initially appointed by God, saw himself as "a god" of sorts. He had exalted himself as equal to God. Why, then, is Lucifer later described in the text? The passage shifts from a man, the king of Tyre, to a spiritual being, Lucifer. I am sure the king of Tyre was not a "*covering cherub*" nor was he "*covered in precious jewels*." He was not in the Garden of Eden as noted in verses 13-19. Ezekiel's words were no longer about a man, but a spiritual being who had overpowered a man. Because the powers and principalities of the second Heaven are stationed over continents, nations, cities, states, regions, and other bodies of people to bring a revolt against God Almighty, we witness in Ezekiel where mere mortals were consumed by such forces waging war against God and His people.

As with Daniel in chapter 10, the angel denotes a battle between himself and the powers of the second Heaven explicitly. The battle was so fierce that the arc angel, Michael, had to step in and lend a hand. Eventually, after twenty-one days from the time Daniel began to pray, the angel made his way to Daniel. What goes on in the spiritual realm is no joke! This leads us to the question, "*Do we pray up to Heaven or forward standing in front of the Almighty?*"

Bold Prayers Standing Before the Lord:

> "Let us therefore come boldly unto the throne of grace, that we may obtain mercy, and find grace to help in time of need (Hebrews 4:16)."

> "...Christ Jesus...who is at the right hand of God, who indeed is interceding for us (Romans 8:34)."

> "Even when we were dead in our transgressions, made us alive together with Christ (by grace you have been saved) and seated us with Him in the heavenly places in Christ Jesus (Ephesians 2:5-6)."

Why do we believe we have to pray upwards as though God is afar? We tend to think of God only as the One seated way up high in the third Heaven noted in—but not limited to—Genesis 1:4-5; 28:12, Deuteronomy 10:14, and I Kings 8:27. The second Heaven is both physical and spiritual according to—but not limited to—Deuteronomy 4:19, Matthew 24:29, and Ephesians 6:12. Physically, the second Heaven is outer space where the sun, moon, and stars reside. Spiritually, it is where the powers and principalities dwell—it is the kingdom of darkness. The skies are the first Heaven—the physical as noted in Genesis 1:8, 14, 16; 6:7. In understanding the Heavens, we can better grasp how to pray, what happens when we pray, and that there is a spiritual encounter between God's angels and Satan's fallen angels. God and His angels are for us. Satan and his legions are against us.

As if the sky isn't far enough away, we reckon that the third Heaven must be untouchable. This is not so. The powers and principalities mentioned in Ephesians 6 are the demonic forces of Satan set in place to war against anything good God sends our way in a speaking manner. Regardless, I Kings 8:27 tells us that God cannot be contained. This is glorious news! Yes, God is in the highest Heaven, but He is also among us and in those who have surrendered to Him through Jesus. *"You are from God, little children, and have overcome them; because greater is He who is in you that he who is in the world,"* is stated in I John 4:4. Through Christ, God is in you. His throne is also in you and me.

Furthermore, most don't understand our position in God the Father through God the Son, or the indwelling of God the Holy Spirit. All my life, I've heard, *"I'll send some prayers up for you,"* as if upwards is the direction those prayers go to be received by God. I want to debunk this theory. For those whose lives are hidden in Christ Jesus, they pray directly to God. There's no need to pray up when, praise God, we pray face-to-face. Hebrews 4:16 tells us we can come boldly before the throne room of grace. How? Because of Jesus who sits at His right hand. Boldly standing before God the Father is a privilege we can access through Jesus, and Jesus alone.

Allow me to explain as simply as possible. You are in Christ. Christ is in you. Christ is both in the third Heaven seated next to God as well as on Earth, where we are physically. You are in Christ here on Earth physically, but, spiritually, you are also in Heaven seated next to God. We don't pray *up* as in our prayers have to float from here to there, passing through the second Heaven where the powers and principalities are. God is in us. He communes with us directly through His Spirit—it is spirit-to-Spirit communion. Our spirits are merged as one with the Holy One of Israel. Contrarily, when God answers, because we reside on a physical Earth, the answers have to pass through the powers and principalities to get to us. We see this in Daniel, along with other poignant elements of Kingdom prayer.

1. The third Heaven is *spiritual*.
2. The first Heaven is *physical*.
3. The second Heaven is both *spiritual* and *physical*. They are the proverbial middle-man who attempt to dictate what man can or cannot receive from God. The powers and principalities are originally spirit-beings from Heaven. They were thrown to the Earth. Hence, they can manifest in both forms.

It is a powerful thing to understand all this, and it's quite simple! Where Christ is, I am. Where I am, Christ is. If He is in Heaven interceding on my behalf, I am with Him as He intercedes. *Answers to prayers* travel differently than *prayers*. Answers—that which is initially spiritual—must manifest in a physical realm where our bodies are. Answers require a transition from spirit to physical. Contrarily, prayers—that which is spiritual—immediately enter the ear of the King of kings because He is spirit. Prayers do not require any transition, unlike answers. It makes a lot of sense to me. The angel who traveled to Daniel had to go to war to reach Daniel, yet he remarked that, on the first day that Daniel prayed, his words were heard. That's because he prayed spirit-to-Spirit—it is instantaneous. The physical man had no participation in the matter. That leads us to the additional information of the angel's words as to how we are all to pray. The angel said, *"From the first day that you set your heart on understanding this and on humbling yourself before your God, your words were heard."*

The reason Daniel's words were received quickly was because of the condition of his heart. He set his heart toward *understanding* God, and he *humbled* himself before Him. These two elements are vital in Kingdom prayer. Yes, we must pray God's Word back to Him, but, additionally, our hearts must be in right-standing before our Sovereign Lord. Far too many people who call themselves "of God" are praying in fear, irritation, and expecting God to give them whatever they want, when and how they desire. This should not be, and these prayers bring only frustration because they do not move the heart of God. James 4:3 confirms this by stating, *"You ask and do not receive, because you ask with wrong motives, so that you may spend it on your pleasures."*

Further, in James 4:6-7, we read, *"God is opposed to the proud, but gives grace to the humble. Submit yourselves therefore to God. Resist the devil, and he will flee from you. Draw near to God, and He will draw near to you. Cleanse your hands, you sinners; and purify your hearts, you double-minded…humble yourselves in the presence of the Lord, and He will exalt you."*

Far too many pray with wrong motives, ill intentions, selfish ambition, and vain conceit. They pray with pride in their hearts with no purpose of glorifying God when their prayers are answered. Whether they are praying for someone not to die, for themselves or someone else to be raised into wellness, financial gain, babies, marriage, or any other prayer, if their hearts are not set on God's perfect and holy will to expand the Kingdom of God here on Earth, their prayers are in vain. These selfish prayers come not from humility, but pride. They do not originate from understanding God, but wanting God to come around to their way of thinking. This is ineffectual and will, without exception, cause the one praying intense frustration. They are left wondering, *"Where's God in all this? His Word is a lie because I prayed in Jesus' name, and nothing happened."* It's a very sad estate to find oneself.

In the beginning of our walk with God, I have found that God answers the silliest of prayers and quickly. I have experienced this. When parents give babies what they want, it is to help them gain our trust and affirm our love for them. As they get older, we must teach them to be wise to become a mature, well-rounded adult. In so doing, we stop giving in to them as easily or quickly. This is how they learn to grow and do what is required of them to meet their needs. They must learn to stand on their own and become more discerning. This is for their good. It is not punishment, but discipline. Likewise, God will answer prayers more quickly when we are young in the Lord, yet, as we grow older in our relationship with Him, our prayers must become refined, and our heart-condition must strengthen in our motives for God. We must weigh everything prior to our requests, think about *why* we're asking, consider *how* we ask, and *when* we should ask. Children have selfish desires, as do young Christ-followers. The way we pray and the way God answers, in the beginning, will, of necessity, morph into an entirely different thing as time passes. Prayers cannot remain the same as nothing in life can. We must be ever-evolving, maturing in Christ. We can either grow with God or fall away in discouragement from not understanding what He's doing or why.

The Lord longs for us to pray face-to-face and spirit-to-Spirit so we can recognize who we are in Christ. He desires us to know our position as a son of God, and to set our attention on Him at all times and in all things. Frivolous prayers are only acceptable in the beginning. A parent is understanding of a child's wants when they're little, but, over time, they grow weary of their childish behavior. So it is with God. He cannot abide our spiritual childishness forever. The mature understand that we pray directly to God the Father because we are seated in heavenly places, not only in the sweet-by-and-by, but in real-time. It is a privilege bestowed us by the grace and mercy of our Lord. Learning to pray in a way that will garner the attention of God's ears and heart comes through self-discipline, studying to show ourselves approved of God, humbling ourselves, and asking with righteous motives.

Our words matter. Life and death are in the power of the tongue. That isn't just about the words we speak in everyday life, but also, and probably more so, in the words we pray to the Father. What and how we pray matters. So many pray unanswerable prayers because we are praying for God to give us what He has already given or to give us that which is unholy, and He simply cannot. Answerable prayers are those centered on the perfect will of God for our good and His glory.

For example, an unanswerable prayer is, *"God be with me."* He already promised He will never leave or forsake you. Therefore, He cannot answer—it's already done. *"God, help me be patient."* God cannot answer this as patience is a matter of self-discipline. Christ is all things, including patient. If Christ is in you, you need to be proactive and tap into the patience of He who is within. He cannot answer such a prayer. Patience has already been granted. The following prayers are taken from the promises and direction of God. Seek the Lord's guidance to discern how to tailor them to your life. He will answer. Please note that some have commentary and some do not. Some have more commentary than others. Some have so many Scriptures and corresponding prayers that they required special attention.

Journaling

SECTION TWO

ONE

Abandoned

Prayer:

Father, I thank You, this day, that You have never left Your people abandoned or ignorant. You give generously to those who knock on the door and seek Your face. Though my mother, father, sister, brother, extended family, friends, co-workers, or other people have left me alone and rejected, You accept me. You receive me as Your own. You never leave me abandoned because You loved me before the foundation of the Earth. Show me Your love that I may embrace it regardless of what mankind has done to me. Help me realize that my real family is in Christ—those who do the will of the Father who is in Heaven. Change the way I see things from assuming You will reject me as have others. I thank You that you love me unconditionally; You have dusted the ash of death and restored my soul unto life (Psalm 23:3). I rejoice even in my sorrow because You have clothed me with garments of salvation. You have wrapped me with a robe of righteousness as a bridegroom decks himself with a garland, and as a bride adorns herself with her jewels (Isaiah 61:10). I will not remain discouraged, depressed, or bitter toward those who have left me. I trust Your exquisite plan for my life. Selah.

Scripture References:

"For my father and my mother have forsaken me, but the Lord will take me up (Psalm 27:10)."

"And one will say to him, 'What are these wounds between your arms?' Then he will say, "Those with which I was wounded in the house of my friends (Zechariah 13:6)."

"It is the Lord who goes before you. He will be with you; he will not leave you or forsake you. Do not fear or be dismayed (Deuteronomy 31:8)."

"Keep your life free from love of money, and be content with what you have, for He has said, "I will never leave you nor forsake you." So we can confidently say, "The Lord is my helper; I will not fear; what can man do to me (Hebrews 13:5-6)?"

Journaling

TWO

Accepting God's Hand

Prayer:

Father, help me to readily recognize Your holy hand on my life, no matter what tactic the enemy uses. Help me to see into the supernatural realm of Heaven to know and accept Your hand. Assist me in understanding, according to Holy Spirit, how to act and react in every situation. Remind me daily to release Your Holy Spirit into every situation so that I will walk in peace through any storm. Your hand made all these things; therefore, all these things came into being. You look to those who are humble and contrite of spirit and who tremble at Your Word (Isaiah 66:2). Your arm is strong, Your hand is mighty, and Your right hand is exalted (Psalm 89:13). No one can ward off Your hand or say to You, "What have I done (Daniel 4:35)?" I trust and place my faith in Your righteous right hand. Amen.

Scripture References:

"The Lord said to Satan, "Have you considered My servant Job?"...Then the Lord said to Satan, "Behold, all that he has is in your power, only do not put forth your hand on him (Job 1:8, 12).""

"Now the Spirit of the Lord departed from Saul, and an evil spirit from the Lord terrorized him(I Samuel 16:14).""

"That men may know from the rising to the setting of the sun that there is no one besides Me. I am the Lord, and there is no other, the One forming light and creating darkness, causing well-being and creating calamity; I am the Lord who does all these (Isaiah 45:6-7).""

Journaling

THREE

Accepting Others As They Are

Commentary:

This is an especially difficult task to achieve, even to the strongest of believers. This is so for several reasons—but not limited to:

1. We're lazy Christians and give what we get.
2. We aren't lazy. We simply don't know how to execute accepting people as they are.
3. We aren't lazy. We know how to execute it, but we are unwilling to surrender to Christ.

I believe these are the top three. If you are someone in category #2, I can help. If you are in # 1 or #3, unless you have a change of heart, this will not help you. We all need to recognize that people are going to be who they are unless or until they choose to be someone different. For me, I chose to change and become something different. I had to lay down my perceptions of how people should be and learn to love them where they are without attempting to change them. People do not change because we will them to, no matter how strongly we will it.

Accepting people as they are will require more than just prayer. Combined with prayer, there must be a shift in perspective of how we see God, how we see others, how we see ourselves. God sees differently than our human nature. Until we see with God's perspective, we will continue to frustrate ourselves by longing for others to change. Change must begin with self. When I see irritating people through the lens of selfishness, I will always be irritated at how they conduct themselves. However, when I say genuinely, *"God, show me how to see them,"* my attitude, perception, perspective, and overall mindset will segue into a heavenly view. Loving people where they are without accepting their sinful conduct is paramount to being able to lead the wayward to Christ. Bullying and shunning will not accomplish God's will for you or them.

Let's look at James 2:1-14. Shunning people who don't look as we believe they ought is sin. This can apply to strangers, friends, family, co-workers, or anyone we deem less than ourselves. This is why we must investigate how we see ourselves, as in, do we see ourselves as better than the one we desire to change? There is such a thing as the sin of partiality. It is real and all too common among so-called followers of Christ. We feel better than murderers, liars, thieves, adulterers, fornicators, addicts, and racists. These are common. But, what about those in our lives who don't believe, handle things, speak, or dress like us? What about those who don't praise and worship in like fashion? It's a hairy situation when we start to observe how judgmental followers of Christ are, and wrongly so. Righteous judgment and unrighteous judgment are entirely different.

It is in our pride that we believe ourselves better than our counterparts. Pride is exposed when we are angered by those who do not conform to our ways, even when, perhaps, our methods are more acceptable by God. But, keep in mind, our pride in feeling superior while resting on our laurels negates whatever right thing we're doing because pride comes just before falling flat on our faces. This is solidified by Romans 12:3, *"For through the grace given to me I say to everyone among you not to think more highly of himself than he ought to think, but to think to have sound judgment, as God has allotted to each a measure of faith."*

Prayer:

Gracious Father, help me to live a life so grateful for your acceptance of me that I perpetually accept others for who and how they are. When I face a family member, friend, co-worker, stranger, or anyone else who rubs me the wrong way, refresh my memory in how patient, kind, and loving You are toward me. Just as Christ accepted me to the glory of God, cause me to accept others before they change or even if they never change. Change *me* from the inside out. I choose humility in which Jesus Himself functioned. When I was Your enemy, You loved me. In the midst of the unloveable, show me how to operate in the love of Christ. Help me to not fall into the trap of pride. Balance me in all my ways so that, even when You direct me to admonish someone, let me do it in humility, love, and mercy as would You to draw all men unto Your bosom. Amen.

Scripture References:

> "Therefore, accept one another, just as Christ also accepted us to the glory of God (Romans 15:7)."

"For if while we were enemies we were reconciled to God through the death of His Son, much more, having been reconciled, we shall be saved by His life (Romans 5:10)."

My brethren, do not hold your faith in our glorious Lord Jesus Christ with an attitude of personal favoritism. For if a man comes into your assembly with a gold ring and dressed in fine clothes, and there also comes in a poor man in dirty clothes, and you pay special attention to the one who is wearing the fine clothes, and say, "you sit here in a good place," and you say to the poor man, "You stand over there, or sit down by my footstool," have you not made distinctions among yourselves, and become judges with evil motives? Listen, my beloved brethren: did not God choose the poor of this world to be rich in faith and heirs of the Kingdom which He promised to those who love Him? But you have dishonored the poor man. Is it not the rich who oppress you and personally drag you into court? Do they not blaspheme the fair name by which you have been called? If, however, you are fulfilling the royal law according to the Scripture, "You shall love your neighbor as yourself," you are doing well. But if you show partiality, you are committing sin and are convicted by the law as transgressors. For whoever keeps the whole law and yet stumbles in one point, he has become guilty of all. For He who said, "Do not commit adultery," also said, "Do not commit murder." Now if you do not commit adultery, but do commit murder, you have become a transgressor of the law. So speak and so act as those who are to be judged by the law of liberty. For judgment will be merciless to one who has shown no mercy; mercy triumphs over judgment (James 2:1-13).

Journaling

FOUR

Armor of God

Prayer:

I choose, this day, to be strong in the Lord and the power of His might. I put on the full armor of God so that I can stand firm against the devil's schemes. For I recognize that my struggle is not against flesh and blood (even though right now it feels like it), but it is against the rulers, against the powers, against the world forces of this darkness, against the spiritual forces of wickedness in the heavenly places. Therefore, I receive God's full armor that I will be able to resist temptation in the evil day and, having done everything, stand firm. I gird my loins with truth, put on the breastplate of righteousness, and place the gospel of peace on my feet. Additionally, I take up the shield of faith with which I will be able to extinguish the evil one's flaming arrows. I also take the helmet of salvation and place it on my head, and I arise with the sword of the Spirit, which is the word of God. With all prayer and petition, I pray, at all times, in the Spirit. With this in view, I will ever be on the alert with all perseverance and petition for all the saints. Selah

Scripture Reference:

> Finally, my brethren, be strong in the Lord, and in the power of His might. Put on the full armor of God, so that you will be able to stand firm against the schemes of the devil. For our struggle is not against flesh and blood, but against the rulers, against the powers, against the world forces of this darkness, against the spiritual forces of wickedness in the heavenly places. Therefore, take up the full armor of God, so that you will be able to resist in the evil day, and having done everything, to stand firm. Stand firm, therefore, having girded your loins with truth, and having put on the breastplate of righteousness, and having shod your feet with the preparation of the Gospel of peace; in addition to all, taking up the shield of faith with which you will be able to extinguish all the flaming arrows of the evil one. And take the helmet of salvation, and the sword of the Spirit, which is the Word of God (Ephesians 6:10-18).

Journaling

FIVE

Attitude of "Want To"

Commentary:

I want to exercise to become lean and fit. I want to, I genuinely do. However, that "want to" has not always been strong enough to cause me to make the time for enacting such a result. It would require a lot of time and sweat, and, frankly, with my busy lifestyle, I am unwilling to give up what little free time I have. My "want to" is insufficient. However, when I came back to Christ after seven years of rebellion, I wanted to get on the path of righteousness, so much that I gave all my time and attention to the Lord. In that, my "want to" was intense and able to guide me where I am today. My attitude toward drawing near unto the Lord was vastly different than my attitude toward becoming lean and fit. I want both, but only one possessed the right attitude. I recognized that drawing near unto the Lord as never before would be eternally life-altering, whereas physical changes would only last in the timeframe of exercising. My attitude toward fitness was, "*Meh, in the long run, will it count for anything?*" My "want to" accounted for nothing. We must have a "want to" that will drive us toward what is holy and spiritually healthy. Without it, you can want God all day and never make a move toward Him. Acknowledgment of the need is insufficient by itself. Our attitude makes all the difference.

Prayer:

Show me how to get out of Your way, Lord, so that Your cleansing blood can wash me and regenerate me into a Kingdom mindset. I recognize You do nothing against my free will. Take me to a place where I no longer say, "*I want to*" then do nothing. I long for an internal "want to," which will ignite such a mighty flame of Holy Spirit that I cannot resist Your will in my life. I choose to grow into the head, where Jesus is that I may fulfill my Kingdom purpose on Earth.

Scripture References:

> "Like newborn babies, long for the pure milk of the word, so that by it you may grow in respect to salvation (I Peter 2:2)."

> "As the deer pants for the water brooks, so my soul pants for You, O God (Psalm 42:1)."

Journaling

SIX

Attitude of Praise

Commentary:

It's easy to praise YHWH in the good times, though, often, this is when we forget God. When difficulties hit, that's generally when we murmur and complain against God, citing how good a person we are and that we don't deserve whatever has befallen us. Nowhere, in either scenario, is praise coming from our lips or overall attitude. Might we consider that praising Him during the good and bad times might bring about God turning our trials into blessings? We are to praise Him no matter the circumstances surrounding us. Praise ushers the hand of God. This is made abundantly clear throughout the Old and New Testaments. Despite what's happening, praise is a sign of faith and true worship.

Prayer:

Father, above all else, allow me to put on a garment of praise at all times and in every situation. Remind me that You are the Great I AM who knows and sees all. You are in all things, through all things. I acknowledge You as the Sovereign Lord over all and that You gave everything so that I may have life and life more abundant (John 10:10). I humble myself in Your presence, knowing that, without You, I am nothing of eternal value. There is nothing too hard for You as You are the Lord of all mankind. I praise You, King of kings, for allowing breath in my lungs. I praise You with thanksgiving that all things work together for good for those who love You – and I love You!

Scripture References:

"Through Him then, let us continually offer up a sacrifice of praise to God, that is, the fruit of the lips that give thanks to His name (Hebrews 13:15)."

"Sing to the Lord a new song, sing His praise from the end of the Earth! You who go down to the sea, and all that is in it you islands and those who dwell on them (Isaiah 42:10)."

For by Him all things were created, both in the Heavens and on Earth, visible and invisible, whether thrones or dominions or rulers or authorities – all things have been created through Him and for Him. He is before all things, and in Him all things hold together. He is also head of the body, the church; and He is the beginning, the firstborn from the dead, so that He Himself will come to have first place in everything. For it was the Father's good pleasure for all the fullness to dwell in Him, and through Him to reconcile all things to Himself, having made peace through the blood of His cross; through Him, I say, whether things on Earth or things in Heaven (Colossians 1:16).

Journaling

SEVEN

Binding Spirits

IMPORTANT NOTE: this is not so much prayer as it is a declaration. One must not bind spirits without spiritual caution.

Commentary:

There is a problem with binding spirits when one is not utterly yielded to God in every area of life. By no means am I saying only perfect people can do it. Only God is perfect. Notwithstanding, such power belongs to those who purpose to live *"perfect as He is perfect and holy as He is holy."* We all make mistakes, but that should be the exception and not the rule. People who justify their sins as, *"I'm only human,"* should not embark upon the binding of spirits. The seven sons of Sceva are a perfect example. The demons knew Jesus and Paul, which translates that they know who truly walks in authority and who does not. Cheap imitations do not fool them.

Matthew 12 is precise information that demons are voracious. They want their home back! If you cast them out, they will seek to return by any means necessary. They will enlist other worse, stronger demons to overtake you. You must be on guard at all times against the infilling of evil spirits. This is why the Word implores us to be sober-minded and vigilant. We cannot be a lax Christian assuming *"God is in control"* and will fix our problems as they arise. He has given His body power and dominion, which means we must take action in His name. We are ambassadors in the Earth representing the King and governing in His name. We speak on His behalf as though we are the King. Only when He truly empowers us does this work. The King did not so embolden the seven sons; therefore, they were devoured and left naked.

Binding spirits should not be taken lightly. I know folks who, when asked, will go to someone's home or office and start commanding spirits to leave simply because they walk with God. The problem, then, is that the person for whom they bound the spirits does not know how to keep themselves clean. Though the one making the demons flee in Jesus' name caused them to depart, the unsuspecting person has no idea they are left vulnerable to worse demons—principalities and powers from the second heaven. This should not be. We must not lightly approach the casting of demons. It is the duty of the one who knows the Lord intimately to steer the other person into righteousness. They must be educated in the matters of the spiritual realm, and how to bind spirits through their walk with the Lord. Never bind spirits unless you know the person knows how to maintain a spiritually clean environment.

Additionally, when we do bind spirits, never leave an opening. Notice in Matthew 12 where it reads, "it finds it *unoccupied, swept*, and *put in order.*" The person or place was cleaned and in order, but it was unoccupied. This is a problem. When you bind spirits, always replace them with Holy Spirit or, more specifically, replace them with the opposite of what was removed. For example, if you cast out fear or doubt, replace them with the spirit of faith in Jesus. If you command a spirit of anger and rage to leave, replace it with the spirit of peace and rest in Christ. Generally speaking, insert that which is of God where there had been that of the evil one.

Warning:

> "Be sober, be vigilant; because your adversary the devil, as a roaring lion, walks about, seeking whom he may devour (I Peter 5:8:)."

> Now when the unclean spirit goes out of a man, it passes through waterless places seeking rest, and does not find it. Then it says, "I will return to my house from which I came"; and when it comes, it finds it unoccupied, swept, and put in order. Then it goes and takes along with it seven other spirits more wicked than itself, and they go in and live there; and the last state of that man becomes worse than the first. That is the way it will also be with this evil generation (Matthew 12:43-45).

> "No, but the sacrifices of pagans are offered to demons, not to God, and I do not want you to be participants with demons. You cannot drink the cup of the Lord and the cup of demons too; you cannot have a part in both the Lord's table and the table of demons (I Corinthians 10:20-21).

> Finally, be strong in the Lord and in the power of His might. Put on the full armor of God, so that you can take your stand against the devil's schemes. For our struggle is not against flesh and blood, but against the rulers, against the authorities, against the powers of this dark world and

against the spiritual forces of evil in the heavenly realms (Ephesians 6:10-12).

Some Jews who went around driving out evil spirits tried to invoke the name of the Lord Jesus over those who were demon-possessed. They would say, "In the name of the Jesus whom Paul preaches, I command you to come out." Seven sons of Sceva, a Jewish chief priest, were doing this. One day the evil spirit answered them, "Jesus I know, and Paul I know about, but who are you?" Then the man who had the evil spirit jumped on them and overpowered them all. He gave them such a beating that they ran out of the house naked and bleeding (Acts 19:13-16).

Commentary:

Above are a few of many texts on the power God gave Jesus who passed His power to the Church. These are a powerful testament of what we, God's righteous seed, are to be in the Earth. With such power, we must heed the warning that we can only use such power under the authority and direct supervision of God through His Spirit. That can only be accomplished when a person is surrendered to God in spirit, soul, and body. This power is not for the average Christian or church-goer. It is not for the faint-of-heart or the fence-straddler who thinks they're a good person. This power can only be ignited when we are functioning in the strength of Jesus, which comes through our humility before God. In other words, if you aren't tapped into God 24/7, do not make such a declaration. Do not bind spirits, not for yourself or others, lest you leave a big mess.

Scriptures of Power and Authority:

"Truly I (Jesus) say to you, whatever you bind on Earth shall have been bound in Heaven; and whatever you loose on Earth shall be loosed in Heaven (Matthew 18:18)."

"Behold, I have given you authority to tread on serpents and scorpions, and over all the power of the enemy, and nothing will injure you (Luke 10:19)."

"And He called the twelve together, and gave them power and authority over all the demons and to heal diseases (Luke 9:1)."

"I also say to you that you are Peter, and upon this rock I will build My church; and the gates of Hades will not overpower it. I (Jesus) will give you the keys to the Kingdom of Heaven; and whatever you bind on Earth shall have been bound in Heaven, and whatever you loose on Earth shall have been loosed in Heaven (Matthew 16:18-19)."

"You, dear children, are from God and have overcome them, because the one who is in you is greater than the one who is in the world (I John 4:4)."

Prayer of Binding Spirits and Releasing Holy Spirit:

In the name of Jesus, I command every demonic force of hell to be bound, gagged, and loosed from its assignment over me and my household. I release the power of the Holy Spirit to be the only spiritual force active in my life. I place His rule over everything with which the Lord has blessed me. I demand every hidden thing to be revealed for what it is. Let no lying spirit remain so that every untruth in my life be exposed for what it is. I command any evil spirit of death, suicide, perversion, lusts of the flesh, depression, oppression, heaviness, self-loathing, insecurities, worthlessness, shame, guilt, condemnation, corruption—list whatever ails you— or anything else to be bound, gagged and loosed from its assignment over myself, my children, spouse, marriage, job, finances and any other place where I have dominion. Father, as I utilize the power with which you have given Your chosen nation, I do this in the name of Jesus. Not of my own power but with the power that raised Jesus from the dead. Because You live in me, I release You to command the spirits through me. Only by Your name and blood do I make such a declaration. I purpose to live according to the Spirit of God so that they cannot return with stronger, more vile demons to overtake me. I triumph, Lord, in Your glory. Selah.

Journaling

EIGHT

Blame Game

Commentary:

Spending life blaming everyone and everything for our misfortunes is a game won by no one. We who are in Christ must humble ourselves to the point of accepting responsibility for our contribution to our trials and become accountable. This does not lend itself to whining, moaning, and groaning around every bend. We must surrender ourselves unto the righteousness of God and become mature to the point of personal accountability. This does not mean we take responsibility for what others have done, but only for our part. Blaming others keeps one in constant turmoil and stunted growth in every area of life.

Prayer:

Father, I choose to be accountable for my messes. I purpose to stop blaming all who have had a hand in my downfall and sin. I do not needlessly take on blame for other people's wrongs, but I also refuse to blame others for my culpability. Help me to be humble. In humility, I can recognize my responsibility and what is someone else's so that I won't needlessly go into shame and condemnation. I will stand before You accountable for me and me alone. I repent of blaming others, and I forgive them for their participation in my pain. I humble myself in Your presence, Lord, that I may walk in freedom and restoration. Amen

Scripture References:

> "And I saw the dead, the great and the small, standing before the throne, and books were opened; and another book was opened, which is the book of life; and the dead were judged from the things which were written in the books, according to their deeds (Revelation 20:12)."

> "Therefore having overlooked the times of ignorance, God is now declaring to men that all people everywhere should repent (Acts 17:30)."

Journaling

NINE

Blessing God

Commentary:

Oh, that the body of Christ would come to a place of blessing the Lord instead of waiting for God to bless them! It is in our contrition toward Yeshua that we purpose to become a walking, living, breathing blessing to the King. When we do, we cannot help but live in peace, love in the face of hatred, forgive for the unforgivable, and much more. Blessing YHWH becomes the source of receiving His blessings.

Prayer:

Father, I thank You for the priceless gift of Your Son, plan, purpose, and Your eternal Kingdom. Show me the way and righteousness of the Kingdom so that everything I need in this Earth will be poured upon me (Matthew 6:33). I pray that, when You pour Your blessings upon me, I will seek to bless You in return, that I will not squander Your help, blessings, promises, or Word. Father, I beseech You to teach me, through Your Spirit, who and what I am, and all You have graciously bestowed upon

Your people. May I no longer wander around the mountain of fear and doubt due to the fleshly man so that I may see Your Kingdom here on Earth (Luke 9:2). I thank You that there is no temptation known to man that You have not already made a way out (I Corinthians 10:13). Show me Your immeasurable love in ways that, no matter the ploy of the enemy, I can see, know, experience, and receive it (Ephesians 3:18). Show me the error of my ways, just as You did with those who have gone before me, so that I may confess, repent, and be made whole (Psalm 139:24). Let me honor You with my body, soul, mind, and spirit (I Corinthians 6:12-20). I choose, this day, to seek first Your Kingdom and righteousness. May I be as a poured out drink offering holy and acceptable in Your sight (Philippians 2:17). Selah

Scripture References:

"While they were ministering to the Lord and fasting, the Holy Spirit said…(Acts 13:2)"
Bless the Lord, O my soul, and all that is within me, bless His holy name. Bless the Lord, O my soul, and forget none of His benefits; who pardons all your iniquities, who heals all your diseases; who redeems your life from the pit, who crowns you with lovingkindness and compassion; who satisfies your years with good things, so that your youth is renewed like the eagle (Psalm 103:1-5).

"Daniel said, "Let the name of God be blessed forever and ever, for wisdom and power belong to Him (Daniel 2:20)."

Journaling

TEN

Blessing Enemies

Commentary:

Blessing our enemies is an offshoot of understanding the love of Jesus Christ. It is in direct contradiction to the nature of the flesh. It is not something we should force ourselves to do. No. Once we are connected intimately to God's heart, it is what we willingly and selflessly do. When we begin to recognize how much we have been forgiven, not based on a sliding scale of sins, but upon the nature of defiled Adam at work in us, we will readily forgive and bless our enemies. The goal is to draw all men unto the Lord. Cursing our enemies is not a display of our Father in Heaven but the father of deceit. Everything God's people do should be a direct display of God's love, bar none. If we are unforgiving and curse those who have cursed us, we are like Satan, like the old nature. This should not be.

Prayer:

Father, You are worthy to be praised, and I give You all praise, honor, and glory due Your holy name. I choose for Christ's death to swallow the hatred of this natural man. I go to Christ's grave. In the place of hatred, I choose to put on love, joy, peace, patience, kindness, goodness, faithfulness, gentleness, self-control (Galatians 5:22), humility (Colossians 3:12), the robe of righteousness (Isaiah 61:10), and forgiveness (Matthew 6:14-16) that can come only from Christ. I choose to deny myself and put aside all hatred, anger, malice, unforgiveness, and things of the like (Ephesians 4:31) to glorify Christ through my body (I Corinthians 6:20). I bless my enemy, and I do not curse him or her. I put on the mind of Christ.

Scripture References:

> But I say to you who hear, love your enemies, do good to those who hate you, bless those who curse you, pray for those who mistreat you. Whoever hits you on the cheek, offer him the other also; and whoever takes away your coat, do not withhold your shirt from him either. Give to everyone who asks of you, and whoever takes away what is yours, do not demand it back. Treat others the same way you want them to treat you (Luke 6:27-31).

Journaling

ELEVEN

Body of Christ

Commentary:

It is vital for the body of Christ to pray for one another, both as individuals and as a collective body. We cannot claim, "God is in control" if we have not purposed to surrender control to Him. Right now, Satan has rule over the Earth and the world's system. It is our responsibility and out privilege to intercede for the Bride of Christ, His Body, ambassadors, kings, priests, and friends. It isn't enough to pray only for our immediate loved ones. We must pray for the Body worldwide. If we are one as Christ says we are, then there are no geographic, racial, social, economic, or other boundaries among us. We must intercede for each other.

Prayer:

Lord, we come humbly before the Throne Room of grace on behalf of the entire body of Christ. I plead Your Son's holy blood over myself as well as all who proclaim the favorable year of the Lord across the globe. Have Your angels camped round about us so that no harm can come near our dwelling place. I thank You that we are blessed coming in and going out; we are blessed in the country and in the city. Bless the fruit of our wombs. You are blessing our basket and kneading trough. You will grant that the enemies who rise against us will be defeated before us. You have established us as Your holy people if we keep Your commands. We will be feared by demons and the disobedient. You will send rain in due season. We are the head and not the tail, the top and not the bottom for Your great name's sake (Deuteronomy 28). No weapon formed against us shall prosper, and every word that comes out against us, You refute and bring down so that they will not prevail against us, for this is the heritage of the servants of the Lord (Isaiah 54:17). May we be a people who do not turn to the right or to the left, but we will keep our faces set like flint toward the God of Heaven and will not be put to shame (Isaiah 50:7). Thank You for giving Your angels charge over us to guard us in all our ways (Psalm 91:11). Command Your angels concerning the body of Christ (Luke 4:10).

We will fear no evil because You are with us (Psalm 23). Amen

Scriptures References:

"Now you are Christ's body, and individually members of it (I Corinthians 12:27)."

"For just as we have many members in one body and all the members do not have the same function, so we, who are many, are one body in Christ, and individually members of one another (Romans 12:4-5)."

"For even as the body is one and yet has many members, and all the members of the body, though they are many, are one body, so also is Christ (I Corinthians 12:12)."

"There is one body and one Spirit, just as also you were called in one hope of your calling (Ephesians 4:4)."

"And He put all things in subjection under His feet, and gave Him as head over all things to the Church (Ephesians 1:22)."

Journaling

TWELVE

Breaking Curses

Commentary:

I recognize that many Christians do not believe there are curses. They cite that, since Jesus bore our curse on the cross, they no longer exist. My perspective is as follows.

Look around you. Look at the body of Christ and the disaster in which she has found herself. Jesus redeemed us from the curse of the Law, having become a curse for us (Galatians 3:13). All types of modern-day curses can be passed from one generation to the next. They are called generational curses. There are spoken or word curses, cultural, witchcraft, geographic, and religious curses, and so much more. For example, with generational curses, you may see things such as suicide, depression, anxiety, premature death, or addiction stemming back many generations. Cultural is broader and can be seen in certain cultures dating back decades and even centuries.

Such curses are cured through *correctly applying* the blood of Jesus, the curse breaker. I liken the blood of Christ to medication. If you are sick, you seek a physician. When that doctor prescribes a cure for what ails you, you must apply it. You cannot expect healing if you merely purchase the medication, have it in your possession, and say, "*Okay, medicine, heal me,*" yet never ingest it. That would be absurd, right? Too many go to church, worship the Lord, and somehow expect the blood of Jesus to work without taking any real action. It's comparable to saying a sinner's prayer and expecting all your problems to dissolve, yet you never do anything to change your lifestyle. God is the One who can turn a curse into a blessing. He did that on the cross. Curses have not been eliminated from the equation. Instead, God gives us a way out from underneath them by the blood of Jesus.

If you have a bacteria, you must swallow the medication, drink lots of fluids, and follow the doctor's instructions. If you have a curse, you seek the Great Physician, drink the blood of Jesus, and then—in addition to—follow His instructions. With the following prayer, you cannot pray it and expect everything to fall away. There must be life-change in you per Scripture. In other words, if you use the blood of Jesus to break a generational curse of obesity, you must also change your diet. If breaking a cycle of bitterness, you must learn to forgive. If breaking the curse of addiction, take the proper steps toward breaking the pattern. We are physical. God is spiritual. This is why we must put to use both the spiritual and physical aspects of healing. One is virtually useless without the other. Man is comprised of spirit, soul, and body; therefore, the road to recovery in any capacity requires we address each aspect.

Prayer:

I plea the blood of Jesus over myself, my children, and my family. I put the blood between (*self or someone else*), and the curse of (*bitterness, addiction, anger, bitterness, whatever*) and I ask that the blood of Jesus break the curse off (*whomever you already named above*) on both my/their mother and father's side of the family back to Adam and Eve. Where there was a curse of (*whatever curse you listed above*), I ask You, Almighty God, to replace it with (*the opposite*). I bless You, heavenly Father, for carrying every curse through Your Son, Jesus Christ, as I never could. I repent of every vow my forefathers have made. I renounce them from my life and the life of my/their family. I forgive those who have hurt me/them or cursed me/them in any way. I receive Your forgiveness, Father, for having judged them in my heart. I ask You to bless my enemies with every spiritual truth in the heavenly realm that they too may be set free. I pull down every word spoken out against me/them so that they cannot prevail against me/them. I pull down every weapon formed against me/them that they not prosper (Isaiah 54:17). I plea the blood of Jesus over my mind, will and emotions, and over every imagination, stronghold, and every high thing that exalts itself above the name of Jesus. I pull it all into the obedience of Christ, our Savior. Amen

Scripture References:

> But it shall come about, if you do not obey the Lord your God, to observe to do all His commandments and His statutes with which I charge you today, that all these curses will come upon you and overtake you…The Lord will send upon you curses, confusion, and rebuke, in all you undertake to do, until you are destroyed and until you perish quickly, on account of the evil of your deeds, because you have forsaken Me (Deuteronomy 28:15, 20).

Journaling

THIRTEEN

Breaking Evil Soul-Ties

Commentary:

Soul-ties can happen with sexual partners as well as non-sexual partners, but the most potent are sexual. When we engage in sexual relations, we become one person with them. That means all their junk—spiritual, mental, emotional—becomes ours. Merely walking away does not negate this fact. Oneness is serious business in the spiritual realm. In correlation to sexual relations, Godly soul-ties come from marriage (Ephesians 5:31; Mark 10:7-9). Unholy sexual soul-ties come from sex outside marriage, whether consensual or through rape (I Corinthians 6:16). Both good and bad non-sexual—mental, emotional, soulish, spiritual—soul-ties can come from strong relationships having nothing to do with sex, for instance, King David and Saul's son, Jonathan, shared a holy soul-tie (I Samuel 18:1). There was a soul-tie between David and Saul, which began well and ended poorly (I Samuel 16:21 & 19:1). Vows—spoken or unspoken—can cause soul-ties and must be broken. Vows are a serious matter to God (Numbers 30:2). Evil soul-ties need to be broken by the blood of Jesus.

Prayer:

In the name of Jesus, I command every evil soul-tie between myself and _____ to be broken as far as the east is from the west. I take up the Sword of the Spirit, which is the Word of God, and sever them by the power and authority You granted me through the blood of Jesus. I thank You for enhancing every holy and good soul-tie in my life. I ask that You, O God, nourish all good soul-ties in my life and break from me all the evil ones, past, present, and future. Stir discernment (I Corinthians 2:13 and 12:10, John 7:24) from within me to know which relationships are from You and which ones are of the evil one. I bind to myself wisdom from above, which is pure, peaceable, easily entreated, without hypocrisy or partiality, and full of grace and mercy (James 3:17). May I always conduct myself in a manner worthy of the gospel of Christ (Philippians 1:27). I thank You, in advance, for the wisdom to recognize things of the spirit-realm that are so much stronger than anything of the natural. I thank You for the wherewithal to apply the tools You've set before me this day. Selah.

Scripture References:

"For this reason a man shall leave his father and mother and shall be joined to his wife, and the two shall become one (Ephesians 5:31)."

"Or do you not know that the one who joins himself to a prostitute is one body with her? For He says, 'The two shall become one flesh (I Corinthians 6:16).'"

"Now it came about when he had finished speaking to Saul, that the soul of Jonathan was knit to the soul of

David, and Jonathan loved him as himself (I Samuel 18:1)."

"Then David came to Saul and attended him; and Saul loved him greatly, and he became his armor bearer (I Samuel 16:21)."

"Now Saul told Jonathan his son and all his servants to put David to death. But Jonathan, Saul's son, greatly delighted in David (I Samuel 19:1)."

"If a man makes a vow to the Lord, or takes an oath to bind himself with a binding obligation, he shall not violate his word; he shall do according to all that proceeds out of his mouth (Numbers 30:2)."

Journaling

FOURTEEN

Children: The Righteous Seed of Abraham

Commentary:

Before my children were conceived, I began praying for them. If you didn't start quite that early, it is never too late. It is both our right and responsibility to pray over our offspring.

Prayer:

Father, I plead the blood of Jesus over my child(ren), grandchildren for a thousand generations. I thank You that they are the righteous seed of Abraham and are richly blessed (Galatians 3:29). I command every demonic spirit of hell to be bound, gagged, and loosed from their assignment over them realeasing Holy Spirit to be the only Spirit active as their life breath (Matthew 18:18; Job 33:4). I call forth the warring angels to war against the demonic spirits attempting to steal from them, kill, and destroy them (John 10:10). By the authority and power given to me by Jesus, I cancel every assignment placed upon their lives (Luke 10:19) and claim them for the Kingdom of God. I send confusion into the enemy's camp (II Chronicles 20:22) that they must flee in seven different directions (Deuteronomy 28:7). I thank You, before it physically manifests, that everything my child(ren) is going through, it will soon turn for their good and the good of the Kingdom of God (Genesis 50:20). No weapon formed against them shall prosper, and no words spoken against them shall prevail (Isaiah 54:17). I rebuke the devourer (Malachi 3:11) and break his teeth (Psalm 3:7), in Jesus' name. Father, I give You all praise, honor, and glory for the person of God You have called and created them to be. They are fearfully and wonderfully made (Psalm 139:14). I stand in faith (I Corinthians 16:13) that nothing will stop them from Your purpose for them. I will not fear the enemy because the plot is already defeated (Philippians 1:28).

Scripture References:

>"Then your houses shall be filled and the houses of all your servants and the houses of all the Egyptians, something which neither your fathers nor your grandfathers have seen, from the day that they came upon the Earth until this day (Exodus 20:6)."

>"You shall not worship them or serve them; for I, the Lord your God, am a jealous God, visiting the iniquity of the fathers on the children, and on the third and the fourth generations of those who hate Me, but showing loving-kindness to thousands, to those who love Me and keep my commandments (Deuteronomy 5:9-10)."

Journaling

FIFTEEN

Children: Righting Wrongs

Commentary:

Parents make mistakes, no exceptions. This prayer points toward making the wrong things right through prayer and taking the necessary steps toward rightness. As in every situation, we must be proactive, both spiritually and physically. We cannot expect one to do the job of both. We live in a physical world. We pray—spiritual—as well as do what is required of us to right wrongs—physical.

Prayer:

Yahweh, I cry out to You for mercy! I desire to correct my wrongs, where my children are concerned. Show me how to lead my children into righteousness, healing, wholeness, purity, forgiveness, and anything of You. I repent of my selfish indiscretions that have dishonored You and my children. Whatever emotions I may have about marriage or divorce, guide me to a place where the feelings no longer run my life. I repent in total humility for making myself an idol before You. Thank You for Your forgiveness and mercy.

Please help me to finish reaping this bad field I've sown that I may, one day, reap the harvest of my new good seed I'm planting in my family and life. Amen.

Scripture References:

"I will go before you and make the rough places smooth; I will shatter the doors of bronze and cut through their iron bars (Isaiah 45:2)."

"Do nothing from selfishness or empty conceit, but with humility of mind regard one another as more important than yourselves (Philippians 2:3)."

"For where jealousy and selfish ambition exist, there is disorder and every evil thing. But if you have bitter jealousy and selfish ambition in your heart, do not be arrogant and so lie against the truth. This wisdom is not that which comes down from above, but is earthly, natural, demonic (James 3:14-16)."

"Train up a child in the way he should go, and when he is old he will not depart from it (Proverbs 22:6)."

"Children, obey your parents in the Lord: for this is right. Honor thy father and mother; which is the first commandment with promise; that it may be well with you, and you may live long on the Earth. And, fathers, do not provoke your children to wrath; but bring them up in the nurture and admonition of the Lord (Ephesians 6:1-4)."

Journaling

SIXTEEN

Character of God

Commentary:

Learning the character of God is vital in a successful relationship with Him. It is too easy to fall away from God when we don't understand His heart toward His people, which is to redeem us through His unfailing love.

Prayer:

O Father, hallowed be Thy name. Your everlasting love, joy, and patience are priceless. Show me, Jesus, how to walk a life of joy, humility, obedience, and patience as Jesus Christ Himself walked this Earth. Bind to me love, joy, peace, patience, kindness, goodness, faithfulness, gentleness, and self-control. May the Lord's joy rule in my heart and life. I pray I will keep my eyes on You, Your Word, and Your work at all times without veering to the right or the left. I pray for Your joy to be made complete in me. Show me Your ways, O Lord, that I may be a poured-out drink offering, holy and acceptable unto You, emptied of self and filled with the Holy Spirit.

Scripture References:

"The Lord appeared to him from far away saying, "I have loved you with an everlasting love, therefore I have drawn you with lovingkindness (Jeremiah 31:3)."

"For God so loved the world that He gave His only begotten Son, that whosoever believed in Him will not perish but have everlasting life (John 3:16)."

Who shall separate us from the love of Christ? Shall tribulation, or distress, or persecution, or famine, or nakedness, or danger, or sword? As it is written, "For your sake we are being killed all the day long; we are regarded as sheep to be slaughtered." No, in all these things we are more than conquerors through Him who loved us. For I am sure that neither death nor life, nor angels nor rulers, nor things present nor things to come, nor powers, nor height nor depth, nor anything else in all creation, will be able to separate us from the love of God in Christ Jesus our Lord (Romans 8:35-39).

Journaling

SEVENTEEN

Circumcise My Heart

Commentary:

Heart circumcision, spiritually speaking, is allowing the Lord to cut away everything pertaining to the nature of the flesh, the natural man. It is a cutting away of selfish desires, wants, and intentions. I never heard this growing up. It was "get saved" without any explanation of what that means or how to go about it. If you want to serve the Lord with a clean heart, there must, of necessity, be a cutting and removal of whatever stands in between you and holiness.

Prayer:

O Jesus, circumcise my heart today. Place in me, O Father, a new heart, and a new spirit (Ezekiel 36:26). I desire with all my heart, soul, mind, and strength to be as You desire, to have a clean, pure, contrite heart before you, O God. Show me the way of righteousness. Show me how to have a heart set on You at all times and in all things. Give me a heart that hates what You hate, loves what You love, goes where You go, and stays where You stay. Teach me, Father, how to be still and quiet in Your holy presence that I may know Your voice better than my own (Psalm 46:10). Instill within me reverent, holy fear of You, Almighty Sovereign. Show me the error of my ways that I may quickly, and without hesitation, confess, repent, and be made clean in Your sight. Reveal every wicked and fruitless deed of darkness within me, Your holy temple. I pray, O Father, to have a sound mind, pure heart, and steadfast spirit all the days of my life. Teach me Your love and how to grow in faith so that You become my trust. I love You, my King. Help me to love You with the pure love You pour upon my head. Separate my spirit from my soul that I may commune with Your Spirit to worship in spirit and in truth (Hebrews 4:12). Thanks be to God in Heaven and Earth. I rejoice in You, Almighty, for You are worthy to be praised!"

Scripture References:

"But he is a Jew who is one inwardly; and circumcision is that which is of the heart, by the Spirit, not by the letter; and his praise is not from men, but from God (Romans 2:29)."

"Moreover the Lord your God will circumcise your heart and the heart of your descendants, to love the Lord your God with all your heart and with all your soul, so that you may live (Deuteronomy 30:6)."

Journaling

EIGHTEEN

Confession

Commentary:

Confession is imperative to clean-living before a holy God. We are to confess our sins to God and to man. Confession leads to repentance, which leads to healing and salvation. Keep in mind that "confess your sins one to another" does not mean you are to tell everyone your dirty laundry. It does, contrarily, mean that we need to be wise in our confessions. If I hurt my brother, I am to confess my sins to my brother, not to every person with whom we come in contact. If we are unwise in our confessions, it is no longer confession, but self-pity. In our self-pity, we begin to seek approval of man because we want them to view us as humble. Unfortunately, it isn't humility, but pride at work. Always confess to God. As for our fellow man, seek the Lord's discernment as to who, when, and where to confess.

Also, we do not need to confess our sins to someone just because they are clergy. Catholicism has led people to believe that their sins cannot be absolved unless they confess to a priest. This is errant on a large scale because man cannot give eternal forgiveness. We are to "call no man 'Father,'" which means we are not to place anyone in the position of God the

Father. It does not translate children cannot refer to their dad as "father." Jesus was speaking to the Jewish leaders who had placed themselves upon a high position. They called people to live in a way they did not live themselves. Priests, pastors, preachers, teachers, prophets, apostles, or anyone in leadership positions are not the ones who can absolve your sins. This is the point. We are to confess to some people, yes, but not necessarily clergy. Confess your sins to one who can lead you to repentance to Jesus. Sometimes it will be clergy, and that's fine, but only as long as Holy Spirit directed it.

Prayer:

Dear Father, show me how to confess my every lie and sin against You. Teach me to walk upright in integrity, wisdom, and faith in who You are. Allow me Your strength to confess the web of lies in which I have allowed myself to become ensnared and to accept the consequences humbly. I desire to be as You, beginning with complete honesty before God and man. Thank You for giving me the courage to endure whatever lies before me. Teach me to know through keen discernment and wisdom, whom to keep in my life, and from whom to separate. Allow the grace and knowledge to see into the heart of every person in my life, that I may know the intention of their hearts. I seek only Your holy, supernatural power to discern right from wrong. Give me Your heart, O God. Give me a pure heart of forgiveness for those who have already offended me and for those who will betray my trust in the future. Allow me the supernatural ability to forgive and heal as well as how to heal those around me. Selah

Scripture References:

"If you confess that Jesus is Lord and believe that God raised Him from the dead, you will be saved. For it is by our faith that we are put right with God; it is by our confession that we are saved (Romans 10:9-10)."

"Then I confessed my sins to You; I did not conceal my wrongdoings. I decided to confess them to You, and You forgave all my sins (Psalm 32:5)."

"Only admit that you are guilty and that you have rebelled against the Lord, your God. Confess that under every green tree you have given your love to foreign gods and that you have not obeyed my commands. I, the Lord, have spoken (Jeremiah 3:13)."

Therefore, confess your sins to one another, and pray for one another so that you may be healed. The effective prayer of a righteous man can accomplish much (James 5:16)."

Journaling

NINETEEN

Conformed Unto God

Commentary:

Being conformed into the image of God is a far cry from being saved from hell. Many people around the world confess Christ as Savior, yet do not conform to His likeness. Though no one is perfect and we're all in progress, there must come a place where we lay down self at the feet of Jesus and live as Christ. This is not about works, though works follow, but about a heart change. It is willingly choosing to deny self with all its wavering emotions and opinions and reside in this world as, *"It is no longer I who live, but Christ who lives in me."*

Prayer:

Place in me, O God, Your ways that I may conform unto You. Pour into me Your very Spirit that is gentle, patient, and humble, so that I may speak on Your behalf as an ambassador in chains. Let Your mighty voice be heard through me in all the territory You have granted. Teach me Your immeasurable patience so that I, like Jesus, will be patient with all mankind. Bless You, O King of kings and Lord of lords. Bridle my tongue that I not defile my whole body, but in everything have knowledge and understanding of Your perfect timing. May I never use Your Word as a tool to tear down others, but rather as the tool for life. Allow me to endure whatever necessary so that patience, gentleness, and humility will freely flow from me in love.

Scripture References:

> "And do not be conformed to this world, but be transformed by the renewing of your mind, so that you may prove what the will of God is, that which is good and acceptable and perfect (Romans 12:2)."

> "As obedient children, do not be conformed to the former lusts which were yours in your ignorance (I Peter 1:14)."

> "Not only so, but we also glory in our sufferings, because we know that suffering produces perseverance Romans 5:3)."

Journaling

TWENTY

Consume Me

Commentary:

God Almighty is the all-consuming fire. Fire does one of two things: it refines, or it destroys. We choose which we allow. It depends on how we approach and receive our Creator. My prayer is to be entirely consumed by God's holy fire. In so doing, I allow Him to refine all the precious elements of Himself within me and to burn out all the rubble of the flesh. Otherwise, I will be destroyed by hellfire. May that never be! If the all-consuming fire of God has overtaken me, what can hell have over me? Nothing.

Prayer:

Oh gracious, heavenly Father, lay Your heart in my body and consume me. Please, let Your supernatural love and holy fire overtake me. Pour Your love upon my head as the healing balm of Gilead (Jeremiah 8:22). Show me how to open myself wholly to You. I desire to be a person of virtue, integrity, honor, love, peace, patience, and boundless generosity. Teach me how to be unashamed of how You made me, fearfully and wonderfully.

Teach me how to be a gracious host for Your Holy Spirit. Let me be a doer of the Word, not just a hearer. Make straight the crooked paths I have laid for myself. Reveal to me who my brothers, sisters, and mothers are as You see them, not as in the natural. Convey to me, O gracious Lord, how to not only forgive those who have sinned against me but also to repent of my judgment against them that I may be forgiven. I desire today to love You with all my heart, soul, mind, and strength. I want all of You in all of me so that my only goal in this life is to be as You have designed me. Father, give me the grace to see the evil I have allowed in my camp. I want my territory clean, unblemished, and spotless before You. Show me which relationships are ungodly and give me the supernatural strength to end them. Bring into my life relationships that are pure and holy. Give me, O gracious, merciful God, clean hands and a pure heart before You, before man and before the demons of hell. I pray, O Sovereign Lord, that You, man, and demons will testify I am a child of the King. Amen and amen. Selah

Scripture References:

> "For the Lord your God is a consuming fire, a jealous God (Deuteronomy 4:24)."

> For this very reason, make every effort to supplement your faith with virtue, and virtue with knowledge, and knowledge with self-control, and self-control with steadfastness, and steadfastness with godliness, and godliness with brotherly affection, and brotherly affection with love. For if these qualities are yours and are increasing, they keep you from being ineffective or unfruitful in the knowledge of our Lord Jesus Christ (II Peter 1:5-8).

Journaling

TWENTY-ONE

Daily Prayer

Commentary:

I pray this daily, no exceptions! My priority of any day is to surrender to God, spirit, soul, and body. If I don't, I will make many more mistakes. Life is complicated enough while in the will of God. There's no sense in attempting to start any day having to face life's challenges outside the purpose and will of God.

Prayer:

I plead the blood of Jesus over my mind, will, and emotions; over every imagination, stronghold, and every high thing that exalts itself above the name of Jesus in my life. I pull it all down into the obedience of Christ. I command every demonic spirit to be bound, gagged, and loosed from its assignment over me. I release Holy Spirit into my life to be the only Spirit functioning (Romans 8:14). I choose to die to my flesh and my soul. Let the mind that is in Christ be also in me (Philippians 2:5). I put on the full armor of God: the helmet of salvation, the breastplate of righteousness, I buckle the belt of truth around my waist, I take up the shield of faith, allow me to take up the Sword of the Spirit which is the Word of God, and I shod my feet with the boots of peace (Ephesians 6:10-18). I choose obedience and humility as I bind from me all forms of rebellion and pride. Amen

Scripture References:

> "We are destroying speculations and every high thing raised up against the knowledge of God, and we are taking every thought captive to the obedience of Christ (II Corinthians 10:5)."

> "For He had commanded the unclean spirit to come out of the man. For it had seized him many times; and he was bound with chains and shackles and kept under guard, and yet he would break his bonds and be driven by the demon into the desert (Luke 8:29)."

> "And He was saying to them all, "If anyone wishes to come after Me, he must deny himself, and take up his cross daily and follow Me (Luke 9:23)."

> "But I say to you truthfully, there are some of those standing here who will not taste death until they see the Kingdom of God (Luke 9:27)."

Journaling

TWENTY-TWO

Discernment

Commentary:

Definition of Discernment: 1) the ability to judge well; 2) (Christian) perception in the absence of judgment with a view to obtaining spiritual guidance and understanding

What would any of us do absent of the discernment of God? Heavenly discernment comes from seeking the face of God, not simply being a good church attendee or merely saved from hell. We must, of necessity, be diligent in seeking the supernatural discernment of God.

Prayer:

I desire, O God of Heaven and Earth, to walk in keen discernment to know how to love whom. I want to properly apply love as You have pre-ordained and not mix emotions with what is true and holy. I desire to keep myself pure in and out of marriage, no matter where I am in life. Reveal to me how to walk in self-discipline always. Selah.

Scripture References:

"Beloved, do not believe every spirit, but test the spirits to see whether they are from God, for many false prophets have gone out into the world (I John 4:1)."

"But test everything; hold fast what is good (I Thessalonians 5:21)."

"But solid food is for the mature, for those who have their powers of discernment trained by constant practice to distinguish good from evil (Hebrews 5:14)."

"But a natural man does not accept the things of the Spirit of God, for they are foolishness to him; and he cannot understand them, because they are spiritually appraised (Corinthians 2:14)."

"And to another the effecting of miracles, and to another prophecy, and to another the distinguishing of spirits, to another various kinds of tongues, and to another the interpretation of tongues (I Corinthians 12:10)."

"As for you, the anointing which you received from Him abides in you, and you have no need for anyone to teach you; but as His anointing teaches you about all things, and is true and is not a lie, and just as it has taught you, you abide in Him (I John 2:27)."

Journaling

TWENTY-THREE

Embodiment of Jesus

Commentary:

When we begin to grasp the magnitude of who we are in Christ, it will change how we think, perceive, pray, and ask. We will long for God to burn us from the inside out. We'll want nothing left in us except that which is the nature of God. God's holy nation is the living, breathing, walking, talking, physical manifestation of the Living God. We are the embodiment of Jesus.

Prayer:

Father, in the name of Jesus, burn me from the inside out. Purify me so that I will become the living, breathing, physical manifestation of Jesus in the world. Reveal every wicked and fruitless deed of darkness hidden deep within me so that I may confess, repent, and be made whole. I pray for nothing of my flesh to stand in the way of Jesus in me. I earnestly desire to be more and more as Jesus with every passing day. Give me the grace to accept what You reveal and the guidance required to move past it. Reveal Yourself to me, O Great God of Heaven and Earth. Burn out the wood, hay, and stubble from my midst, and refine all the precious metal You have planted in me. I thank You, Father, that, since all of You is in all of Jesus, and all of Jesus now resides within me, I am equipped to be as Jesus in this dark and dying world. I thank You that, in Your power, the same power that raised Jesus from the dead resides within me.

Scripture References:

"For it was the Father's good pleasure for all the fullness to dwell in Him (Colossians 1:19)."

"For in Christ all the fullness of the Deity dwells in bodily form, and in Christ you have been brought to fullness (Colossians 2:9-10)."

"When Christ, who is your life, appears, then you also will appear with Him in glory (Colossians 3:4)."

"Now if any man build upon this foundation gold, silver, precious stones, wood, hay stubble; every man's work shall be made manifest; for the day shall declare it, because it shall be revealed by fire; and the fire shall try every man's work of what sort it is (I Corinthians 3:12-13, KJV)."

"But if the Spirit of Him who raised Jesus from the dead dwells in you, He who raised Christ Jesus from the dead will also give life to your mortal bodies through His Spirit who dwells in you (Romans 8:11)."

Journaling

Fear Scriptures and Commentary

"Now hear this, O foolish and senseless people, who have eyes but do not see; who have ears but do not hear. *Do you not fear Me?*" declares the Lord. "Do you not tremble in My presence? For I have placed the sand as a boundary for the sea, an eternal decree, so it cannot cross over it. Though the waves toss, yet they cannot prevail; though they roar, yet they cannot cross over it. But this people has a stubborn and rebellious heart; they have turned aside and departed. They do not say in their heart, 'Let us now fear the Lord our God, who gives rain in its season… your iniquities have turned these away, and your sins have withheld good from you. For wicked men are found among my people, they watch like fowlers lying in wait; they set a trap, they catch men. Like a cage full of birds, so their houses are full of deceit; therefore they have become great and rich. They are fat, they are sleek, they also excel in deeds of wickedness; they do not plead the cause of the orphan, that they may prosper; and they do not defend the rights of the poor. Shall I not punish these people?" declares the Lord. "On a nation such as this shall I not avenge myself? An appalling and horrible thing has happened in the land; the prophets prophesy falsely. And the priests rule on their own authority; and my people love it so. But what will you do at the end of it?"

Jeremiah 5:21-31 (NAS)

All words of correction and rebuke are for the benefit of the child of God, not for condemnation, but restoration and deliverance. As a whole, the body of Christ does not know or even desire to fear the Lord. *Fear the Lord* is a term grossly tossed about to many, but few understand or heed. When a person begins to fear God reverently, transformation comes. In the text above, God states that His people are foolish and senseless because of a lack of fear. Please read it carefully.

As you and I seek holiness and putting God first, He wants us to know that it all starts with this reverent fear, not with skipping to doing good deeds. Without this fear, you will not understand how to transition into the love God has for His people as a bride to her husband. We are not to fear Him as one who holds His proverbial thumb over you like a rigid disciplinarian.

Allow me to explain in brief. Remember, per God's design, an earthly husband is supposed to be the protector to his wife. God is our heavenly Father to His children, but He is equally our heavenly husband to His bride; you and I are the Bride of Christ. A true husband loves his wife so much that he would do whatever is best for her.

For example, I am in love with my husband, Michael. I have a reverent fear of him out of respect for who he is as my covenant covering. This does not mean I am consciously going around thinking how afraid I am of him; on the contrary. I have an inner reverence for him not to disrespect him. Because I know how in love he is with me and that I have this reverent fear, I do not come against him if he makes a decision I do not like or understand. I am more focused on *love* rather than *fear*.

This is because perfect love casts out fear (I John 4:18-19) – love takes precedence over fear. In other words, though the fear is ever-present, the love is dominant. Through love, I recognize that Michael's decisions for this family and me are always for our good, whether or not I initially recognize it. To properly teach the love of God, one must first address the fear, which is only the beginning. We must all begin at the starting point to transition into the next phase of Christ.

That being understood, let's further delve into the passage in Jeremiah 5. God continues to talk about people with a stubborn and rebellious heart. Anyone who continually disobeys Yeshua's commands is rebellious in the sight of God. Everyone knows, on some level, right from wrong, yet we do not seek Him; we have sought only the things that bring us personal pleasure from the vantage point of "God is love so He should give me what I want." This, to be sure, is remiss.

The Lord goes on to say that they did not say in their heart, "I fear you, Almighty God." When God said that, because of the people's sin, He could not bless them as He wished to do. God always desires to bless His people. The Great I AM has always loved us so completely that He wants to bless us, but our rebellion will stop His hand from blessing our lives.

He further states that these peoples' houses (their inner spirit man and heart) are full of deceit. This does not mean we are merely deceitful, but we have allowed ourselves to be deceived. We have, for a long time, deluded ourselves into believing that what is sin is okay. The world says, "Follow your heart." God says, "Never trust your heart, for it will lead you astray." You, I and the body of Christ are to be moved only by the Spirit of the Living God, not the emotions of our heart. Only a heart set on God will be trustworthy, because it has been consigned to Him and not the desire of the fleshly man.

The Lord continues by asking the rhetorical question, "Should I not punish this wickedness?" One can sin for a long, long time as far as man's timeframe is concerned. However, God watches until the people (or person) nearly destroy themselves and then He disciplines. It is for His holy and pure name's sake and the well-being of the individual.

Whose Authority Rules?

An excellent case in point is the lives of many of the men and women to whom I minister in prisons. Many of them went about their daily lives sinning by selling drugs and themselves. They had no concept of a holy God, or if they did, they paid no heed. In each of their lives, a day came where they were captured and incarcerated—some after many years of disobedience. They were enraged that God put them in prison. Many have said that they were mad that God did not show them mercy in their situation.

Nonetheless, for those who sought Him, they realized that they had to be stopped for their own sake and for those they were hurting. It was in prison that they came to a place of brokenness. This is the best place to be in the eyes of our Savior. He disciplined them because of the wicked acts and to get their attention. It was the only way to help them see the error to guide them to turn to repentance and newness of life.

Let us look at the latter part of the text in Jeremiah. We read, "The priests rule on their authority, and my people love it so." First, once you accept Christ through repentance, you are now of a royal priesthood. Since you are a priest, you must seek *God's* authority instead of the authority you think you have over your body. By conducting yourself in a manner unworthy of the gospel of Christ, you are overriding His authority. This, too, equals rebellion.

Many appear to succeed as the world considers success, but He asks, "What will come of it all in the end?" He says that you need to stop doing what pleases your fleshly man, turn your heart toward Him, have it set on Him at all times and in all seasons, and your heart's desires will change. The sin in your life that currently pleases you for a moment does not please you; instead, it brings about destruction and curses upon your head.

The excellent news is that, as you begin to recognize God for who He is, *fear* of Him will overtake you. As you set your heart like flint toward God and His righteousness, *love* will override the fear, and the blessings will begin to abound endlessly in your life. It is a promise to Abraham's righteous seed, but you haven't lived a life that depicts it. Throughout the Word, God scorns the wicked but then says, "Turn from your wicked ways, and I will bless you."

Steps to Holy Spirit:

1. Believe (Romans 10:9-10, John 1:12)
2. recognize the fleshly man was crucified with Christ (Galatians 2:20) and was, therefore, rendered dead pre-conception
3. repent and turn from wickedness (Matthew 4:17)
4. be baptized in the Holy Spirit (Acts 2:38)
5. receive the life of Christ as your own (Romans 10:9-10)
6. make your body a slave to Holy Spirit (I Corinthians 9:27)

The fear of God will turn your heart away from wickedness and toward holiness as you come into this new place. You will care more about pleasing him than yourself. It means that no matter what your *flesh* desires, your desire to please him will override. This is sacrifice. He sacrificed everything that you may live. What are you willing to *sacrifice* that you may please such a holy God? I say this to bring you into a higher place of freedom than you can ever imagine. You will begin to surely have "eyes that see, ears that hear, and a mind that truly understands and comprehends the Lord." Obedience will become, in time, a pleasure to you and not a burden. When you fear the Lord, you will both allow and desire His hand to rule because you will see that He is in love with you beyond measure.

Journaling

TWENTY-FOUR

Fear to Love

Prayer:

You promise that perfect love casts out fear. Father, I don't exactly know how to receive Your love, but I want it. This wicked flesh, in which I currently dwell, is full of doubt, fear, and unbelief, yet You promise that Your love casts all that aside. Jesus, reveal to me how to deny myself and to replace the fleshly nature with the perfect love only You possess and can give. I submit myself to You as a poured out drink offering and desire to be holy and acceptable to You (Philippians 2:17). I choose to allow all that You are to overtake all that I am. I reject fear and anxiety because You care for me (I Peter 5:7) and have already defeated my greatest foe (John 16:33) and made me more than an overcomer (Romans 8:37)

Scripture References:

> "There is no fear in love; but perfect love casts out fear, because fear involves punishment, and the one who fears is not perfected in love (I John 4:18)."

"Above all, keep fervent in your love for one another, because love covers a multitude of sins (I Peter 4:8)."

"But even if I am being poured out as a drink offering upon the sacrifice and service of your faith, I rejoice and share my joy with you all (Philippians 2:17)."

Journaling

TWENTY-FIVE

Fear No More

Prayer:

Our most gracious Savior, hallowed be Thy name in all the Earth. Continually show me Your will that I may step in faith when You open the doorway. Open every door that no man can close, and close every door that no man can open. Teach me Your ways, O God, that I become so merged with You that I won't flinch in the face of the enemy (Psalm 86:11). I will no longer be led by fear of failure. I thank You, Christ my Sovereign, that as my heart is set on You, You will lead, guide, direct, and orchestrate my path every step of the way. I surrender spirit, soul and body. I freely give myself away to You. May nothing and no one hinder Your sovereignty. Selah

Scripture References:

> "I know your deeds. Behold, I have put before you an open door which no one can shut, because you have a little power, and have kept My word, and have not denied My name (Revelation 3:8)."

"Then I will set the key of the house of David on his shoulder, when he opens no one will shut, when he shuts no one will open (Isaiah 22:22)."

"Say to those with fearful hearts, "Be strong, do not fear; your God will come, He will come with vengeance; with divine retribution He will come to save you (Isaiah 35:4)."

"Peace I leave with you; My peace I give you. I do not give to you as the world gives. Do not let your hearts be troubled and do not be afraid (John 14:27)."

"These things I have spoken to you, so that in Me you may have peace. In the world you have tribulation, but take courage; I have overcome the world (John 16:33)."

Journaling

TWENTY-SIX

Financial Trouble

Prayer:

Father, in the name of Jesus, I plead His holy blood covenant over my finances. First, I repent of mishandling the money You have provided. Secondly, I purpose to align myself with Your perfect plan for my finances and life as a whole. Show me the way out of the debt I find myself. Allow me to be wise in all my ways so that, eventually, things will work out. I trust You that what Satan has meant against me for evil to kill and destroy me, You will turn for good because I love You. I purpose to, from here and forevermore, live in accordance to Your desires. I will spend where You desire and refrain from purchases not of You. Guide me in the ways of the Kingdom of God. I will seek You first and Your Kingdom in all things, and, in so doing, I know all things needed for this life will be added unto me.

Scripture References:

> "But seek first the Kingdom of God and His righteousness and then all these things will be added unto you (Matthew 6:33)."

"And God is able to bless you abundantly, so that in all things at all times, having all that you need, you will abound in every good work (II Corinthians 9:8)."

"His divine power has given us everything we need for a godly life through our knowledge of Him who called us by His own glory and goodness (II Peter 1:3)."

"Keep your lives free from the love of money and be content with what you have, because God has said, "Never will I leave you; never will I forsake you (Hebrews 13:5)."

"Consider the ravens: they do not sow or reap, they have no storeroom or barn; yet God feeds them. And how much more valuable you are than birds (Luke 12:24)!"

Journaling

TWENTY-SEVEN

Focus on God

Prayer:

Since You, Lord, have so graciously given all of mankind the wonderful opportunity to be graphed into the Living Vine, may I personally never disengage myself from You for any reason (Romans 11:11-24). The things and ways of this condemned world are foolish and fruitless. Direct me to keep my focus ever upon You and Your majesty so that I will not be lured away by the fool's gold of this age. You are the Vine, and I am Your branch. My life is found and sustained only when attached to You. I purpose to set my face like flint refusing to look to the right or the left. Selah.

Scripture References:

> "Do not participate in the unfruitful deeds of darkness, but instead even expose them (Ephesians 5:11)."

"For the Lord God helps Me, therefore, I am not disgraced; therefore, I have set My face like flint, and I know that I will not be ashamed (Isaiah 50:7)."

Journaling

Forgiveness Scriptures and Commentary

My strong desire, as from the Lord, is to teach people how to deal with their issues so they can live a life set apart unto our Holy God. We cannot tell a person how to live correctly if we don't know how ourselves. This is where personal accountability enters. Most want to blame their problems on everyone and everything around them. Yes, some people and circumstances make life complicated.

However, when we begin to *choose to change our vantage point* from the earthly to the heavenly, we won't be able to stop ourselves from seeing things differently. We will begin to understand that what Satan intends against us for evil, God, in His sovereignty and wisdom, purposes it for our good for those who love Him. Satan has no authority to do anything without consent from God (Romans 8:28; Job 1; Genesis 50:20), and this knowledge, at least for me, changes the game.

Joseph's life is a great example. Look at all the adverse encounters that came his way. By chapter fifty and verse twenty, he tells his brothers—who were afraid he would return evil to them, "*As for you, you meant evil against me, but God meant it for good to bring about this present result, to preserve many people alive.*" The bottom line in this message is that, although times can be tough and bring much travail, God always has something excellent and bountiful on the other side.

All of God's people have made mistakes. Regardless, we know that we can do all things through Christ who gives us strength, so long as we are doing that which is pleasing to God. The only irreversible things are those not surrendered to God's hand that cannot be shortened. The longer there has been a problem, the longer it will take to resolve. There is a process to everything. It took time to get in the mess, and it will take time to come out. This is why *now* is the best time to begin. The hope is *knowing* and *trusting,* through faith, that God is greater than the situation. Learn to become patient as He is patient. Don't seek God one day and, if things don't change overnight, throw our hands in the air in defeat and go back to that which is familiar. *Impatience* is a crucial factor in Satan's success in our downfall.

Bitterness and Unforgiveness:

> "*You have no excuse*, you who pass judgment on someone else, for at whatever point you judge the other, you are condemning yourself, because you who pass judgment do the same things (Romans 2:1)."

> "For if you forgive others for their transgressions, your heavenly Father will also forgive you. But if you do not forgive others, then your Father will not forgive your transgressions (Matthew 6:14-15)."

> "There is no fear in love; but perfect love casts out fear, because fear involves punishment, and the one who fears is not perfected in love. We love, because he first loved us (1 John 4:18-19)."

With this foundation, let's look at some basics about God and His Word so we can analyze whatever junk may be in us that stems back to our birth and before. Unforgiveness and judgment against others are vital elements that keep us forever bound. They are the opposite of love. They stand as barriers between us and the blessings of God. They are a blockade between us and healthy relationships with those in our lives.

As we can see in the above verses, *unforgiveness* and harbored *judgment* are our downfall. Hebrews 12:15 reads, "*See to it that no one misses the grace of God and that no bitter root grows up to cause trouble and defile many."* Resentment, as mentioned in Job 36:21, is the equivalent of godlessness. I challenge us to dig deeper into our past and inspect our hearts. Only God can reveal the condition of anyone's heart. Seek Yeshua to expose all roots of bitterness, unforgiveness, and judgment that have been allowed to take hold and defile not only you as an individual, but also family and other relationships. As hard as this may be, the outcome is far superior to the current condition.

Bitterness Explanation:

1. **Bitterroot expectancy:** *emotionally* charged, expecting that whatever happens to you at one point will always happen—it is psychological. People are often drawn to someone like their abuser.

2. **Bitterroot judgment:** driven by *law*, and it is more potent than expectancy – it is the law God set in the Earth. The Law of God is that you will be judged as you judge (Romans 2:1). We see in Matthew 7:1-2: *"Do not judge so that you will not be judged. For in the way you judge, you will be judged; and by your standard of measure, it will be measured to you."* (To learn more of bitter roots, check out John and Paula Sanford of *Elijah House Ministries*. Recordings can be found on YouTube.)

Bitter root judgment is not the same as *righteous judgment* to which the body of Christ is called; that is an entirely different message. In a case where a husband and wife were both abused or neglected in childhood, early in life they passed judgment against their parents. They did not realize what they were doing, but it happened nonetheless. No one can blame them given the circumstances, but it is no less against the law of God. As the two became one flesh, they merged all their bitter roots. There was a multiplication—not addition—of internal rubbish that had been packed in the basements of their hearts. Not only were the judgments multiplied, but so were the penalties. At whatever point they judged their parents, they eventually turned to do the same things.

Taking Action:

Hebrews 12:15 begins with an action statement: "See to it..." This means *you* are to take care of it. It is *your* responsibility to keep yourself cleansed of bitterness and unforgiveness. Forgiveness is two-fold. On some level, most people realize that they must forgive whoever hurt them. Unfortunately, after extending forgiveness, they are not aware that they must go a step further and *repent* of their judgment against their offender. It is part of the filth that must be removed before purity takes hold. Most forgive begrudgingly out of obligation because it is the *right thing to do*.

Matthew 18:35 reads, "...you must forgive *from the heart.*" This translates that idle words of forgiveness are useless. Unless we forgive with the boundless love of Christ, we have not been set free. A heart genuinely set on pleasing the Father is a heart ready at all times to forgive. This is the essence of true love. It is a *sacrificial forgiveness*, just as God's forgiveness is 100% sacrificial.

Until we *see to it* to cleanse our hearts of hatred, unforgiveness, and judgment against parents, grandparents, siblings, bosses, strangers, spouses (ex or current), or whomever, we will continue to conduct ourselves in undesirable ways. We won't be able to stop being like those we hate. It is the law of God in effect. As a result, those around us will also, on some level, hate us. The supernatural love of Christ can only override the generational patterns of hatred in action through our person.

If we want our children to stop being like us, we must stop being like our old nature. One cannot do this on their own. Only a supernatural move of God can incite an otherwise impossible change of character. A friend of mine called me some time ago asking how to get her six-year-old to stop acting with ingratitude and arrogance. As lovingly as possible, I told her the only way she could teach humility and gratitude was to change her conduct and ask the Lord to teach *her* gratitude and humility. She didn't like that at all. She expressed her difficulty with humility and gratitude toward others. I insisted that her efforts to instill these Christ-like attributes in her child were useless because children live what they see, not what they hear. They were both living under unbroken, unrepented generational patterns.

You, the individual parent, must humble yourself in a childlike manner before Almighty God. To do this with efficacy, ask the Lord to expose every wicked way within so *you* may confess, repent, and be made whole. Until *you* let Christ transform you, *you* cannot fix your child. No amount of yelling, belittling, restriction, beating, or insults will change them. No matter how many times *you* start a sentence with, "*When I was your age...*" or, "*Don't be like me,*" or, "*If you only knew what I know,*" or, "*It was good enough for me,*" they will continue on the wrong path. Without repenting of personal judgment and bitterness held in *your* heart, *you* will continue to fuel the fire of rebellion in your children. *You* need to take the time to look within, allowing Holy Spirit to do a work of love in *you* and be patient upon the Lord to do a work in them.

Journaling

TWENTY-EIGHT

Forgiveness of Others

Prayer:

Father, in the name of Your Son, Jesus, thank You for revealing how to forgive. I make a choice today to forgive my offender(s). I also repent of my judgment against (*whomever*) with a sincere heart. Remind me always that I need the same amount of grace and mercy as they. May I never lose sight of the boundless forgiveness I have required. Thank You for the gift of Your Son and the loving forgiveness You continuously extend toward me. Show me how to daily keep my heart pure from the evil of judgment and all unrighteousness. May I never allow any person or demon to sever my communion with You, my precious Savior and Redeemer. Selah.

Scripture References:

> "Bear with each other and forgive one another if any of you has a grievance against someone. Forgive as the Lord forgave you (Colossians 3:13)."

"For if you forgive other people when they sin against you, your heavenly Father will also forgive you. But if you do not forgive others their sins, your Father will not forgive your sins (Matthew 6:14-15)."

"For in the way you judge, you will be judged; and by your standard of measure, it will be measured to you (Matthew 7:2)."

Journaling

TWENTY-NINE

Forgiveness of Self

Prayer:

Oh, Father, I pray in the holy name of Jesus that You will begin to show me how to forgive myself as You have forgiven me. Bestow understanding of how to apply Your grace in my life to be free of my past sin. With all my heart, soul, mind, and strength, I desire to please and love You completely. I praise You that peace, which passes all understanding, is bound to me as I align my life with Yours. I thank You that, as I forgive those who have sinned against me, You have forgiven me. Give me a God-consciousness at all times and in all things. The moment I begin to enter temptation, You are free to rebuke, correct me, and allow me to confess, repent, and be made complete again in You. Bless You, O heavenly Father, for Your everlasting love and patience with me. You have removed my sins as far as the east is from the west. Remind me to not continuously beat myself for that which I have repented and been forgiven. Show me how to correct my wrongs with my fellow man. I humble myself before God and man. I humbly receive the forgiveness I do not deserve, and I purpose to go and sin no more. Amen.

Scripture References:

"But if we confess our sins to Him, He is faithful and just to forgive us our sins and to cleanse us from all wickedness (I John 1:9)."

"If you forgive those who sin against you, your heavenly Father will forgive you. But if you refuse to forgive others, your Father will not forgive your sins (Matthew 6:14-15)."

"She said to Him, 'No one, Lord.' And Jesus said, 'I do not condemn you, either. Go and sin no more'…So if the Son makes you free, you will be free indeed (John 8:11, 36)."

Journaling

THIRTY

Forgiveness of Anger, Hatred, and Malice

Prayer:

Father God, I recognize that to be angry is not, in itself, sin. However, when it festers unchecked, it turns into hatred, and hatred turns to malice. I repent of unchecked anger, hatred, and malice within my spirit. I forgive those who have been the surface cause of such things, and I ask that You lovingly reveal to me the root of such emotions so that I can address them according to Your Spirit, dig it up, and be set free from it. I intend fully to comply with the love of God. Help me to love people with the supernatural love that I, in and of myself, do not possess. May the love of Christ compel me to come out of that which is grounded in Satan. You have stripped off the old nature with its practices and clothed me with the new nature. Thank You. Amen.

Scripture References:

Then you'll call, and the Lord will answer; you'll cry for help, and He'll respond, "Here I am." If you do away with the yoke among you, and pointing fingers and malicious talk; if you pour yourself out for the hungry and satisfy the needs of afflicted souls, then your light will rise in darkness and your night will be like noonday. And the Lord will guide you continually, and satisfy your soul in parched places, and they will strengthen your bones; and you'll be like a watered garden, like a spring of water, whose water never fail (Isaiah 58:9-11).

But now you must also get rid of anger, wrath, malice, slander, obscene speech, and all such sins. Do not lie to one another, for you have stripped off the old nature with its practices and have clothed yourselves with the new nature, which is being renewed in full knowledge, consistent with the image of the one who created it (Colossians 3:7-10).

Slander no one, to be peaceable and considerate, and always to be gentle toward everyone. At one time we too were foolish, disobedient, deceived and enslaved by all kinds of passions and pleasures. We lived in malice and envy, being hated and hating one another. But when the kindness and love of God our Savior appeared, He saved us, not because of righteous things we had done, but because of His mercy. He saved us through the washing of rebirth and renewal by the Holy Spirit, whom He poured out on us generously through Jesus Christ our Savior (Titus: 3:2-6).

Journaling

THIRTY-ONE

Forgiveness of Bitterness and Resentment

Prayer:

Father, as I choose to disembowel all ungodly characteristics, I continue stripping away the old man. I surrender all bitterness and resentment held in my heart against others. I choose to look at other people through God's eyes instead of my limited, earthly, fleshly man. As I want to be forgiven, I purposefully forgive those who have harmed me, no matter how greatly they have done so. I set aside resentment and bitterness and forgive them with my whole heart. I desire earnestly to take every measure to live in peace with all mankind and to be holy—I want to see You, Lord. By the power of the Spirit of God, I am uprooting bitterness and resentment so that no one else is troubled or defiled by my hand. Heal me from the inside out. Selah

Scripture References:

"Make every effort to live in peace with all mankind and to be holy; without holiness, no one will see the Lord. See to it that no one misses the grace of God and that no bitter root grows up to cause trouble and defile many (Hebrews 12:14-15)."

"Get rid of all bitterness, rage, and anger, brawling and slander, along with every form of malice. Be kind and compassionate to one another, forgiving each other, just as in Christ God forgave you (Ephesians 4:31-32)."

Journaling

THIRTY-TWO
Forgiveness of Greed and Jealousy

Prayer:

My Father, who art in Heaven, sacred is Your name in all the Earth. I repent of all greed and jealousy I have harbored in my heart against my fellow man. I know that neither greed nor jealousy comes from You but from the world. Before I die, there are two things, Lord, I want You to do: 1) Make me honest, and 2) don't let me be too poor or too rich. Give me just what I need. If I have too much to eat, I might forget about You; if I don't have enough, I might steal and disgrace Your name (Proverbs 30:7-9). I recognize, Jesus, that, since there is still jealousy in me, I am still worldly (I Corinthians 3:3). I no longer want to be worldly but heavenly-minded. I understand that a heart at peace gives life to the body, but envy rots the bones (Proverbs 27:4). I thank You, Abba Father, that I no longer have to give way to jealousy or greed. I purpose to be a cheerful giver content with what I have, thankful You have not forsaken me. Amen.

Scripture References:

"For everything in the world – the lust of the flesh, the lust of the eyes, and the pride of life – comes not from the Father but from the world (I John 2:16)."

"Whoever loves money never has enough; whoever loves wealth is never satisfied with their income. This too is meaningless (Ecclesiastes 5:10)."

"Keep your lives free from the love of money and be content with what you have, because God has said, "Never will I leave you; never will I forsake you (Hebrews 13:5).""

Journaling

Freedom Scriptures and Commentary

"So if the Son makes you free, you will be free indeed (John 8:26)."

Definition of Freedom:
1. the quality or state of being free
2. the absence of necessity, coercion, or constraint in choice or action
3. liberation from slavery or restraint or from the power of another
4. independence
5. the quality or state of being exempt or released usually from something onerous <*freedom from care*>

Freedom from What?

So the questions on everyone's minds must be, "*What, exactly, is freedom in Christ? Freedom from what? Is it merely freedom from hell?*" Yes, of course, freedom from hell, but much more. It's freedom from all things burdensome. Freedom from the heavy yoke of slavery birthed through the sin of Adam. The "yoke of slavery" is more about the mind than physical slavery. As we all know, we're all enslaved physically in one way or another: e.g., enslaved by the burden of finances, jobs, spouses, children, addictions, emotions, habits, greed, lust, anger, rage, hatred, prejudice, gossip, and so on. Bondage is the way of the world's corrupt system and run by ole slew foot, Satan.

I know men and women locked in physical prisons freer than most sitting every Sunday in church pews. Why? Because they know the freedom of the mind that can come only from Christ, from total surrender to the One True God. Having the appearance of freedom isn't the same as experiencing it. Anyone who calls upon the name of the Lord shall be saved. This ushers freedom from hell eternal. Surrendering to the God who rescued you from hell is a whole other level.

As I've written in numerous books, surrender to Christ is not the same as being saved from hell. Surrender ushers freedom because it is death of self. A dead man is 100% free from the plight of this life. When we are tossed to and fro by varying people's opinions, unsure of who we are, or of the God-purpose for our life, self is active, and we cannot differentiate right from wrong, or wisdom from opinion. When tossed in such a fashion, we are bound, in a sense, to the confusion that besets us.

When we consign ourselves to the Kingdom of God, we're throwing away everything. That includes the need and want to people-please, any man-made course we've set for ourselves or by others, and any purpose contrived by the flesh. We're saying, in essence, *"Father, in my bondage, I cannot make right and godly decisions. I recognize I cannot please all people—or any fully; therefore, I defer to Your life, purity, clarity, sovereignty, and purpose for my life. Show me Your way, and I will not deter from it no matter what anyone says."*

This alone is how people locked in physical prisons can be so free, free from worry, guilt, shame, condemnation, what others think of them, and so on. Freedom is exclusively a matter of the mind, not the body. Case in point, countless people live in large homes with unlimited finances to go and do whatever, whenever, but, in their minds, they are bound by sorrow, hurt, pain, confusion, turmoil, opinions of others, and much of the like. They are prisoners.

Christ has called us to freedom—freedom from everything of this world, everything man-made, and everything not of God. Freedom is not for the faint of heart! It requires boldness married to humility and integrity. Some may say this is an oxymoron attempting to combine such contrasting attitudes, but I assure you, since Christ walked in them simultaneously, so can all who have become one with Him.

First, freedom requires a boldness to not back down in a decision that is in direct opposition to what those around you are doing. Secondly, it requires humility to not be prideful in our stance against the norm. Thirdly, freedom insists on being unswervingly undivided and incorruptible.

When I was initially called to write and publish my first book, *What was God Thinking*, believe me, there was scoffing from many locations, including my family. After all, I have no formal education, only what I've learned through the power of intimacy with Holy Spirit. Certainly, and thankfully, there were those select few who saw the vision and assisted, but it was not from outlets that were otherwise close to me. I was surprised both by those who stood beside me with encouragement and financial aid, as well as with families who couldn't wrap their brains around me as an author.

Because I was confident in the calling upon my life, I was neither offended nor swayed by the naysayers. They were people I loved dearly, but God's directive trumped their opinions. Not for a moment did I allow myself to become double-minded, thinking, "*What if they're right? What if I can't write? What if I royally flub it? What if no one wants to read my books? What if people think I'm a joke?*" It never crossed my mind *not* to do as God instructed. Sometimes I'm so oblivious to anything outside my goal that I don't recognize negativity.

When I think of grown adults taking poles to attain the most popular opinion amongst their friends and family, I think of middle-school students who are so immature they don't know what they're about, what they like and dislike, or for what they stand. A free, mature person in Christ who daily seeks the heart of God need not go with the majority. Because they are so attuned to how God created them, they are secure and are stopped by nothing. They do not base their decisions on emotions—their own or others—but on what is right. They know the difference between opinion and true godly counsel. This is freedom in Christ.

Journaling

THIRTY-THREE

Freedom

Prayer:

Thank You, my Redeemer, that You have given me freedom from bondage. You, majestic Lord of lords, have taken my entire sin-nature that afflicted me and transferred me into the Kingdom of light and life everlasting. I can't give enough gratitude to You that, though men and demons attempt to hold me in darkness, You, the God of liberty, have given me freedom from my past, freedom from condemnation, freedom from lies, fear, and shame, and freedom from man's fickle opinions. I repent as dust and ash recognizing my worthless estate, and I receive all Your worth that You so graciously share. I bless You for not only removing the shackles, but shattering them. I receive my liberty. Selah

Scripture References:

> "For He rescued us from the domain of darkness, and transferred us to the Kingdom of His beloved Son, in whom we have redemption, the forgiveness of sins (Colossians 1:13-14)."

"I am the Lord, I have called You in righteousness, I will also hold You by the hand and watch over You, and I will appoint You as a covenant to the people, as a light to the nations, to open blind eyes, to bring out prisoners from the dungeon, and those who dwell in darkness from the prison (Isaiah 42:6-7)."

"Therefore I retract, and I repent in dust and ashes (Job 42:6)."

Journaling

THIRTY-FOUR
Freedom from Religious Bondage

Prayer:

Father, I pray for my spiritual eyes to be opened, deaf ears unstopped, and the veil from my mind to be lifted. Show the way out of the ceremonial, religious traditions made by the hands of man. Transition me into Your holiness, righteousness, love, and freedom. May nothing stand in my way from walking the path of liberty You paved before me. I thank You in advance for nothing to keep me from Your freedom, love, wisdom, knowledge, and guidance. Lead me not into temptation but deliver me from evil, in Jesus' name. Open Your Word to me and illuminate the eyes of my understanding that I may know the hope of my calling in Christ Jesus. When I start to feel the shackles of life, remind me I don't need to get free—I am already free. Amen.

Scripture References:

"But their minds were hardened; for until this very day at the reading of the old covenant the same veil remains unlifted, because it is removed in Christ. But to this day whenever Moses is read, a veil lies over their heart; but whenever a person turns to the Lord, the veil is taken away. Now the Lord is Spirit, and where the Spirit of the Lord is, there is liberty (II Corinthians 3:14-17)."

"Then the eyes of the blind will be opened and the ears of the deaf will be unstopped. Then the lame will leap like a deer, and the tongue of the mute will shout for joy. For waters will break forth in the wilderness and streams in the Arabah (Isaiah 35:5-6)."

Read Matthew 23

Journaling

THIRTY-FIVE

Freedom from Rejection

Prayer:

When I, the righteous, cry for help, You hear and deliver me out of all my troubles. You, LORD, ARE near to the brokenhearted and save the crushed in spirit. Right now, that is me. Many are my afflictions, but You deliver me out of them all. You keep all my bones; not one of them is broken. For You will not forsake Your people. You will not abandon Your heritage, and I am Your heritage and Your people. For I am a people holy to YOU. You have chosen me to be a people for Your treasured possession of all the peoples who are on the face of the Earth. My people have rejected me, but You, the Almighty, have received me (Ezekiel 16). Thank You for loving me unconditionally and without measure. May I come to know the height, width, length, and depth of Your everlasting love and reciprocate it back to You (Ephesians 3:18).

Scripture References:

"The righteous cry, and the Lord hears and delivers them out of all their troubles. The Lord is near to the brokenhearted and saves those who are crushed in spirit. Many are the afflictions of the righteous, but the Lord delivers him out of them all. He keeps all his bones, not one of them is broken (Psalm 34:17-20)."

"For the Lord will not abandon His people, nor will He forsake His inheritance (Psalm 94:14)."

"For you are a holy people to the Lord your God, and the Lord has chosen you to be a people for His own possession out of all the peoples who are on the face of the Earth (Deuteronomy 14:2)."

"But God demonstrates His own love toward us, in that while we were yet sinners, Christ died for us (Romans 5:8)."

Read Ezekiel 16

Journaling

THIRTY-SIX

Freedom from Shame and Condemnation

Prayer:

Father, because of the blood shed for me on Calvary, I release every ounce of shame, lies, fear, guilt, and condemnation over to You. Remind me who I am in You. Jesus, You gave Your life that I could walk as a free person on this Earth. May I never forsake or reject that which You have given to me as a gift. May I walk upright in heart and spirit, knowing that I have been redeemed from my sins, past, present, and future. I thank You that I no longer have to carry the load of guilt and reproach I brought upon myself. I release it all to You and receive the new robe of righteousness set aside by You just for me! Blessings to You, great God of Heaven and Earth! There is now no condemnation in those who love the Lord, who walk not according to the flesh but according to the Spirit, and since that is the life I choose, I am grateful that I don't have to walk in shame and condemnation any longer. Though my past is tainted immeasurably, my present and future are clean because of Jesus' blood transfusion within me. Since I have been redeemed and Christ is my life, there is no condemnation or shame for me because there is none for Christ. Amen

Scripture References:

"Therefore there is now no condemnation for those who are in Christ Jesus. For the law of the Spirit of life in Christ Jesus has set you free from the law of sin and of death (Romans 8:1-2)."

"For the Scripture says, "Whoever believes in Him will not be ashamed (Romans 10:11)."

"So if the Son makes you free, you will be free indeed (John 8:36)."

"There is therefore now no condemnation to them which are in Christ Jesus, who walk not after the flesh, but after the Spirit...And we know that all things work together for good to them that love God, to them who are called according to His purpose (Romans 8:1, 28, KJV)."

"I put on righteousness, and it clothed me; my justice was like a robe and a turban (Job 29:14)."

"It was given to her to clothe herself in fine linen, bright and clean; for the fine linen is the righteous acts of the saints (Revelation 19:8)."

"I will rejoice greatly in the Lord, my soul will exult in my God; for He has clothed me with garments of salvation, He has wrapped me with a robe of righteousness, as a bridegroom decks himself with a garland, and as a bride adorns herself with her jewels (Isaiah 61:10)."

Journaling

THIRTY-SEVEN
Governing Authorities

Commentary: (from *Extinguishing the Inferno of Anger*, chapter 19)

I dare say that people's jobs cause daily anger more than most things. Dealing with fellow employees who don't see or do things as us can certainly cause dissension and irritation, but I want to discuss bad bosses specifically. Bad bosses can rile the most calm of temperaments! As with anything, the best and most productive approach to dealing with bad bosses is through the written Word of God. There the Lord instructs us precisely how we are to handle situations where our "masters" are ungodly and unfair.

Ephesians 6:5 begins with the words, "Slaves..." When we are employed, we are, in essence, a *slave* to those who compensate us for certain tasks. We are to be obedient in their instruction lest it goes against our morals, integrity, or overall well-being. I often think of Joseph and Daniel when dealing with this subject matter. Both had to submit to rulers and rules set against God. Joseph did not argue or defend himself to Potiphar when falsely accused of rape. He went to prison, trusting that God had a better plan in store. Daniel did not openly mock the king or his rules; he stayed on course, praying as he always did. He did not do it to rebel against human authority, but in his home, quietly. In the end, the king who set a "stupid" rule in motion did everything possible to get Daniel out of harm's way as he respected Daniel.

Humility in tough situations is something entirely supernatural – of Holy Spirit; it is not of the fleshly man. Humility will be the best combatant against anger and its counterparts. Few accomplish this because most Christians allow their flesh to rule instead of Holy Spirit within. It requires prayer and supplication (constant communion with and focus on the Lord) at all times and in all things. Humility is being willing to submit to God and trusting in His ways instead of seeing it only as unto the unreasonable boss, person(s) or set of earthly rules.

For those of us who are in Christ, we must submit to God first and foremost. If we are "Christian" in title only, that shallow title will not aid us in our conflict with unruly authority or anyone else. Ephesians 6 above goes on to state, "…be obedient to those who are your masters according to the flesh, with fear and trembling, in the sincerity of your heart, as to Christ; not by way of eye-service, as men-pleasers, but as slaves of Christ, doing the will of God from the heart…" We must work as *unto God*, not as *unto man*. This is a terribly difficult concept for people to understand. We live in the fleshly nature, which earnestly desires to fight and to stand against that which is annoying, irritating, and otherwise unbearable for us.

But God (that's a bold statement in itself). But God calls us to obedience to *Him*, and, in our God-obedience, we must be respectful, honorable, and humble. "Slaves, in all things, obey those who are your masters on earth, not with external service, as those who merely please men, but with sincerity of heart, fearing the Lord. Whatever you do, do your work heartily, as for the Lord rather than for men, knowing that from the Lord, you will receive the reward of the inheritance. It is the Lord Christ whom you serve. For he who does wrong will receive the consequences of the wrong which he has done, and that without partiality," reads Colossians 3:22-25. Here again, the passage begins with "slaves" and going further to say we are to obey those who are our masters on earth and how we are to do it. Reading along, we find we are reminded that we reap whatever we sow into our lives, into the earth, and into the kingdom of heaven.

Humility is foreign to this natural estate. The Word of God must be applied on purpose with intense focus on the humility of Jesus. Knowing Judas would betray Him, he kissed him and broke bread with him; He even washed his feet! Joseph, knowing the treacherous deeds of his brothers, forgave, blessed, and protected them. Both Jesus and Joseph were able to tap into the heart of God the Father so deeply that they reacted according to the bigger picture. Jesus saved the entire human race. On a smaller scale, Joseph saved an entire population spanning the entire world at that time. They did not rally against their oppressors. Jesus allowed Himself to be taken by the authorities of the land. Joseph honored the rulers over him: Potiphar, the prison authorities, and Pharaoh. In each place, Joseph, through his humility, ended up ruling in their stead because they trusted and respected Joseph (their servant).

We must, at least we who are called of Christ, insist that humility rule where our employers are concerned (and every other area of life). If and when we do not, rage will build like a fiery inferno. We will retaliate in word and deed. We will cease completing our appointed jobs with integrity feeling our bosses owe us something. Our unrighteous judgment of them will lead down a bad road, to be sure.

Judging Our Authority:

"Do not judge so that you will not be judged (Matthew 7:1)."

"For rebellion is as the sin of divination (witchcraft), and insubordination is as iniquity and idolatry (I Samuel 15:23)."

It is exceedingly difficult, nay, impossible, for the flesh of mankind to not pass judgment on those who offend us, namely our authority. However, exclusively, it is in the Spirit of God that we are supernaturally capable of refraining from passing such judgment. Suffice it to say, there is no one who can say honestly that judgment does not cross their mind and heart occasionally. It is, after all, human nature. We must remember that we who are in Christ are no longer of the human race, but of the heavenly race. We are but strangers and aliens in the earth sent from heaven to bring heaven down to earth.

Because of the nature of man in which we were born and currently reside, it is altogether a necessity to hone in on the Spirit of God within the born-again believer through the spirit-man. If we do not daily (moment to moment sometimes) purposefully tap into Holy Spirit, we will find ourselves in the midst of fleshly judgment. We can defend it all day long, especially when it comes to bosses but, unless we choose to recognize that we have indeed passed judgment in our hearts, that judgment will lead to fierce animosity, anger, and wrath. It will cause us to become rebellious against God and our authority.

When I speak of rebellion, I am speaking of rebellion against God because, when we rebel against our set authority, we are, in fact, going against God Himself. Whether it is our direct authority on the job, our governing officials, parents, or anyone else set above us, we must oblige them; again, unless it goes against God or our walk with God. Although your boss may appear as an enemy, we're back to engaging them as unto God, not as unto their unreasonable demands. It's time to tackle our anger against our authorities with a kingdom-of-God perspective instead of flesh and blood. Remember, our war is not against mankind but rulers and evils of darkness.

When you feel yourself steaming over a dumb move of your boss, pause, breathe, and wait upon the Lord. Pray and seek His guidance rather than act on biased judgment or the heat of a moment. Study the Word to show yourselves approved of God. We must intend to be an "unashamed workman." II Timothy 2:14-16 reads, "Remind them of these things, and solemnly charge them in the presence of God not to wrangle about words, which is useless and leads to the ruin of the hearers. Be diligent to present yourselves approved of God as a workman who does not need to be ashamed, accurately handling the word of truth. But avoid worldly and empty chatter, for it will lead to further ungodliness, and their talk will spread like gangrene…"

I love the words, "Be diligent to present yourselves approved of God" because, in this condition, we will become a "workman who does not need to be ashamed." Refrain from getting together with co-workers and trash-talking your boss. Keep your lips from idle and empty words, which would serve only to fan the flame of rage. Pray for your boss. Pray for guidance on whether or not you should seek new employment, but whatever you do, don't be rash in your decision to stay or go, to confront your boss, or to remain silent. Always keep the emotion of anger in its rightful place, share it with the Father, wait upon the prompting of Holy Spirit, and then, and only then, go forward with the plans He lays on your heart. This will keep your anger from becoming sin.

Prayer:

In the name of Jesus, I thank you, Father, that I have the power to submit to the governing authorities because You have placed them in office. Show me how to pray diligently in allegiance to Your holy will for them. Guide me into all righteousness so that I do not rebel against You. Show me when to and how to obey. I choose not to sin against Your holiness. Give me eyes to see authority as You see them. Teach me the humility of Christ, my Savior and Lord, so that I do not arise in my emotions and sin against You. When dealing with evil authority, help me to pray and respond like Daniel. Help me to pray out those who are evil and pray in those anointed in holiness. Amen

Scripture References:

> Every person is to be in subjection to the governing authorities. For there is no authority except from God, and those which exist are established by God. Therefore whoever resists authority has opposed the ordinance of God; and they who have opposed will receive condemnation upon themselves. For rulers are not a cause of fear for good behavior, but for evil. Do you want to have no fear of authority? Do what is good and you will have praise from the same; for it is a minister of God to you for good. But if you do what is evil, be afraid; for it does not bear the sword for nothing; for it is a minister of God, an avenger who brings wrath on the one who practices evil. Therefore *it is necessary to be in subjection, not only because of wrath, but also for conscience' sake.* For because of this you also pay taxes, for rulers are servants of God, devoting themselves to this very thing. Render to all what is due them: tax to whom tax is due; custom to whom custom; fear to whom fear; honor to whom honor (Romans 13:1-7).

> Now when Daniel knew that the document was signed, he entered his house (now in his roof chamber he had windows open toward Jerusalem); and he continued kneeling on his knees three times a day, praying and giving thanks before his God, as he had been doing previously. Then these men came by agreement and found Daniel making petition and supplication before his God. Then

they approached and spoke before the king about the king's injunction, "Did you not sign an injunction that any man who makes a petition to any god or man besides you, O king, for thirty days, is to be cast into the lion' den?" The king replied, "The statement is true, according to the law of the Medes and Persians, which may not be revoked." Then they answered and spoke before the king, "Daniel, who is one of the exiles from Judah, pays no attention to you, O king, or to the injunction which you signed, but keeps making his petition three times a day."

"For rebellion is as the sin of divination (witchcraft), and insubordination is as iniquity and idolatry (I Samuel 15:23)."

Slaves, be obedient to those who are your masters according to the flesh, with fear and trembling, in the sincerity of your heart, as to Christ; not by way of eye-service, as men-pleasers, but as slaves of Christ, doing the will of God from the heart. With good will render service, as to the Lord, and not to men, knowing that whatever good thing each one does, this he will receive back from the Lord, whether slave or free. And masters, do the same things to them, and give up threatening, knowing that both their Master and yours is in heaven, and there is no partiality with Him (Ephesians 6:5-9).

Journaling

THIRTY-EIGHT

Grief

Prayer:

My Husband, Comforter, and Savior, bless Your holy name in all the Earth. You know my heartbreak, pain, and sorrow in this very moment. I feel so utterly alone, abandoned, and without hope. Nevertheless, I place my full faith and confidence in You that, no matter the anguish I am currently experiencing, I know You are the Healer and lover of my soul. O God, You are my God, earnestly I seek You; my soul thirsts for You; my flesh faints for You, as in a dry and weary land where there is no water. So I look upon You in the sanctuary, beholding Your power and glory. Because Your steadfast love is better than life, my lips will praise You. I will bless You as long as I live; in Your name, I will lift my hands (Psalm 63). The Lord is my rock, my fortress, and my deliverer; my buckler, and the horn of my salvation, and my high tower. I will call upon the Lord, who is worthy to be praised: so shall I be saved from mine enemies and grief. The sorrows of death compassed me, and the floods of ungodly men made me afraid. The sorrows of hell compassed me about: the snares of death prevented me. In my distress, I call upon the Lord, and cry unto my God: You hear my voice out of Your temple, and my cry comes before You, even into Your ears. It is God who saves me. You gird me with strength, and make my way perfect. You make my feet like hinds' feet and set me upon high places (Psalm 18). Father, thank You for seeing me through this extremely difficult time of anguish. I am expecting great things through this tragedy because of Your great and mighty promises. I trust Your sovereignty. I praise You in all things and every circumstance (Romans 8:28). Selah

Scripture References:

"He will wipe away every tear from their eyes. There will be no more death or mourning or crying or pain, for the old order of things has passed away (Revelation 21:4)."

"And we know that in all things God works for the good of those who love Him, who have been called according to His purpose (Romans 8:28)."
"The Lord is close to the brokenhearted and saves those who are crushed in spirit (Psalm 34:18)."

"He heals the brokenhearted and binds up their wounds (Psalm 147:3)."

"Do not let your hearts be troubled. You believe in God; believe also in Me (John 14:1)."

Read Psalm 63 and 18

Journaling

THIRTY-NINE
God's Will Above All

Prayer:

Our Father, who art in Heaven, hallowed be Your name. Your Kingdom come, Your will be done, on Earth as it is in Heaven. Give me this day my daily bread and forgive me my debts, as I also have forgiven my debtors. Do not lead me into temptation, but deliver and give me the strength to run from evil. For Yours is the Kingdom, and the power, and the glory forever (Matthew 6:9-13). Allow me the privilege of having unity of heart with You. You replace my life. May I go nowhere You are not leading; may I leave every place where You are not in control. Supernaturally help me to remove myself from my comfort zone. Take me to the places of discomfort so that You will be able to teach me to grow beyond what I can see with my natural eyes. I thank You, Lord, that I see as You see, hear as You hear, and think as You think. Change my perspective from the earthly to the heavenly. I love and adore You, O King of kings. May I never leave You nor forsake You till the end of eternity. Amen

Scripture References:

"Our Father who is in Heaven, hallowed be Your name. Your Kingdom come, Your will be done, on Earth as it is in Heaven (Matthew 6:9-10)."

"Father, if You are willing, remove this cup from Me; yet not My will, but Yours be done (Luke 22:42)."

"For I through the law died to the law that I might live to God. I have been crucified with Christ; it is no longer I who live but Christ who lives in me; and the life which I now live in the flesh I live by faith in the Son of God, who loved me and gave Himself for me (Galatians 2:19-20)."

Journaling

FORTY

Holiness

Prayer:

Show me, Lord, how to be holy as You are holy. Establish me in faith so that I will not be tossed about by every wind of doctrine. Daily guide my footsteps so I will walk the straight and narrow path set by Your dear Son, Jesus. I love You. Continue to grow me in love so that my walk may be pure and holy, forgiving, and without spot or wrinkle. Let love and faith work in my life that I may be pleasing to You, O gracious Savior. Reveal my temptations so that I will be quick to flee from them and slow to go near them. Let me have a God-consciousness at all times so, when I sin, I will be quick to recognize, repent, and allow communion with You to be restored. Bless You, O my Lord God and Redeemer, in all the Earth. May Your name be proclaimed forever and ever. Amen.

Scripture References:

"Therefore, since we have these promises, dear friends, let us purify ourselves from everything that contaminates body and spirit, perfecting holiness out of reverence for God (II Corinthians 7:1:)."

"But just as He who called you is holy, so be holy in all you do; for it is written: 'Be holy, because I am holy I Peter 1:15-16: (I Peter 1:15-16).'"

"How can a young person stay on the path of purity? By living according to Your word (Psalm 119:9)."

"Search me, God, and know my heart; test me and know my anxious thoughts. See if there is any wicked way in me, and lead me in the way everlasting (Psalm 139:23-24)."

Do everything without grumbling or arguing, so that you may become blameless and pure, children of God without fault in a warped and crooked generation. Then you will shine among them like stars in the sky as you hold firmly to the word of life (Philippians 2:14-16).

Holy Spirit Scriptures and Commentary

"And do not get drunk with wine, for that is dissipation, but be filled with the Spirit (Ephesians 5:18)."

"…Lord Jesus, who appeared to you on the road by which you were coming, has sent me so that you may regain your sight and be filled with the Holy Spirit (Acts 9:17)."

"Then Peter, filled with the Holy Spirit, said to them… (Acts 4:8)."

"And when they had prayed, the place where they had gathered together was shaken, and they were all filled with the Holy Spirit and began to speak the word of God with boldness (Acts 4:31)."

"For the flesh sets its desire against the Spirit, and the Spirit against the flesh; for these are in opposition to one another, so that you may not do the things that you please (Galatians 5:17)."

"By this we know that we abide in Him and He in us, because He has given us of His Spirit (I John 4:13)."

"For the mind set on the flesh is death, but the mind set on the Spirit is life and peace (Romans 8:6)."

"Then he said to me, This is the word of the Lord to Zerubbabel saying, 'Not by might nor by power, but by My Spirit,' says the Lord of hosts (Zechariah 4:6)."

Time and time again, we see "filled with the Spirit." We need to be "filled with the Spirit," not just in words, but in truth. The Spirit of God must immeasurably flow and overflow through us. How can one appropriately pray lest they are filled with the Spirit who knows God, is God, and has complete faith in Himself? How can one trust in utter confidence lest they are filled with the Spirit who trusts Himself?

Without Holy Spirit, can God's mouth, hands, and feet, continue to do this ceremonial church-thing we've been practicing for centuries? How long until we recognize we've been doing a lot with excellent intentions but utterly the wrong way? We cannot be generous without Holy Spirit. We cannot be holy, lest the Spirit who is holy is allowed to rule through our otherwise tainted person. Holiness can stem only from one who is holy. Beauty can come only from the root of One who is beautiful. Love can blossom only from the root of love—and that is the Holy Spirit. *"The fruit of the Spirit is love..."* and so on.

Let us purpose to be filled and driven to the fullest measure of God's Spirit. If we do not, we will continue to exhaust ourselves, attempting with futility to be "good" absent of the One who is good; we'll continue to be defeated. Thistles and thorns (the fleshly man) cannot produce anything good—fruit of the Spirit. "And behold, I am sending forth the promise of My Father upon you; but you are to stay in the city until you are clothed with power from on high (Luke 24:49)."

> "As for me, I baptize you with water for repentance, but He who is coming after me is mightier than I, and I am not fit to remove His sandals; He will baptize you with the Holy Spirit and fire. His winnowing fork is in His hand, and He will thoroughly clear His threshing floor; and He will gather His wheat into the barn, but He will burn up the chaff with unquenchable fire." Then Jesus arrived from Galilee at the

Jordan coming to John, to be baptized by him. But John tried to prevent Him, saying, "I have need to be baptized by You, and do You come to me?" But Jesus answering said to him, "Permit it at this time; for in this way it is fitting for us to fulfill all righteousness." Then he permitted Him. After being baptized, Jesus came up immediately from the water; and behold, the Heavens were opened, and he saw the Spirit of God descending as a dove and lighting on Him, and behold, a voice out of the Heavens said, "This is My beloved Son, in whom I am well-pleased (Matthew 3:11-17).

Do not let your heart be troubled; believe in God, believe also in Me. In My Father's house are many dwelling places; if it were not so, I would have told you; for I go to prepare a place for you. If I go and prepare a place for you, I will come again and receive you to Myself, that where I am, there you may be also. And you know the way where I am going…I will ask the Father, and He will give you another Helper, that He may be with you forever; that is the Spirit of truth, whom the world cannot receive, because it does not see Him or know Him, but you know Him because He abides with you and will be in you…but the Helper, the Holy Spirit, whom the Father will send in My name, He will teach you all things, and bring to your remembrance all that I said to you (John 14:1-5, 16-17, 26).

We're back to the point that, if Jesus couldn't fulfill His mission without Holy Spirit direction, we need Holy Spirit leading. Jesus had to be water baptized as a representation of His spiritual baptism. He had to be "baptized" into His Spirit for God to say, *"This is My beloved Son, in whom I am well pleased."* If such baptism was required of Jesus to hear those words from the Father, we are no different today.

Everywhere I look, I see our garden-variety of denominations whose congregants are very, very busy. They're busy doing a lot of "good stuff," but, at the root, most are not Holy Spirit led. I do not say this to insult or belittle anyone. I only desire that the body of Christ will learn how to be instructed by God's Spirit. When we begin to hear Him, we'll be a lot less exhausted and worn to a frazzle.

"My yoke is easy and My burden is light" are Jesus' words in Matthew 11:30. I've said it many times over, yet it bears repeating. If our yoke is hard and our burden is heavy, it is not of God. It's one of the easiest ways to determine if something we're doing is of Holy Spirit or the flesh. Perpetually, we do things because someone says, *"Hey, you'd be really good at this"* or *"I really, really need your help"* or some variation thereof. We hear these words and immediately feel compelled by guilt or flattery— emotionalism— to enter the plea of man.

Unfortunately, though our intentions are good in desiring to help someone or some project, we are still not being led by the Spirit. We are being strung by the nose and influenced by emotions, emotions that make us feel obliged, yet, all the while, know our plate is too full of other, more critical tasks. How many times have we begun something and almost immediately thought, *"Oh, dear. Into what have I gotten myself?"* It isn't that we don't sometimes feel that when it *is* of the Spirit, but there is an inner "knowing" as to whether it is of God or another source.

With the baptism of Holy Spirit, He is made alive within us so much that we can profess, *"It is no longer I who live, but Christ who lives in me."* We have it backward when we instruct someone to get "saved" and then get baptized by water emersion. The instruction should be as that of the Word of God: *"Peter said to them, 'Repent, and each of you be baptized in the name of Jesus Christ for the forgiveness of your sins; and you will receive the gift of the Holy Spirit* (Acts 2:38).'"

We have made things far too complicated. One needs to repent and then be baptized spiritually in the Holy Spirit. With such baptism, when we read or hear the Word, Holy Spirit will supernaturally make it understandable and relatable. As it is in the modern-day church, we tell one to repent, get saved, get baptized with water, read the Word, and then follow the Word. Yikes! I did it that way, and, though fulfilling some biblical instruction seemed attainable, most did not, especially as I grew older.

We comprehend that the only way to accomplish such a daunting task of holiness is to die to self. Dying to self allows us to have the life of the Spirit, not only living in us, but also being allowed to become the air we breathe; I cannot state that enough. This is a level of accountability and responsibility most do not want. Few want to give up self. Most people want to retain a portion of self and Christ, but it does not work that way. It is to be zero self and 100% God. Many charismatic believers miss this vital part. They errantly assume that being *filled* with the Spirit automatically causes them to be *led* by the Spirit. This is inaccurate and dangerous.

Kingdom-living is not commonly what we witness in the churches. The Lord isn't interested in busy work. It is a place of total rest where we are not working, but, instead, allowing the completed work of Christ to pour through us while in a state of rest. This can only come through the baptism of Holy Spirit.

Sons and Holy Spirit:

> However, you are not in the flesh but the Spirit, if indeed the Spirit of God dwells in you. But if anyone does not have the Spirit of Christ, he does not belong to Him… *for all who are being led by the Spirit of God, these are sons of God*…the Spirit Himself testifies with our spirit that we are children of God (Romans 8:9, 14, 16).

We read above in Romans 8:14, "*All who are being led by the Spirit of God, these are sons of God.*" I like to look at the opposite of any statement, promise, or command. It lends a better grasp of what is being said. The opposite of the above statement would read, "*All who are not led by the Spirit of God; these are not sons of God.*" Likewise, it could read, "*All who are not being led by the Spirit of God, these are sons of Satan.*" If that doesn't get our attention, I certainly do not know what would! It's a daunting thought, indeed.

I believe, as I have stated in other writings, most people who think themselves "saved" are not saved at all. I don't know who formulated the "sinner's prayer," but I don't see it anywhere in the Bible, at least not the way we approach the concept. As we've already read, we are to repent and be baptized in the Holy Spirit. With that baptism, I don't see anyone praying our traditional "sinner's prayer."

I realize it is derived from Romans 10:9 "*...if you confess with your mouth Jesus as Lord, and believe in your heart God raised Him from the dead, you will be saved,*" but we must also take account of the entire instruction, not just one or two texts. After all, to believe in our heart, authentically believe, is to place all faith in the One in whom we believe. Far too many mutter the man-made "sinner's prayer," yet no transition from death unto life has occurred. They have yet to be transformed by the renewing of their minds. Just because someone speaks words, those words are empty without actions to follow from a heart set on obedience to God.

The only way to have actions to follow such an expression of faith is for the person to be baptized into the Holy Spirit, which means they surrender—lose, give away—their own life to receive Christ's new life. Some have argued, "*I desire to be led by the Spirit, but I know I falter from time to time*" as if to invalidate the above statement in Romans 8:14.

My response is per the Word. The Bible tells us that we all falter as there is a constant battle between the flesh and the Spirit.

God tells us that He chastens those who are His sons, and He does so because we *are* His sons, albeit we go astray from time to time (Hebrews 12:7-8). He wouldn't have to correct those who never make a mistake, assuring us that we all make mistakes and are still sons. That being said, we ought not to make excuses for blatant and continual sinful behavior. We should not seek to excuse the flesh but try to find the voice and instruction of Holy Spirit on a deeper level from where we are.

Instead of posing the excuse, *"I'm just human,"* we must recognize we are no longer human but altogether supernatural of the heavenly realm. In so doing, we will begin to seek God's face and His perfect will through Holy Spirit while living in the fleshly temple. Holy Spirit breaks all chains of the traditions of man and, once we follow the true spirit (Holy Spirit vs. the spirit of man and Satan), we'll cease struggling as we once did. The flesh will always want to override Holy Spirit, but the Spirit will cause more ease of obedience.

It is with the utmost urgency that we believe we are saved and understand what it is to be saved, both from hell and this perverse generation. We also need to understand *into* what we have been transitioned—the Kingdom of Heaven. The transition into the Kingdom of God should be emphasized far more than whence we have been transferred *out*—hell and the flesh.

Whose Child are You?

> By this we know that we love the *children of God*, when we love God and observe His commandments. (I John 5:2)."

> By this the *children of God* and the *children of the devil* are obvious: anyone who does not practice righteousness is not of God, nor the one who does not love his brother. (I John 3:10)."

"Blessed are the peacemakers, for they shall be called *sons of God* (Matthew 5:9)."

"But *love your enemies*, and do good, and lend, expecting nothing in return; and your reward will be great, and you will be *sons of the Most High*; for He Himself is kind to ungrateful and evil men (Luke 6:35)."

"'While you have the Light, believe in the Light, so that you may become *sons of Light.*' These things Jesus spoke, and He went away and hid Himself from them (John 12:36)."

"Therefore, be sure that it is those who are of faith who are *sons of Abraham*...you are all sons of God through faith in Christ Jesus (Galatians 3:7, 26)."

In the above Scriptures, we see with crystal clarity that the evidence of the *sons* of God:

1. love God
2. obey God's commands
3. practice righteousness
4. love our brother
5. are peacemakers
6. love our enemies
7. do good to our enemies
8. expect nothing in return
9. believe the Light
10. walk in faith

These are merely a few of the evidences of the sons of God. Keep in mind that being a "son" is not about the male gender, but position, just as being the "Bride" of Christ is not about the female gender, but position. For anyone who is a son of God, being driven exclusively by the Spirit is the way to do good to someone who curses us. It is the Spirit within who was kind to evil people, which allows His power to do the impossible. After all, the firstborn Son gave His life for the entire evil human race. We can't do more good than that.

Still, knowing what Christ did, we have already reviewed that Christ could not have made such an accomplishment against the nature of the flesh lest the Spirit of God was leading, directing, and instructing. He even prayed, *"If this cup can pass from Me, nevertheless, Thy will be done."* Only the Son of God could have been able to see beyond the realm of the here-and-now, yet He still required the third person of the Trinity to aid His obedience.

A son of God will be a peacemaker and not a troublemaker; they will give expecting nothing in return, even when they are giving to someone who steals from them. A *child* of God practices righteousness. Notice the first two texts cited above say "*children* of God," but the others following say "*sons* of God." My book, *Thy Kingdom Come: Kingdom vs. Religion*, expressly details the difference between being a child, saved from hell, and a son who is mature and ready to rule.

> However, you are not in the flesh but in the Spirit, if indeed the Spirit of God dwells in you. But if anyone does not have the Spirit of Christ, he does not belong to Him…*for all who are being led by the Spirit of God, these are sons of God*…the Spirit Himself testifies with our spirit that we are children of God (Romans 8:9, 14, 16).

Journaling

FORTY-ONE

Holy Spirit: Fan the Flame

Prayer:

Father, I pray for Your endless flame to burn me from the inside out; that You will purposefully set ablaze all the wood, hay, and stubble in my life that it be removed as ash and dust. Purify the precious stones, gold, and silver You graciously planted in me before the foundation of the Earth that I may turn and bless You. Allow me the privilege of holiness that I may expand Your Kingdom here on Earth so that You may take back Your land. I welcome Your fire and the trials with which the burning comes. Thank You, Jesus, for loving me enough to burn the iniquity from my midst. Selah.

Scripture References:

> "For this reason I remind you to fan into flame the gift of God, which is in you through the laying on of my hands (II Timothy 1:6, NIV)."

"Beloved, think it not strange concerning the fiery trial which is to try you, as though some strange thing happened unto you; but rejoice, in as much as you are partakers of Christ's sufferings; that, when His glory shall be revealed, you may be glad also with exceeding joy (I Peter 4:12-13, KJV)."

Journaling

FORTY-TWO

Holy Spirit Leading

Prayer:

Father, I call upon Your holy name to be a person who is led by Your Holy Spirit. Show me who You are and how You move through Your Spirit in the Earth. I pray I am a person who understands that, outside Your Spirit, I am powerless and cannot tap into Your holy Kingdom. Reveal Yourself to me with refreshment and invigoration so that I begin to recognize You in all things. May I stop missing You due to a religious spirit and begin to experience You in the freedom from religiosity. I bind a spirit of churchianity and rigid religiosity from my presence and release Your Spirit of liberty and life to be the only Spirit active as my life's breath. Rejuvenate me, and the body of Christ, so that we may serve You in spirit and truth and be washed by the water that ran from the side of Jesus. I desire to see, know, hear, feel, and express Your holiness into the four corners of the Earth. Selah.

Scripture References:

"For all who are being led by the Spirit of God, these are sons of God (Romans 8:14)."

"Teach me to do Your will, for You are my God; let Your good Spirit lead me on level ground (Psalm 143:10)."

"And He will lift up a standard for the nations and assemble the banished ones of Israel, and will gather the dispersed of Judah from the four corner of the Earth (Isaiah 11:12)."

"After this I saw four angels standing at the four corners of the Earth, holding back the four winds of the Earth, so that no wind would blow on the Earth or on the sea or on any tree (Revelation 7:1)."

Journaling

FORTY-THREE

Holy Spirit: Weighing According to the Spirit

Prayer:

Oh, God, how I cry out to You to allow me to see You behind the storm. Help me to be so centered and balanced in every way that I will not react through my flesh, but through Your Spirit, who dwells within me. Teach me, merciful Savior, to be considerate and non-judgy in every situation of life, to weigh everything according to truth and not according to half-truths. Father, I command every lying, deceitful spirit to be bound, gagged, and loosed from its assignment over my family and me. I release Your Holy Spirit to be the only spirit in activity in my life. Reveal everything hidden so that I can get to the root cause of the problem and handle it with grace. As You are merciful and forgiving toward me, show me how to be merciful and forgiving toward others (Exodus 34:6-7). Amen

Scripture References:

"You of little faith, why are you so afraid?" Then He got up and rebuked the winds and the waves, and it was completely calm (Matthew 8:26)."

"Therefore from now on we recognize no one according to the flesh; even though we have known Christ according to the flesh, yet now we know Him in this way no longer (II Corinthians 5:16)."

"A false balance is an abomination to the Lord...the integrity of the upright will guide them, but the crookedness of the treacherous will destroy them (Proverbs 11:1, 3)."

"Differing weights and differing measures, both of them are abominable to the Lord...differing weights are an abomination to the Lord, and a false scale is no good (Proverbs 20:10, 23)."

Journaling

Humility and Pride Scriptures and Commentary

The First Sin:

"The fear of the Lord is to hate evil: I hate pride and arrogance, evil behavior and perverse speech (Proverbs 8:13, NAS)."

"Pride goes before destruction, a haughty spirit before a fall… (Proverbs 16:18, NAS)."

"Do you think the Scripture says without reason that the Spirit He caused to live in us envies intensely? But He gives more grace. That is why the Scripture says: "God opposes the proud, but gives grace to the humble (James 4:5-6, NAS)."

"All of you, clothe yourselves with humility toward one another (I Peter 5:5, NAS)."

Pride was the first sin. As David E. Taylor points out in His book *Victory Over Pride,* Lucifer manifested the only sin that can get in when everything else has been set in order. Pride is the only sin that can attack while in the presence of perfection. Pride is one of the hardest enemies to see or detect. The Scriptures say that pride goes before destruction. That means that pride itself is not destruction, but is sent as an ambassador before the destruction comes. Pride destroys God's people daily. Things such as rebellion, unforgiveness, rage, malice, slander, boasting, self-abasement, and coveting are a few manifestations of pride. To be frank, anything in the form of rebellion against God's

Word all stems from P.R.I.D.E, bar none. All expressions of sin derive from it.

We must allow God to reveal the hidden fruitless deeds of darkness buried deep within us. Pride causes God's grace to be rejected in our lives, even though it has been activated in other areas. Grace comes only in the presence of humility. Look at the next passages.

> "I, Nebuchadnezzar, was at home in my palace, contented, and prosperous (Daniel 4:4, NAS)."

> "While people are saying, 'Peace and safety,' destruction will come on them suddenly, as labor pains on a pregnant woman, and they will not escape (I Thessalonians 5:3, NAS)."

The Scripture in Daniel 4 reads that the king, just before the wrath of God came against him, was content in his home. He had no consciousness of God whatsoever, though he had been warned by Daniel. He thought himself superior, self-sufficient, self-sustaining, self-made. He commended his own hand for having brought himself such superiority among the nations. Pride only seems to be good for a season, but that season will end abruptly. Destruction came in an instant though it took 12 months for it to manifest from the time Daniel spoke the prophecy of destruction. Just when Nebuchadnezzar became comfortable in the luxury of his home, the penance of Pride arrived. Prideful people rest in their wickedness when they need to be warring against the evil in their midst. Pride would not allow the king to humble himself to repent before God, a decision for which he paid dearly.

It's time for God's royal priesthood to take this application and put it to use in our individual lives. Have *you* allowed Pride in your heart? Are *you* allowing Pride to destroy your family, job, health, finances, or, more importantly, your relationship with God? If so, begin to seek inwardly and allow God to reveal all Pride within and then expunge it from your person.

Pride is very tricky and manifests differently from person to person. Since it was the first accounted sin, don't think for one moment anyone is exempt. For the one who shows it outwardly, once they become aware of it, it is relatively simple to remove. Contrarily, for the rest of the Body of Christ, it is not so easily detected; those doing good deeds, going to church regularly, dressing modestly, not stealing, lying, cursing, drinking, smoking, doing drugs, etc. These are the people most susceptible to the lures of Pride. Because Satan is deceptive, he slinks into God's people unawares. He does not come in with forked tail and pitchfork or some ornate Halloween costume – he is beautiful and intensely alluring. II Corinthians 11:14 makes evident he masquerades as a beacon of light, as an angel.

Again, to quote David E. Taylor in *Victory Over Pride*, "Pride always leads you to the high place. Humility leads you to a low place. Pride is whatever makes your head too big for a room… in the world, the leader in a chain of authority is positioned at the top. The pyramid is right-side up. Everyone at the bottom serves the one at the top. However, in the Kingdom of God, the pyramid is upside down. The person who is the greatest is servant to all. The pinnacle is still pointing toward the leader, but the leader is at the bottom serving all. Jesus lowered Himself and served others and exalted all others above Himself, including His enemies. Even on the cross, He prayed for those who hung Him."

World's Authority
Prideful purposing to rise to glory
   having others serve them

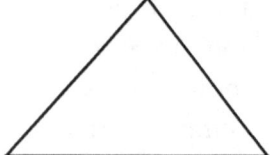 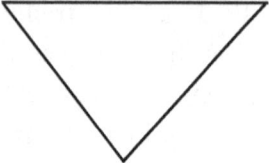

                        Jesus' Authority
               Humbled Himself to serve others and
                  to love His neighbor as Himself

Remain Broken:

> But Jesus called them to Himself and said, "You know that the rulers of the Gentiles lord it over them, and their great men exercise authority over them. It is not this way among you, but whoever wishes to become great among you shall be your servant, and whoever wishes to be first among you shall be your slave; just as the Son of Man did not come to be served, but to serve, and to give His life a ransom for many."
> Matthew 20:26-28 (NAS)

> "But the greatest among you shall be your servant. Whoever exalts himself shall be humbled; and whoever humbles himself shall be exalted (Matthew 23:11, NAS)."

We who are within the Body of Christ are not here to be served but to serve, the same as Jesus, since it is Jesus living through us. Those who desire to be great will be brought down. Christ states that those who serve are the greatest among His people, but those who purpose in the name of Christ Jesus to serve the Body will be highly exalted in due season. Many misunderstand, but there is a vast difference between a slave and a servant. A *slave* is in bondage to his master and has no choice, therefore becomes easily embittered. A *servant,* on the other hand, is employed by choice by his superior. He serves with diligence because his payment is imminent.

A *bondservant* is a person released from slavery by their master, yet chooses to remain out of dedication and love. This person is willing to do anything they are asked without hesitation or grudge. God's bondservants, who serve with a grateful heart, will be rewarded in the Kingdom of Heaven. The lower we humble ourselves before Christ and His people, the higher we are moved toward Christ. We become more of a servant as time goes by, not less. This is the way of the King, and the Father is honored.

Our most significant purpose in this life is to love and glorify the Father. When we are focused on ourselves, we shift the focus from Him. Pride can be very subtle. Remember what I said about those most at risk? It is very easy to find ourselves out of spiritual sync with God because we forget who we serve and who gives us the ability to do what we do. We can easily allow the praises we receive from those around us to puff us internally. Miss Barder, the mentor of the most humble, Watchman Nee, a man of God who suffered intensely for China, spoke this way of humility in the book, *Watchman Nee: Sufferer of China*, page 30:

> "Stay broken. Don't believe all the good things people say about you. You must stay broken. His Word says that if your ways are pleasing to the Lord, He will make your enemies to be at peace with you. He is most pleased with your brokenness. Remember the cross, To-sheng (Watchman Nee). You must stay broken."

When we are in a place of servitude, we must remember there is no good but God. Therefore, if there is good coming from us, it is not us, but Christ through our mortal bodies. Human nature can tend to look down in judgment on those not doing what we are or conducting themselves as well as us. To be judgmental comes from a spirit of pride, and no one is exempt; we've all done it at some point. The key is to be so aware that we don't allow it to remain and take root.

We must be quick to repent of a judgmental spirit and remove that foothold of the enemy. Keep in mind that the Body of Christ is to judge things according to the Spirit of God; this is righteous judgment. That differs significantly from being judgmental (viewing ourselves better than another). We, God's holy people, also need to be careful about starting a *life story* wanting to exalt God yet talk endlessly about ourselves and what *we* did or said in a particular situation. Once again, human nature is to glorify self and get people to be in awe of how humble and selfless we seem to be. This is not behavior indicative of Christ.

(My) Definition of Pride:
Pushing
Righteousness
Into
Dire
Elimination

> "Take My yoke upon you and learn from me, for I am gentle and humble in heart, and you will find rest for your souls (Matthew 11:29, NAS)."

> "For if you forgive men when they sin against you, your Heavenly Father will also forgive you. But if you do not

forgive men their sins, your Father will not forgive your sins (Matthew 6:14-15, NAS)."

The Chair:

"My heavenly Father will also do the same to you, if each of you does not forgive his brother from your heart (Matthew 18:35, NAS)."

According to the Word, pride is an issue everyone somehow, somewhere, needs to confront. Pride takes constant pruning because it grows like weeds and spreads itself as fast and as far as it can. It is unrelenting. One must not assume that, once we have dealt with pride, it is never to be faced again. Our hearts require constant supervision. The fleshly nature is driven by pride; therefore, we all need to be alert regularly.

We all need to be so heavily clothed in the spirit of humility that we can walk in a perpetual internal condition of forgiveness. This translates we are to have forgiveness readily available for those who have *not yet* offended us. Many years ago, I was taught a great technique about alleviating unforgiveness and judgment, which we form against others. The method is to put people in "the chair."

The process is to pull up an empty chair imagining the offender is sitting there. Begin to tell them what they have done to hurt, offend or anger you. Once you have released your irritations, frustrations and heartache, forgive them from the heart. The next step is to confess to God and repent of all judgment forged against them. Pray and ask God to apply His forgiveness to you for the judgment you've held in your heart against them.

This is an excellent technique for purging oneself of hidden unforgiveness and judgment. Pride is the only thing standing in the way of forgiveness. Getting *our* hearts clean is *our* issue, not whether or not they hear our plea or receive our forgiveness or apology for what they did wrong. It has nothing to do with the other person at all.

I have heard, "*Well, I think putting people in the chair is a cop-out. Every time I repent of my unforgiveness, I should go to those people directly to the one who offended me. How they react does not matter, only that I tell them what they did wrong, how it affected me, what is going on with me, and that I forgive them anyway.*" There are times when we should go to an actual person. If the one who hurt or offended us is a friend, they should be able to listen, apologize for their action, and forgive us for whatever we've held in our hearts against them.

If they are a friend, the question we should ask ourselves is, "Why am I offended?" Then we should ask, "Are they someone that would purposely hurt me?" If not, consider they did not mean to hurt us and don't let their misstep offend any longer. Otherwise, maybe they aren't someone with whom we need to remain in relationship. We should control our emotions and be slow to get angry and offended (Psalm 119:165).

Please understand that putting people in "the chair" is strictly for the purpose of keeping our hearts clean before God. The attitude of "*I have to confront the offender*" is erroneous because what may seem humble on our part by confessing to the offender is, in reality, an act of revenge. It is having the perspective of, "*I'm going to tell them what they did to me because they need to know.*" However, in actuality, people with this attitude want to tell the offender what they did wrong so that they will hurt like the offended as well as recognize how "big" the forgiver is. It's all quite selfish and prideful at heart.

This person's so-called "confession" of unforgiveness and judgment to the offender is not an act of humility. In response to such a confession, more anger and judgment are going round and round in both people. If the offender did not accept the so-called apology and became angry at the offended, both the offended and the offender grow ever more angry. By going to the actual person, fire is being fueled when it all could have been avoided simply by keeping mouths closed and dealing with personal issues in our quiet time with Yahweh. This requires genuine humility.

There may be someone who attempts to annoy or upset us regularly. In this instance, it is not necessary to go to them every time. If we did, we would irritate the situation by making them irritated. *We* then are the ones who make our brother or sister fall, and the guilt lies on us. Be very mindful and discerning about whom to apologize in person or privately to an empty chair. Nine times out of ten, privately, is the best resolution.

Remember, the person who has offended may be very fragile in their heart. If we, thinking only of ourselves, go to them when they upset us, we may make them feel worse about themselves because they did not know what they did. Another scenario could be that the offender has confirmation they accomplished their task of annoying us, and they will continue all the more. Some people are full of evil spirits, and it is their mission to wreak as much havoc on others as possible. Be careful with people. We are a fragile creation, and we need tender, loving care that can only be given through obedience to Holy Spirit within.

The Attack of Pride:

> (Lucifer) You had the seal of perfection, full of wisdom and perfect in beauty. You were in Eden, the garden of God; every precious stone was your covering; the ruby, the topaz, and the diamond; the beryl, the onyx, and the jasper; the lapis lazuli, the turquoise and the emerald; and the gold, the workmanship of your settings and sockets, was in you. On the day that you were created they were prepared...your heart became proud on account of your beauty, and you corrupted your wisdom because of your

splendor. So I threw you to the Earth; I made a spectacle of you before kings (Ezekiel 28:12-17).

(King Belshazzar) "But when his heart became arrogant and hardened with pride, he was deposed from his royal throne and stripped of his glory (Daniel 5:20, NAS)."

See, I will make you small among the nations; you will be utterly despised. The pride of your heart has deceived you, you who live in the clefts of the rocks and make your home on the heights, you who say to yourself, 'Who can bring me down to the ground?' Though you soar like the eagle and make your nest among the stars, from there I will bring you down," declares the Lord (Obadiah 1:2-4).

Satan was cast out from Heaven by God, specifically due to his pride, which led him to rebel against Yahweh. When Lucifer stood next to God, His light would shine upon Lucifer's jewels placed upon him by God. It was *God's* beauty reflecting off the jewels set on Lucifer, which made him appear beautiful, yet Lucifer's beauty was not his own. In like fashion, any beauty you or I may possess is not ours; we have nothing of our own to be proud. Lucifer became blinded by the brilliant light reflecting off him. His wisdom became corrupt and ineffective and caused him to determine greater things about himself than what was real.

Everyone wants to be God or like God and to have all His power, but *few* want to be like Jesus, *lowly, and humble.* Jesus is the only connection humans have to God, the Father, His Kingdom, and His glory. To quote David E. Taylor once more from his book, *Victory Over Pride*, "*One can never crush an invisible enemy; neither can we crush him if we do not know he is attacking. Satan has strategically tricked mankind into attributing many behavioral patterns in our lives to reasons other than what is true. It is pride that hinders us from seeking the Lord and praying, hence causing us to walk in discord with others...pride also hinders us from receiving correction, blessings, reproof, instruction, wisdom, knowledge, and the fullness of God. It is pride that hinders people from looking at others the way Jesus does, which is with single vision. Pride binds and blinds. A sign of a mature Christian is one who can humbly receive correction or rebuke, deserved or undeserved."*

> "And so all Israel will be saved, as it is written: 'The deliverer will come from Zion; He will turn godlessness away from Jacob. And this is My covenant with them when I take away their sins' (Romans 11:26-27, NAS).'"

If there is a way into a situation, there is a way out. Regardless of our weaknesses, if we are humble enough to deal with them through Holy Spirit, when the weaknesses arise, we will grow stronger in Christ. This is what is meant in II Peter 3:18, *"grow in grace."* The Father can exalt us as we walk humbly, as did Jesus. Many ministries have fallen from the place God ordained because of the division and strife caused by pride. We would all get further in life, relationships, businesses, ministry, etc., if we humbled ourselves to walk as Jesus and approach situations as He.

"God has exalted Jesus and gave Him a name above all names," reads Philippians 2:9. We are to make ourselves of no reputation, of no account. Watchman Nee is quoted as having said in *Watchman Nee: Sufferer for China*, *"The lower we put something, the safer it is. It is safest to put a cup on the floor, meaning that the more a Christian is humbled, the safer it is for him. In fact, the safest place this side of Heaven is the cross."*

We need to allow God to make our name great versus trying with futility to do it ourselves. If we humble our name, He will make it great. If we exalt our name, He cannot. Jesus never got into arguments, contentions, or disagreements with people or even with His enemies. He retained peace that surpassed all understanding and knowledge (Philippians 4:7). He has left us that same peace; we need to choose to retain it.

Journaling

FORTY-FOUR

Humility

Commentary:

The body of Christ seems to be in short supply of humility and it's destroying her. There are far too many Scriptures to place them all here, but, to be sure, we need desperately to humble ourselves if we want to see any healing personally or collectively.

Prayer:

Yeshua, I humble myself before You seeking understanding and wisdom from above. I pray to attain understanding of Your original intent for mankind, that I begin to learn to die to self that You, the King of kings, will rule the Earth through me. Reveal to me how to walk humbly in a Kingdom-mindset. Show me every wicked way in me that I may confess, repent and walk in the wholeness that Adam forfeited. I choose, this day, to die that I may walk in the newness of genuine life. I desire, with all my spirit, heart, soul, and body, to be humble as Christ Himself was humble as He walked the Earth. Show me the difference between timidity and humility, righteous judgment and being judgmental, discernment, and emotionalism. I thank you that you have given me a new heart and a new spirit. Lay your heart of humility, grace, mercy, and compassion within me so that I never stray from truth. Show me how to be obedient as you see obedience, Jesus. I love You. Show me how never to forsake You as You never forsake me." Selah

Scripture References:

> "Therefore, as God's chosen people, holy and dearly loved, clothe yourselves with compassion, kindness, humility, gentleness and patience (Colossians 3:12)."

> "Be completely humble and gentle; be patient, bearing with one another in love (Ephesians 4:2)."

> "But He gives more grace. That is why Scripture says, "God opposes the proud but shows favor to the humble (James 4:6)."

> "If My people, who are called by My name, will humble themselves and pray and seek My face and turn from their wicked ways, then I will hear from Heaven, and I will forgive their sin and will heal their land (II Chronicles 7:14)."

Journaling

FORTY-FIVE

Pride

Prayer:

Father, may the very humility in which Jesus walked as a perfect human being dwell richly within me. I surrender my prideful nature to You today and every day. Remind me that I have life only by the grace of the One who did not deserve to die. Remind me that pride is the strongest of all lies and that humility is my only recourse if I want a life of peace. Selah.

Scripture References:

> "But He gives us more grace. That is why Scripture says, "God opposes the proud but shows favor to the humble."…humble yourselves before the Lord, and He will lift you up (James 4:6, 10)."

> "This is what the Lord says, 'Let not the wise boast of their wisdom or the strong boast of their strength or the rich boast of their riches (Jeremiah 9:23).'"

> "When pride comes, then comes disgrace, but with humility comes wisdom (Proverbs 11:2)."

Journaling

Identity Scripture and Commentary

Definition of Identify:

1. to know, discover or reveal who someone is or what something is
2. to cause to be or become identical
3. to conceive as united (as in spirit, outlook, or principle)

Most people do not identify with God. Years ago, I asked the Lord to show me how I can convey how to walk in total freedom in Christ and from the cares of this world. He revealed that I could teach and counsel all day, every day, but until the individual desires to come into a friendship relationship with Him, they will always be slaves in some capacity.

Most people serve God out of a slavery-mindset, even though He desires us to serve Him out of friendship. Abraham could "call the things that were not as though they were" (Romans 4) because He was such great friends with God—it was a mutual relationship. He knew God's character and trusted it. Abraham served God because he loved God. In the natural, you help—serve—your closest friends because you love them and desire to make them happy, not because you see yourself as their slave. A true friend serves out of love, not obligation.

When you know a person only through a mutual friend, you cannot trust that person's word because you have only heard that they are trustworthy. You have not experienced it firsthand. You may even tell others that the person is reliable, but you don't know it firsthand. So it is with God. You talk a good talk about how trustworthy and faithful God is, yet you do not know it on an intimate level. In reality, you fall due to doubt and fear.

One can only realize their identity in Christ when they begin to identify with and relate to His pure love. Until then, you do not identify with His Spirit. Flesh cannot identify with spirit. They cannot "relate," therefore, a relationship cannot properly mature. Choosing to hold to any aspect of the flesh separates you from God and keeps you from identifying with Him on His supreme level. It is the flesh that says, *"You aren't good enough. He isn't good enough."* You have to *identify* with people before you can formulate a friendship; the same applies in relation to Christ.

To *identify* is to *connect* or *to relate; to become identical*. Most relationships with God are shallow and meaningless. You say, *"Have faith,"* yet you are faithless yourself. You say, *"I am a friend of God,"* yet hold to worry, stress, anxiety, sorrow, fear, anger, greed, lust, bitterness, and anything else not of God. As your best, closest, dearest friend, He wants to and has the supernatural capacity to alleviate all those burdens. You do not allow Him because of your identity crisis. If your identity is not resting entirely in the perfection of the blood of the Lamb, you are in spiritual-identity crises, whether you know it or not. No matter how many good acts you perform, no matter what superior religious title you hold or how long you have been saved or in ministry, there is a crisis.

When your identity is grounded in Christ, you will fully be able to laugh at the days ahead (Psalms 2:1-5)! You can laugh because you have the future-mindset and not the past or present. You have an eternal view of the Kingdom instead of your here-and-now circumstances. The future is already God's past. When distress, conflict, or opposition come against you in any form, you will be able to laugh heartily. Your trust will be founded on and grounded in The Rock of all ages. The enemy will not shake you. You won't care that you are being stolen from because you will know that the enemy has to give back to you seven times what he steals (Proverbs 6:31). Praise God!

Knowing you have full right to claim this Scripture allows you to love your enemy and your neighbor as yourself. You can give your coat when your shirt is stolen because you see, hear, know, and understand that God is so in love with you that nothing can be stolen. Everything belongs to His people because everything belongs to God. You are His inheritance, and His estate is yours. You are His child, and He protects His own. This is Kingdom understanding.

Circumstances are Irrelevant:

> "He will not fear evil tidings; his heart is steadfast, trusting in the Lord. His heart is upheld, he will not fear, until he looks with satisfaction on his adversaries. (Psalm 112:7-8)."

Your circumstances will no longer have any effect on your walk with Christ. Your circumstances will no longer make you or break you. Your circumstances will no longer dictate how you conduct yourself. You will begin your victory in Jesus once you realize that:

1. His love is unfailing, and His eye is on you always.
2. He has defeated the enemy.
3. Everything the evil one does against you for evil; God has already turned around for your good.
4. The world is condemned and has no power over you.
5. The evil one *is* defeated and has been overthrown and is acting on borrowed time.
6. You *are* more than a conqueror.
7. Yahweh is a friend that sticks closer than a brother.

Once I identified with Christ and related to Him on a personal level, I was able to come to a place where I laugh when adversity comes. As stated in Psalm 112:7-8, I have *no fear of bad news*, and neither should you. I know immediately that Satan cannot succeed against my family or me. I laugh, even through tears, knowing that the situation has already worked in my favor. I could write a book merely on the blessings of God, turning things around for my favor! Let's stop giving Satan a foothold by worrying about everything that appears bad. Begin to praise His holy name that it—whatever "it" is—has already become a benefit to you and not a liability. Deny that old Adamic, fleshly nature that Christ overcame on the cross.

You are your own worst enemy when you do not fully know or understand who God has made you through the blood and the water. Peter refers to those in Christ as *"aliens and strangers."* He does so because your origin has changed from the earthly to heavenly. Christ was a stranger on Earth. Therefore, since He is your life, you too are a stranger. When you were in your sin, you were born into and of the Earth.

You can be born anew through the water and the blood of Christ, who is *of Heaven*. If you are in Christ, you now originate *from Heaven*. The Earth is not your home. You are an alien on this planet (I Peter 2:11). You can identify with Christ because He is your blood relation.

Identity in Christ

> For You formed my inward parts; You wove me in my mother's womb. I will give thanks to You, for I am fearfully and wonderfully made; wonderful are Your works, and my soul knows it very well. My frame was not hidden from You, when I was made in secret, and skillfully wrought in the depths of the Earth; Your eyes have seen my

unformed substance; and in Your book were all written the days that were ordained for me, when as yet there was not one of them (Psalm 139:13-16).

"Just as He chose us in Him before the foundation of the world, that we would be holy and blameless before Him. In love He predestined us to adoption as sons through Jesus Christ to Himself, according to the kind intention of His will (Ephesians 1:4-5)."

"When you were dead in your transgressions and the uncircumcision of your flesh, He made you alive together with Him, having forgiven us all our transgressions, having canceled out the certificate of debt consisting of decrees against us, which was hostile to us; and He has taken it out of the way, having nailed it to the cross (Colossians 2:13-14)."

"For you are all *sons of God* through faith in Christ Jesus. For all of you who were baptized into Christ have clothed yourselves with Christ (Galatians 3:26-27)."

Take No Pride, Keep No Shame:

"For by grace you have been saved through faith, and this is not from you; it is the gift of God; it is not from works, so no one may boast (Ephesians 2:8-9)."

"These are matters which have, to be sure, the appearance of wisdom in self-made religion and self-abasement and severe treatment of the body, but are of no value against fleshly indulgence (Colossians 2:23)."

There are so many other references than these about our new identity in Christ, and they are profoundly magnificent! Once the fleshly nature is out of the way, we are free to have our only identity rooted in Christ; in this, nothing of the flesh, either good or bad, will determine our worth. Our identity should be neither in the great things we accomplish, nor the failures of life, not in our Earthly origin, but of our heavenly origin. This is why I coined the phrase, *"Take no pride, keep no shame."* Our past wrongdoings are irrelevant, at least in as much as who God has created us to be. Anything good we perform can only come from Christ. Therefore, it is not our credit to pridefully receive.

When you are dead to yourself, the false identities of this fallen world will no longer stick. You, as a believer through faith, need to be so sure of who you are in the Lord that nothing makes you waiver from what He has spoken over you. I heard it said that your reputation is your photograph, but your character is your face. How's your face? When people get to know you, what do they find? When you conduct yourself in Jesus' character, there is nothing that can successfully come against you.

Allow me to elaborate. If you are a renowned scientist and discover a cure for cancer, that could tend to make you think very highly of yourself, more highly than you ought. One day someone does not recover from cancer after receiving your treatment. The same world that praised you now calls you a fraud and failure. What would happen to your false identity of greatness other than crumbling quickly? You would go down in flames, and now, where there was arrogance, shame is its replacement. Both arrogance and shame are a product of pride, and we know that pride always comes before the fall.

On the other hand, say you are an inmate as a result of having committed some crime. The world labels you as a stain upon the Earth. If your identity is in that label, though you gave your life to Christ, you never seem able to rise above that identity.

Your mind is fixed on the natural instead of the supernatural. A mindset on self will always cause arrogance, or guilt and shame. A "poor me" mentality is as much pride as the one who boasts in themselves. When in a condition of pride, the labels of this world will most assuredly stick to your heart because, since self is your focus, all you can focus on is what others think of you.

The only way to overcome the world's identities is to be transformed by the renewing of your mind. It is the mind that tells you who you are or are not. You hear the world around you whispering in your ear and, unless you have committed the flesh to its rightful place of death, you believe the lie. Anything that gives you identity other than the blood of Christ Jesus is a lie, good or bad. This reiterates the validity of being able to hear from God. You have to be tuned in to Him to recognize His voice to how Yahweh identifies you.

I had a lot of labels cast upon me as a child, teen, and young wife: lazy, slow, accident-prone, ugly, painfully shy. Much later came identities of divorce', adulterer, and much more. Some were valid, and others not. The most significant flaw with these identities is that they are based on what man—including self—decided about me based on how things appeared. They had nothing to do with what God decreed over me long before my conception.

The next problem the labels brought was that I carried them simultaneously, and they became quite a heavy burden to bear well into adulthood. They just mounded, one on top of the other. It was not until I submitted completely to Holy Spirit that He was free to break these falsehoods from my head and heart, and usher truth and revelation. Well, technically, they were broken at the cross, but I had to learn truth and how to apply it correctly.

The world—influences and voices other than from God—are the ones that say things such as, "Have a good time. Sleep with whomever you want. Do drugs. Smoking is fine. Embezzle money, no one will notice. Murder the one who hurt you because they deserve it," and so on. They are the same voices that turn their back on you and call you a harlot, addict, disgusting, grotesque, thief, and murderer. The world view will always lead you into false labeling leading to sin and death eternal.

Seek Transformation:

> "When You said, "Seek My face," my heart said to You, "Your face, O LORD, I shall seek (Psalm 27:8)."

> "And do not be conformed to this world, but be transformed by the renewing of your mind…(Romans 12:2)."

> "But He said, "You cannot see My face, for no man can see Me and live (Exodus 33:20)."

The Body of Christ must seek real transformation, not just a few characteristics of Christ. In other words, you must be changed into the likeness of Christ at your root. At the Mount of Transfiguration, Holy Spirit came upon Jesus. He transformed into the image of the Father. He was already God in physical manifestation; He was in every way "like God," yet He still had to be transformed.

If Jesus had to experience transformation, you, too, must undergo this metamorphosis. The root problem with Adam and Eve is that, although they were created in God's image and placed in the center of perfection, they had yet to be transformed. They were, as we've discussed at length, of the Earth. It was required of them to fall and then, knowing good and evil, choose to be transformed from the inside out. Just because you're saved from hell, that does not equate transformation from earthly to heavenly and living as such.

Interestingly enough, we're instructed to "seek His face," yet He told Moses, *"No one can see my face and live!"* If you seek and find God's face, you will be broken and changed forever at a mere glimpse. You won't be able to live! Since we're called, post-resurrection, to die to self, seeking His face and finding Him will accomplish that quite well. If, on the other hand, you seek only His attributes or characteristics, you will only *appear* changed for a time, but without your internal man being changed. This translates as a farce. Seeking only to mimic His characteristics is likened unto seeking sex, yet skipping the proper order of marriage and covenant, or seeking to worship the Lord without first falling in love with Him.

You must seek the deepest part of Him—His heart, His face, His Spirit—to know who you are in Him. It is vital to know who He is to recognize who He is in you and through you. He is your life, not a part of your life. Otherwise, the world and all its charming deception will lie to you and lead to destruction.

Fear, guilt, condemnation, and shame have overwhelmed Christ's Bride to such a degree that pastors and ministers of the Word are committing physical suicide, fornication, and adultery of every kind, and all are set against God. Their identity became blurry, and they were easy targets for Satan to deceive them into thinking that what is good wasn't that great, and what is wrong wasn't that wrong. Blurred and foggy spiritual vision is an anointing-killer.

Journaling

FORTY-SIX

Identifying with God

Prayer:

My Father, Husband, and faithful Friend, I long to identify with You. I want to relate to You as You identify and relate to me, a mere human. Help me to see Your heart so that I can commune with You on Your heavenly level. As You chose to live as a man on Earth to be able to identify with my plight, and then die for me that I may live with, in, and through You, I give You my life. I hide myself in Thee, O Lord, so that all I know of my identity is that of Jesus. Neither worthlessness nor wholeness is about who *I think* I am, but who *You* have created me to become. I am a son, ambassador, king, priest, and all that Christ is. As Jesus is in this world, so am I. It is no longer I who live. I pray, Almighty God, that I will begin to see myself as You see me. I bless You that, when You look upon me, you see only the pure blood of Your Son, Jesus. Show me how to be led only by You, who is within, and not by my fleshly, soulish desires. Reveal to me Your holiness that I, too, may be holy. Remind me that I am a stranger in this land because I am of Heaven and not of Earth; that I am of the royal, holy priesthood, O God. I bless Your name, El-Olam, the everlasting God, that my old self is dead to sin, and I am now alive to purity and life everlasting. I love You, Jesus, and thank You for giving me the honor and privilege of being seated at the right hand of the Father with You. Give me heavenly insight to live in peace, though the world around me is in chaos. Selah

Scripture References:

"…But when you are tempted, He will also provide a way out so that you can endure it (I Corinthians 10:13)."

"…God is light; in Him there is no darkness (I John 1:5)."

"The Lord is not slow in keeping His promise, as some understand slowness. Instead He is patient with you, not wanting anyone to perish, but everyone to come to repentance (II Peter 3:9)."
"Every good and perfect gift is from above, coming down from the Father of heavenly lights, who does not change like shifting shadows (James 1:17)."

"God is not human, that He should lie, not a human being, that He should change His mind. Does He speak and then not act? Does He promise and not fulfill (Numbers 23:19)?"

Journaling

FORTY-SEVEN

Identity in Christ

Prayer:

Father, I implore You, reveal to me who You are that I may know who I am in You. As I get to know You, I will begin to realize, recognize, and accept who You have made me. I thank You that I am no longer an "old dirty sinner" needing to wallow around in self-pity. I have been redeemed by the blood of the spotless Lamb of God, and I have been healed and made completely whole through You. I am an heir to the throne of the Most High God. I am seated at Your right hand, where Jesus is because I am hidden in Jesus. I will walk only in the identity of Jesus Christ because I have consumed Him, and He has consumed me. As I accept that we are one, no longer do I have to, nor shall I accept the Earth's labels. I will no longer take pride in the Earth's false flattering identifiers, nor will I keep shame from the Earth's false negative labels. I am not who anyone says I am except who the Lord of Heaven and Earth says I am. My identity is Jesus Christ. My identity is Jesus Christ. My identity is Jesus Christ. I lose myself in You, and I thank You for such a grand gift. May I never take such a priceless gift for granted. You are my all-in-all as You should be. Take Your rightful place as King of my heart—You are my heartbeat. Selah.

Scripture References:

"By this, love is perfected with us, so that we may have confidence in the day of judgment; because as He is, so also are we in this world (I John 4:17)."

Journaling

FORTY-EIGHT

Life without Lack

Prayer:

Thank You, Thank You, Thank You, Yahweh, that there is nothing You have not already provided and will manifest in perfect season (Philippians 4:19). I thank You that, no matter how much I appear to be in debt, I lend and never borrow because the floodgates of Heaven are opened to me (Deuteronomy 28:12). I give and expect nothing in return even to my enemies (Luke 6:35) because You are the One who brings return (Romans 2:6). I thank You that You are revealing to me how to walk in humility and obedience to position myself to receive all You have already supplied. I look forward, in total faith, for the physical manifestation of what is stored in the heavenlies for me and my household. Amen

Scripture References:

> "And my God will supply all your needs according to His riches in glory in Christ Jesus (Philippians 4:19)."

"The Lord will open for you His good storehouse, the Heavens, to give rain to your land in its season and to bless all the work of your hand; and you shall lend to many nations, but you shall not borrow (Deuteronomy 28:12)."

"But love your enemies, and do good, and lend, expecting nothing in return; and your reward will be great, and you will be sons of the Most High; for He Himself is kind to ungrateful and evil men (Luke 6:35)."

"Who will render to each person according to his deeds (Romans 2:6)."

Journaling

FORTY-NINE

Love

Prayer:

Jehovah-Rapha, my Lord, who heals, lay Your heart in my body and consume me. Please, allow me to be overtaken by Your supernatural love. Pour out Your love upon my head as the healing balm of Gilead. Let me open and expose myself to You completely. I desire to be a person of virtue, integrity, honor, love, peace, patience, and endless generosity. Teach me how to be unashamed of how You created me, fearfully and wonderfully. Show me how not to be prideful based on looks or possessions. I am saved by Your grace like all those before and after me. Teach me how to be a gracious host for Your Holy Spirit. Father, give me the grace to see the evil I have allowed in my camp. I want my territory clean, unblemished, and spotless before You. Show me which relationships are ungodly and give me the supernatural strength to end them. Bring into my life relationships that are pure and holy. Give me, O gracious, merciful God, clean hands and a pure heart before You, man, and the demons of hell. I pray, O Sovereign Lord, that You, man, and demons will testify that I am a child of the King. Amen and amen. Selah.

Scripture References:

From whom every family in Heaven and on Earth derives its name, that He would grant you, according to the riches of His glory, to be strengthened with power through His Spirit in the inner man, so that Christ may dwell in your hearts through faith; and that you, being rooted and grounded in love, may be able to comprehend with all the saints what is the breadth, length, height and depth, and to know the love of Christ which surpasses knowledge, that you may be filled up to all the fullness of God (Ephesians 3:15-19).

"And now these three things remain: faith, hope and love; but the greatest of these is love (I Corinthians 13:13)."

Journaling

Marriage Scriptures and Commentary

"The wife does not have authority over her own body, but the husband does; and likewise also the husband does not have authority over his own body, but the wife does (I Corinthians 7:4)."

Submitting yourselves one to another in the fear of God. Wives, submit to your own husbands, as unto the Lord. For the husband is the head of the wife, even as Christ is the head of the church; and He is the Savior of the body. But as the church is subject to Christ, so also the wives ought to be to their husbands in everything. Husbands, love your wives, just as Christ also loved the church and gave Himself up for her, so that He might sanctify her, having cleansed her by the washing of water with the word, that He might present to Himself the church in all her glory, having no spot or wrinkle or any such thing; but that she would be holy and blameless. So husbands ought also to love their own wives as their own bodies. He who loves his own wife loves himself; for no one ever hated his own flesh, but nourishes and cherishes it, just as Christ also does the church, because we are members of His body. For this reason a man shall leave his father and mother and shall be joined to his wife, and the two shall become one flesh. This mystery is great; but I am speaking with reference to Christ and the church. Nevertheless, each individual among you also is to love his own wife even as himself, and the wife must see to it that she respects her husband (Ephesians 5:21-33).

"So God created man in His own image, in the image of God He created him; male and female He created them. And God blesses them. And God said to them, "Be fruitful and multiply and fill the Earth and subdue it and have dominion…(Genesis 1:27-28)."

"For your Maker is your husband, the Lord of hosts is His name; and the Holy One of Israel is you Redeemer, the God of the whole Earth He is called (Isaiah 54:5)."

"Two are better than one, because they have a good return for their labor: if either of them falls down, one can help the other up. But pity anyone who falls and has no one to help them up. Also, if two lie down together, they will keep warm. But how can one keep warm alone (Ecclesiastes 4:9)?"

I wrote three books on marriage and divorce, which are:

1. *How to Get It Right: Being Single, Married, Divorced, and Everything in Between*
2. *Marriage Beyond Mediocrity*
3. *Wrecked by My Ex: Finding Peace Amid the Rubble*

Within these three, I discuss, at length, holy covenant with God. By understanding such a holy covenant with our Creator, we will better comprehend holy covenant between a husband and wife. I defer to those books if you want an extensive version of this subject. The following is the opening chapter of *Marriage Beyond Mediocrity*.

Definition of Marriage:

1. the legally or formally recognized union of a man and a woman (recently also potentially two people of the same gender) as partners in a relationship

2. a combination or mixture of two or more elements such as mixing music styles

***God's* Definition of Marriage:** a union creating covenant between one man and one woman causing the two individual people to become one new creation

Marriage is a great many things and serves positive purposes beyond imagination—when, of course, it is approached and handled correctly. When handled poorly, Satan has not only a foothold to climb into your bed but also an open invitation to destroy what may very well have been ordained by God. We who walk with Yeshua on purpose, knowing full well that Satan has come to kill, steal and destroy and his destruction applies very must against God's ordained unions. Satan knows that "where *two or three* are gathered in His name, there He will be in the midst of them (Matthew 18:20)."

This promise in Matthew can be used for any number of people groups such as friends, business partners, classmates, and many others, but I genuinely believe, as it pertains to marriage, this "2 or 3" is the equation of:

1. husband + wife + Holy Spirit (1 + 1 + 1 = 3)
2. husband/wife + Holy Spirit (1 + 1 = 2)

Depending on how you count—husband and wife considered as one or as two individuals, it's still *"two or three gathered together."* This text goes along with the statement, *"And if one can overpower him who is alone, two can resist him. A cord of three strands is not quickly torn apart,"* found in Ecclesiastes 4:12. This is unprecedented power, ladies and gentlemen! When an ordained man and woman—not just *any* man and *any* woman—unite as one in marriage under the holy covenant of God, yikes! They are an unstoppable force that can withstand the storms of any magnitude. Marriage is covenant, and covenant is protection, and protection is so many things. Protection ensures confidence, grace, mercy, joy, happiness, unity, power, and so much more.

Marriage, to me personally, is nothing short of bliss. That doesn't mean there aren't hard times, difficult situations, perplexing problems, and obstacles that are seemingly impossible to withstand and overcome; no one lives in utopia. It does, however, mean that when the couple is truly of one mind as God intends marriage to be, you can confidently stand together and brave the weather until it passes.

When you are in a marriage of unity, even when you disagree, and you will, you possess the confidence to know that, no matter how long it takes to get to the other side of something, divorce or abuse isn't awaiting you. God-ordained marriages are breathtaking, they are peaceful, and they are God-honoring. Again, that doesn't mean that either the husband or the wife conduct themselves perfectly at all times. Still, it ensures that, at the end of the day, you will resolve the struggles without worrying about impending doom to the marriage.

As a person thrice married and twice divorced, I have the insight of both good and bad marriages, holy and unholy marriages. There is a vast difference between God-ordained marriages and those we enter just because we wanted to for whatever plethora of reasons. My first dramatically horrific marriage appeared correct but wasn't. My second marriage was with someone pretty impressive, but he wasn't the one for whom I was created, not to mention I married from a place of having been crushed by marriage number one.

Michael is, adversely, the one for whom I was created, and it's a beautiful thing. We don't argue, fuss, fight, go silent against one another, withhold privileges to get our way, or anything of the sort. We have had adversities but, through it all, we stand stronger than ever, and that is what marriage is. Marriage is not pretending to be okay. It's loving one another through every circumstance with the assurance that your vows cannot and will not be broken by either party.

Marriage is a privilege and not something for which we should take so lightly as to enter without the go-ahead from our Creator and King. When we enter so lightly, we make our own Ishmael's and hence land in quicksand. It's this very self-inflicted quicksand that causes the general population to turn away from marriage, assuming that all marriages are bad and that they are, in fact, outdated and unnecessary. The following chapter on covenant should help clarity what marriage is and why it is as valuable today as in the beginning.

Marriage is intended to be a gift, a blessing from God; a place of protection, comfort, security, provision, help, encouragement, admonishment in love, growth, maturity, and a representation of our spiritual marriage with Christ and a supernatural tool of expanding the Kingdom of God here on Earth.

Journaling

FIFTY
Marriage: Surrender

Prayer:

Father, I surrender my marriage, attitude, anger, disappointment, judgment, and life to You. I thank You for displaying and extending Your supernatural, eternal, unfailing love toward me personally. I ask that You stir within me that same love that comes only from above so that I will walk, talk, eat, drink, and breathe that love in my marriage. Help me to love my spouse as You love me. Allow me to think before I speak and never act in anger. Teach me Your ways, O Lord, that I will always give mercy instead of punishment, grace instead of malice, love instead of hatred. Show Me Your love so that I can first receive it for myself and then, as an extension of myself, grant such eternal love toward my spouse. Fill me with Your love and give me eyes to see as You see, ears to hear as You hear, and a mind to understand and process as do You. I love You, Yeshua, and I thank You for my marriage. Rule this marriage through me lest I make a huge mess. Selah.

Journaling

FIFTY-ONE

Marriage: Loving with God's Love

Prayer:

Father, in the name of Jesus, show me the frailty of my fleshly love so that I can come to You a broken vessel. As I commit my limited love to You, fill me with Your limitless, supernatural, abounding, abiding love. Reveal to me exactly how You have ordained marriage between my spouse and me, and that which is between my new family and me. Help me to understand in my mind, heart, and spirit that they are as much my family as my spouse's, no matter how they treat me. Allow me to move, think, act, and speak according to Your Holy Spirit and never according to my fleshly man. I release myself and all of my frailty and failures to You, O God, so that You are free to move through me according to Your way, will, plan and purpose. Expose to me every wicked way within me so that I can confess, repent, and be made whole in You. Give me eyes to see, ears to hear, and a mind to comprehend Your heart, Jesus. For only in You can anything good come from this worthless, earthen vessel. You are the Potter, and I am the clay. Mold me, make me, and take me as You desire, O Lord. May I never shame You by conducting myself in a manner unworthy of Your Gospel. In Jesus' name, I pray and claim that I will walk according to the Spirit rather than the flesh. Amen.

Journaling

FIFTY-TWO

Marriage: Taking Dominion

Prayer:

Allow me to discover deep spiritual truths so that my marriage will become healthy and a testament to our relationship, marriage, and covenant with You, my Husband. Place Your heart in my body so that all You are will be expressed to my spouse. Give me Your eyes that I may see clearly and Your ears that I may properly hear what You are revealing and saying. Illuminate the eyes of my understanding so that Your compassion, patience, wisdom, and desires will overtake my spouse and me. I pray for us to be unified instead of divided. I take authority over myself and my marriage, and command, in the name of Jesus, every demonic spirit of division, confusion, wrath, depression, sorrow, despair, depravity, perversion, and any other evil spirit released from their assignment over my marriage. In their place, I release the Spirit of the Living God. He is given all authority and power to rule, once again or for the first time. I give You every leeway to move in me and my marriage according to Your perfect will. Show me every wicked way in me that I may become whole through repentance and surrender. Direct my path and my marriage according to Your perfect plan. I repent of _____ leading my marriage in the wrong direction. I receive Your forgiveness and accept Your leading from here. I bless You, King and Savior, for your patience and renewed love between my spouse and me. I call my spouse out of the darkness and into the light of Christ. I take my God-given authority over their body for the righteousness of the Lord. I declare that we will walk in accordance with God's will all the days of our lives. Strengthen our marriage on every level. Knit our hearts together with Yours so that we will be a three-strand cord that cannot be ripped apart. Selah.

Journaling

FIFTY-THREE

Marriage: Husband's Prayer

Prayer:

Father, I pray with all my being that You reveal to me what is holy in Your sight. I thank You that, because of Your Holy Spirit who dwells within me, You have already given me wisdom from on high to love my wife as You love the church. You have readily supplied me with everything required to walk in self-discipline to be faithful, loving, and kind to her. Grant me the wherewithal to utilize, to the fullest extent, the power of Holy Spirit instead of my flesh to be the husband required for an exceptional marriage. Just as You, O God, are my Husband, reveal to me how to be a husband to my wife as You are a Husband to the body of Christ. I desire to marry only she whom You have designed for me, and only me. I desire to work through every issue of life with her as one entity instead of standing as two individuals. Help me to put You above all else and then love my wife above myself. Knit our hearts together as one. Allow me the privilege to view marriage as it is and not as I wish it were. Remind me that my wife and I are a physical representation of our marriage to You. I choose today to honor You in spirit, soul, mind, body, and marriage, whatever that sacrifice requires. I no longer belong to myself, but I belong to You and my wife. I love You, O Lord, above all else. Because my body belongs to her, direct me to pray fervently over her as I would pray for myself. Allow me to apply Your love to my wife properly. Bless her, Lord. Allow me to be a blessing and a compliment to her. Show me how to encourage and not discourage her; how to build her and not break her. Show me how to not "work harder" at a good marriage, but to learn to be so at peace with You that we begin to flow together effortlessly. Selah

journaling

FIFTY-FOUR

Marriage: Wife's Prayer

Prayer:

Father God, You are my first love, my Husband, the lover of my soul. As I surrender myself to You, You are teaching me how to submit to my earthly husband. Reveal to me, in the innermost parts of my being, how to respect and honor my husband as You respect and honor mankind. I recognize that, as I have become one with him, I no longer have authority over my own body. Since I have authority over his body, teach me how to pray for and encourage him. Reveal to me how to help him become the man You have called and created him to become. You have readily supplied me with everything required to walk in self-discipline to be faithful, loving, and respectful toward him. Grant me the wherewithal to utilize, to the fullest extent, the power of Holy Spirit instead of my flesh to be the wife required for an exceptional marriage. Remind me that my husband and I are a physical representation of our marriage to You. I choose today to honor You in spirit, soul, mind, body, and marriage, whatever that sacrifice requires. I desire to work through every issue of life with him as one entity instead of attempting to stand as two individuals. Help me to put You above all else and then honor my husband above myself. Knit our hearts together as one. Show me how to not "work harder" at a good marriage, but to learn to be so at peace with You that we begin to flow together effortlessly. Selah

Journaling

Mindset Scriptures and Commentary

For though we walk in the flesh, we do not war after the flesh: for the weapons of our warfare are not carnal, but mighty through God to the pulling down of strongholds; casting down imaginations, and every high thing that exalts itself against the knowledge of God, and bringing into captivity every thought to the obedience of Christ; and having in a readiness to revenge all disobedience, when your obedience is made complete (II Corinthians 10:3-6).

"For who has known the mind of the Lord, that He will instruct him? But we have the mind of Christ (I Corinthians 2:16)."

"Set your mind on things above, not on things on the Earth (Colossians 3:2)."

"Rejoice always, pray without ceasing, give thanks in all circumstances; for this is the will of God in Christ Jesus for you (I Thessalonians 5:16-18)."

"Therefore, if anyone is in Christ, he is a new creation. The old has passed away; behold, the new has come (II Corinthians 5:17)."

"Let this mind be in you, which was also in Christ Jesus… (Philippians 2:5, KJV)."

Definition of Double-Minded:

1. wavering in mind: undecided, vacillating
2. marked by hypocrisy

People all over the globe, from generation to generation, both within and without the body of Christ, have suffered mercilessly with double-mindedness. Indecisive people, in extreme cases, lose their sanity. In lesser cases, they appear to live a normal life, yet, in reality, they are tossed to and fro within the recesses of their minds and never find peace. Jeremiah refers to this type of person as a tumbleweed tossed to and fro.

This is a horrific place for anyone because there is no peace, joy, or stability of mind. James 1 states that a double-minded man—though it is explicitly referencing asking for wisdom—ought not to expect anything from the Lord. That is a harsh statement, but a reality nonetheless. Because God is exceedingly generous, He allows us to understand the rules. If we're hoping for anything from Him, He lays out the plan for us to be positioned to receive. Nothing is hidden as to how the Kingdom of Heaven functions in the Earth.

Becoming double-minded in this life is relatively standard. With all the turmoil, religions, denominations, and divisions, it's simply too easy to be tossed about by every wind of doctrine as are small children, mentioned in Ephesians 4:14. "Doctrine" is not necessarily a religion; it can be anyone's voice in your ear telling you any number of differing opinions on literally any topic known to man.

Among professing followers of Christ, to God's chagrin, it is commonplace to witness multitudes entangled in it, though Christ Himself made a way out. The problem, as I see, enters when people who have walked with God any length of time hit a roadblock. They go along teaching the Word and living it when things are well and secure, yet, once they enter a time of wilderness, turmoil, or turbulence of any kind, they begin to doubt God. This causes anxiety, fear, and sometimes a complete turning away from Christ.

These people become ensconced in doubt and cannot land on a firm foundation of wisdom, so they're left floundering like a fish out of water. These folks don't know the Lord as much as they thought. I was that person during my mid-twenties. I had accepted the Lord as my Savior at the age of six. By the time my first husband walked out, I had become a spiritual basket case. I lost my identity—or instead, it became apparent I never knew it—and began to go the way of Cain in many respects. I doubted God, who He is, how He is and, especially, I questioned, *"Why did You do this to me? I served you faithfully, witnessed to people, etc., etc., etc."* I spoke to God the litany of reasons why these troubles should not have come upon me.

Until we know through and through who we are in Christ, double-mindedness will cause anxiety, stress, frustration, fear, condemnation, doubt, panic, anger, hatred, and more. Today, the world-traveling chef, Anthony Bourdain, died at 61 from an apparent suicide. Yesterday, world-renowned designer, Kate Spade, age 55, died from an apparent suicide. On February 11, 2012, Whitney Houston, world-renowned singer, died at age 48. Robin Williams, a world-renown actor and comedian, died August 11, 2014, from an apparent suicide.

My point, or rather, God's point is this: life-altering anxiety will come upon anyone who does not have their mind purposefully set on the God who created us; on His promise, purpose, will, life, and Kingdom. This struggle is real because we don't know who we are in Christ Jesus. The sooner we realize that being immersed into the life of Jesus does not exempt us from various trials and that God has a purpose in each one of them, the sooner we will be freed from the captivity of anxiety and its counterparts.

Consider it all joy, my brethren, when you encounter various trials, knowing that the testing of your faith produces endurance. And let endurance have its perfect result, so that you may be perfect and complete, lacking in nothing (James 1:2-4).

For though we walk in the flesh, we do not war according to the flesh, for the weapons of our warfare are not of the flesh, but divinely powerful for the destruction of fortresses. We are destroying imaginations and every high thing raised up against the knowledge of God, and we are taking every thought captive to the obedience of Christ, and we are ready to punish all disobedience, whenever your obedience is complete (II Corinthians 10:3-6).

"For who has known the mind of the Lord, that he will instruct Him? But we have the mind of Christ (I Corinthians 2:16)."

Multiple times, the Bible instructs, *"Do not walk according to the flesh,"* because the Lord knew, from the beginning, that, after we come into our newness of life, there would be intense temptation to do so. Romans 8:5 states, *"For those who are according to the flesh set their minds on the things of the flesh, but those who are according to the Spirit, the things of the Spirit."* Galatians 5:16 says, *"But I say, walk by the Spirit, and you will not carry out the desire of the flesh."*

People walking according to the desires of the flesh do not know or care that God has given instructions on how to live according to the Spirit. For me, growing up in a standard denominational church, I did not know. Emotions led me daily, and it led to anxiety. My first marriage was based on emotions, not Holy Spirit instruction. I did not know how to surrender the flesh while living in it. I did not know how to avoid anxiety by pulling down imaginations and strongholds and every high thing that exalts itself above the name of Christ. I did not understand how to take every thought captive or to punish my disobedience before acting upon it readily.

Every single sin, past, present, or future, begins in the mind. When we can get our minds right, the rest will follow suit. My friend, who has lived a life full of anxiety, now grasps the concept that, if her mind is focused on the Spirit, the rest of her person will align with God. For example, in the last 20+ years since returning to Christ, I have purposed to live a surrendered life unto Yahweh. I choose to live, not according to the flesh, but unto the Spirit. I have poured over the Bible cover to cover, taught in prisons, conferences, TV and radio, and have counseled countless people. I have twenty-five published books. In all that, I, too, have moments where my thoughts are not aligned with God. I have to pull down purposefully—remove—thoughts that are not of God, cast them out of me, and battle in the spirit-realm through prayer. I demand of myself that my disobedience is brought into captivity to Christ. I remind myself such conduct is unholy, unwise, and altogether a disastrous minefield. When left unchecked, all those bad feelings become fortresses within me, internally barricading me, and imprisoning my mind.

No matter how closely I walk with God, I still, on occasion, experience feelings of anger, resentment, fear, hatred, jealousy, and things similar. These emotions can come so quickly it's shocking. Notwithstanding, once I feel them, I must attend them immediately lest I run amuck with them. I cannot allow them to drive me to action. I have heard of children and adults who have been mercilessly abused by their parents, relatives, spouses, neighbors, or strangers who suffer from severe PTSD—post-traumatic stress disorder. Many of these people, though pulled out of their hostile environment, never overcome the aftermath because they can't seem to release the memories of their abuse or their abusers. When I counsel, I hear this regularly, "*I just can't get it out of my mind.*" Everything begins in the mind, freedom and bondage, obedience and disobedience.

Imagine having Christ's mind free from anxiety. It seems impossible, yet it is altogether made available to the surrendered person of God. With such a mind, we have the supernatural ability to:

1. See the end from the beginning, as does God (Isaiah 46:10)
2. Discern people's hearts and intentions, as did Jesus while in the flesh (Luke 5:22; Matthew 12:25: Luke 11:17)
3. Function in wisdom from above (James 3:17; Romans 10:17; John 8:47)
4. Hear the audible voice of God (John 10:27)
5. Be fearless (Isaiah 35:4; John 14:27; Joshua 1:9)
6. Speak the things that are not as though they already exist (Romans 4:17)
7. Discern the times (I Chronicles 12:32; Luke 12:56; John 7:24)
8. Be as Jesus on the Earth (I John 2:6; I Corinthians 11:1; I Peter 2:21)
9. Possess a hope that is alive based on the promises of God (I Peter 1:3-9; Jeremiah 29:11; Romans 15:13)
10. When surrounded by anxiety and fear, stand firmly in peace, faith and confidence (Colossians 3:15; Galatians 5:22; James 3:18; Matthew 8:23-27)

Journaling

FIFTY-FIVE

Mindset: New and Improved

Prayer:

Father, I plead the blood of Jesus over my spirit, soul, body, and mind. In the name of Jesus, I have a "want to" for a new mindset. I willingly surrender myself to receive the mind of Christ. I reconcile my chaotic, stressful, unsolvable situation to You because You are my only solution. Show me daily who I am in You and who You are in me. I pray for Your identity to become my own so that I may come out of this trial better than I entered. I receive Your mercy, grace, wisdom, discipline, correction, and forgiveness. I will rejoice in all things because I think with the mind of Christ. Thank You, Jesus, for saving me from hell, this perverse generation, myself, and my enemies. I am what and who You say I am. Nothing more and nothing less. Selah.

Journaling

FIFTY-SIX

Mind Set on Heaven

Prayer:

Father, help me set my mind on things of Heaven and not on the things of this Earth. Move through me, even in the hardest of times, that You may speak and act through me. I thank You, Holy Father, that You have given me everything I need for life; that I will speak as the oracles of God and not as my flesh directs. In the name of Jesus, I command every demon spirit of anger, greed, malice, anxiety, sorrow, depression, chaos, confusion, cowardliness, and every demon of hell to be bound, gagged, and loosed from their assignment over my mind, will, emotions, intellect, and memories. I declare that I am not led by anything or anyone other than Holy Spirit. Even in my grief and pain, I choose You, O Lord, and not my selfish nature of vengeance, since vengeance belongs to You alone. I thank You that You have given me a sound mind, pure heart, and steadfast spirit, and I will walk with You all the days of my life. I will turn neither to the right nor to the left, and I will not be double-minded. I stand with, in, and through You. I release everything to You, and I trust You and You alone. Selah.

Journaling

FIFTY-SEVEN

Mindset: Taking Every Thought Captive

Prayer:

Father, I plea the blood of Christ Jesus over my mind, will, and emotions; over every imagination and stronghold that exalts itself above the name of Jesus in my life, and I bring it into the obedience of Christ (II Corinthians 10:5). I take every thought captive and proclaim that all fear, doubt, rage, worthlessness, depression, sorrow, (<u>name your issue</u>) has to leave now, in the name of Jesus Christ. I praise You, Father, that the only life in me is Your Holy Spirit communing with my spirit. I glory in You that I have the mind of Christ (I Corinthians 2:16). Show me how to be entirely led by You, and not the old Adamic, fleshly way of thinking. I praise You that Holy Spirit is blowing into my life in such a way that my entire atmosphere is shifting. Show and remind me of my Kingdom destiny. Reveal my calling and direct my path that I may honor You always. Make straight every crooked path (Isaiah 40:4). I thank You, in advance, that everything Satan has meant against me and the Kingdom ministry for evil, You have already, in the spirit-realm, turned it all for Your good and mine because I love You (Romans 8:28). I praise You that the natural ways of this world will become unnatural, and God's supernatural ways will become natural to me. Thank You, Jesus! I stand in awe of You, and I enter Your gates with praise, expectation, and thanksgiving! Selah.

journaling

FIFTY-EIGHT

Mindset: Natural to Supernatural

Prayer:

Father, in the name of Jesus, I pray that the natural life becomes unnatural, and that the supernatural of God become altogether natural to me. I pray that when I get off track, Your Holy Spirit will quickly correct me and give me the grace to humble myself, repent, and realign myself (Proverbs 12:1). Give me eyes to see, ears to hear, and a mind to understand Your Word. Show me how to be led only by and through the power of Holy Spirit within. Burn everything within me that was not planted by You, O Lord. Show me how to walk, talk, and think as Christ. Let the mind that is in Christ be also in me. Reveal to me my Kingdom purpose on this planet that I may, through Your power, fulfill it. You are my heart and my desire. On Your word, I meditate day and night. Always correct me when I take a misstep. Teach me, O God, to move past the elementary things of Your Word so that I will move into the richness of all You have ordained for, by, and through me. Help me not to focus on the fear of losing salvation or forfeiting it, but rather, help me to focus entirely on falling in love with and pleasing You. I love You, Lord. Allow me the privilege of falling in love with You as You are in love with me. Show me how to reciprocate Your love. Selah

Scripture References:

> Therefore there is now no condemnation for those who are in Christ Jesus. For the law of the Spirit of life in Christ Jesus has set you free from the law of sin and of death… the Spirit of God, who raised Jesus from the dead, lives in you. And just as God raised Christ Jesus from the dead, He will give life to your mortal bodies by this same Spirit living within you (Romans 8:1-2, 11).

Journaling

FIFTY-NINE

Mindset: PTSD

Prayer:

Father, we know that every good and perfect thing comes from You (James 1:17). We also know that there is no real healing outside Your righteous right hand. On the shoulders of Jesus, You bore my griefs and sorrows. You were stricken, afflicted, and smitten for my transgressions. You were pierced and crushed for my iniquities. The chastening for my well-being fell on Jesus. By His scourging, I am healed. All of us, me included, like sheep, have gone astray. I have turned to my way, but the Lord has caused my sins to fall on Him. As Jesus was oppressed and did not open His mouth, teach me to walk in His healing and humility (Psalm 23). I cast my cares of PTSD and all I've experienced upon the strong shoulders of the Lord God Almighty. If Jesus could carry the load and cares of all humanity, surely He can bear the weight I carry. Teach me how to alight myself from these burdens of shame, woes, trauma, and wounds inflicted upon me. Your yoke is easy, and Your burden is light. I release my memories and false inclinations onto You, Sovereign Lord. Remind me that You are in love with me, the whole of me, regardless of the sins and crimes I have committed against You, and the sins committed against me. You are no respecter of persons, and You receive me just as I am. Settle my mind, calm my fears, put out the flames of desperation and despair as only You can. I pray to surrender my thoughts to You every single day. I pray for Your peace, which passes all understanding, to cover me. Pour Your holy blood over me from the top of my head to the soles of my feet so that the enemy's fiery darts cannot prevail against my mind or body. Amen.

"Fear not, for I am with you; be not dismayed, for I am your God; I will strengthen you, I will help you, I will uphold you with my righteous right hand (Isaiah 41:10)."

"But he was pierced for our transgressions; he was crushed for our iniquities; upon him was the chastisement that brought us peace, and with his wounds we are healed (Isaiah 53:5)."

"But this I call to mind, and therefore I have hope: The steadfast love of the Lord never ceases; his mercies never come to an end; they are new every morning; great is your faithfulness (Lamentations 3:21-23)."

"For our sake he made him to be sin who knew no sin, so that in him we might become the righteousness of God (2 Corinthians 5:21)."

"The Lord is the one who goes ahead of you; He will be with you. He will not fail you or forsake you. Do not fear or be dismayed (Deuteronomy 31:8.)"

"So that He sets on high those who are lowly, and those who mourn are lifted to safety (Job 5:11)."

The Lord is my shepherd, I shall not want. He makes me lie down in green pastures, He leads me beside quiet waters. He restores my soul; He guides me in the paths of righteousness for His name's sake. Even though I walk through the valley of the shadow of death, I will fear no evil, for You are with me; Your rod and Your staff, they comfort me. You prepare a table before me in the presence of my enemies; You have anointed my head with oil; My cup runneth over. Surely goodness and loving-kindness will follow me all the days of my life, and I will dwell in the house of the Lord forever (Psalm 23).

"God is our refuge and strength, a very present help in trouble (Psalm 46:1)."

"Blessed be God, even the Father of our Lord Jesus Christ, the Father of mercies, and the God of all comfort (II Corinthians 1:3)."

"The things I have spoken unto you, that in me you might have peace. In the world you shall have tribulation: but be of good cheer. I have overcome the world (John 16:33)."

Journaling

SIXTY

Navigating the Word

Prayer:

Help me to navigate Your Word that I may know the hope of my calling in Christ Jesus. Reveal hidden truths so that I may utilize them to the fullest. Help me to be a Kingdom-minded person to meet the maximum of my calling for the Kingdom of God. Show me how to learn the Word and then how to apply it to everyday life properly. Make it known to me what is Your perfect will in each situation I face. Amen

Scripture References:

> "However, there is a God in Heaven who reveals mysteries…the king answered Daniel and said, "Surely your God is a God of gods and a Lord of kings and a revealer of mysteries, since you have been able to reveal this mystery (Daniel 2:28, 47)."

"and pray on my behalf, that utterance may be given to me in the opening of my mouth, to make known with boldness the mystery of the gospel (Ephesians 6:19)."

"to whom God willed to make known what is the riches of the glory of this mystery among the Gentiles, which is Christ in you, the hope of glory (Colossians 1:27)."

Journaling

SIXTY-ONE

Nightly

Prayer:

I plea the blood of Jesus over my conscience, unconscious, and subconscious mind so that nothing can enter me that is not of You. I take full authority over my mind and place it in Your righteous right hand. I thank You that no dream, vision, spirit, or thought come to me from any demonic force, but let only that which is from God come to me. Let me remember and understand that You have given me supernatural ability to rightly discern what is revealed and to walk in obedience. Allow me to grow ever stronger in You and in my identity in You, in the name of Jesus. Amen

Scripture References:

> "We are destroying speculations and every lofty thing raised up against the knowledge of God, and we are taking every thought captive to the obedience of Christ (II Corinthians 10:5)."

"Every person is to be in subjection to the governing authorities. For there is no authority except from God, and those which exist are established by God (Romans 13:1)."

"But examine everything carefully; hold fast to that which is good; abstain from every form of evil (I Thessalonians 5:21-22)."

"For Christ also died for sins once for all, the just for the unjust, so that He might bring us to God, having been put to death in the flesh, but made alive in the spirit (II Peter 3:18)."

Journaling

SIXTY-TWO

No Longer an "Old Dirty Sinner"

Prayer:

I cannot thank You enough, heavenly Father, for allowing me to come out of darkness and into Your holy light. I thank You that, in and of myself, I have zero eternal worth (Galatians 2:20), but You have given me a name with the name above all names by giving Your Son to make me a son (John 1:12). Because of the blood of Your Son, making my dead man alive in You (Galatians 2:20), I am of a chosen people, a royal priesthood, and a holy nation. Remind me of who I am in You so that I no longer allow myself and its emotions to control anything; I refuse to allow myself to dictate my condition either way as I am nothing without You. Thank You for the honor and privilege of being called by the name of God. I thank You that old things are gone, and I have been made new in Christ. I am not an old dirty sinner. In Christ, I am redeemed and clothed in a robe of righteousness. I am an heir to the Kingdom of Heaven, and ambassador in chains, a son of God, the bride of Christ, a friend of God's. I am forever transformed. Selah

Scripture References:

"For God, who said, 'Light shall shine out of darkness,' is the One who has shone in our hearts to give the Light of the knowledge of the glory of God in the face of Christ (II Corinthians 4:6)."

"But now He has obtained a more excellent ministry, by as much as He is also the mediator of a better covenant, which has been enacted on better promises…when He said, "A new covenant," He has made the first obsolete. But whatever is becoming obsolete and growing old is ready to disappear (Romans 8:6, 13)."

"But you are a chosen race, a royal priesthood, a holy nation, a people for God's own possession, so that you may proclaim the excellencies of Him who has called you out of darkness into His marvelous light (I Peter 2:9)."

Journaling

SIXTY-THREE

Obedience

Prayer:

O merciful Savior, show me the simplicity of obedience with a heart wholly given over to Yours. I pray to know the freedom of obedience instead of the burden of it. Reveal to me, in any way You desire, how true obedience looks so that I may never cease to please You. I want to be as a poured out drink offering holy and acceptable to You. Burn me from the inside out, so I will be as a sweet, fragrant aroma to Your nostrils. I pray that obedience will be a blessing to me instead of a curse. Amen

Scripture References:

> "Now if you obey me fully and keep my covenant, then out of all nations you will be my treasured possession... (Exodus 19:5)."

> "This calls for patient endurance on the part of the people of God who keep His commands and remain faithful to Jesus (Revelation 14:12)."

"Through Him we received grace and apostleship to call all the Gentiles to the obedience that comes from faith for His name's sake (Romans 1:5)."

"You are My friends if you do what I command (John 15:14)."

"If you love Me, keep My commands (John 14:15)."

Journaling

SIXTY-FOUR

Outside the City Gate

Prayer:

Allow me the privilege of having unity of heart with You. I desire that You replace my life. May I go nowhere You are not leading; may I leave every place where You are not in control. Help me supernaturally to remove myself from my comfort zone. Take me to the places of discomfort so that You will be able to teach me to grow beyond what I can see with my natural eyes. I thank You, Lord, that I see as You see, hear as You hear, and think as You think. Change my perspective from the earthly into the heavenly. I love and adore You, O God, and King of kings. May I never leave You nor forsake You till the end of eternity. Amen

Scripture References:

> "For your husband is your Maker, whose name is the Lord of hosts; and your Redeemer is the Holy One of Israel, who is called the God of all the Earth (Isaiah 54:5-6)."

"For I through the law died to the law that I might live to God. I have been crucified with Christ; it is no longer I who live, but Christ lives in me; and the life which I now live in the flesh I live by faith in the Son of God, who loved me and gave Himself for me (Galatians 2:19-20)."

"Open my eyes, that I may behold wondrous things out of Your law (Psalm 119:18)."

"But blessed are your eyes, because they see; and your ears, because they hear (Matthew 13:16)."

"Therefore Jesus also, that He might sanctify the people through His own blood, suffered outside the gate. So, let us go out to Him outside the camp, bearing His reproach (Hebrews 13:12-13)."

Journaling

SIXTY-FIVE
Overcoming Evil with Good

Commentary: (from *Extinguishing the Inferno of Anger*, chapter 22)

"Do not be overcome by evil, but overcome evil with good (Romans 12:21)."

This is quite a simple statement yet full of power! In this one verse in Romans, we see that evil is running rampant; otherwise, God would not give us such a command. He understands that evil is the way of this Satan-driven world. The earth and mankind were condemned because Adam allowed Satan to dethrone him from his position in the Lord. There are innumerable types of evil in the world which can, at a moment's notice, turn us from our peace toward anger and, in our anger, devastation is the outcome. So how do we overcome evil with good? How do we accomplish that which is impossible for the natural man?

For starters, II Timothy 2:22-26 tells us, "Now flee from youthful lusts and pursue righteousness, faith, love, and peace, with those who call on the Lord from a pure heart. But refuse foolish and ignorant speculations, knowing that they produce quarrels. The Lord's bond-servant must not be quarrelsome, but be kind to all, able to teach, patient when wronged, with gentleness correcting those who are in opposition, if perhaps God may grant them repentance leading to the knowledge of the truth, and they may come to their senses and escape from the snare of the devil, having been held captive by him to do his will." So as to simplify, here is a list of instruction listed here:

1. Flee youthful lusts (sinful, incontrollable desires)
2. Pursue righteousness (holiness)
3. Pursue faith (in God)
4. Pursue love (God's immeasurable, supernatural love)
5. Pursue peace (contentment in all circumstances)
6. Pursue godliness alongside those who call on the Lord with a pure heart
7. Reject foolish speculations (guesswork)
8. Reject ignorant speculations (theorizing)
9. Understand speculations produce quarrels
10. Do not be quarrelsome (argumentative, contentious)
11. Be kind to all (everyone regardless of differing opinions, race, religion, background, etc.)
12. Be able to teach (while in blatant sin, you are disqualified to teach – know the Word and live it)
13. Be patient when wronged (don't allow your anger to cause you to lose your cool and snap)
14. Correct those in opposition to you but do so in gentleness (do not harshly slam people who don't agree with you)
15. Correct with the purpose of leading them to repentance (not to shame them)
16. Correct with the purpose of leading people into the knowledge of truth (not to belittle or scorn them)
17. Correct people with the purpose of directing them to come to their [God] senses (lead them into the mind of Christ)

18. Correct people with the purpose of helping them escape the snare of the devil (not condemning making them feel they'll be forever evil)
19. Correct people with the explicit purpose of setting them free from the chains of darkness and evil (not pushing them further into the grip of Satan through criticism)

This is a pretty detailed list of what we are to do and, as I've mentioned numerous times, it cannot be done in the strength of our flesh. The greatest strength of our natural man is no match for the supernatural power of evil and perversion. This goes back to the fact that our true enemy is not our fellow man but the devil and his legion of fallen angels (evil spirits, demons). Once we understand with whom is our fight, we will have a completely new outlook. With that new vantage, we will approach the worst with an altered sense of priority. No longer will our main objective be to retaliate against an oppressor but it will be to look beyond the veil.

The instruction, "Therefore be careful how you walk, not as unwise men but as wise, making the most of your time, because the days are evil. So then do not be foolish, but understand what the will of the Lord is," are found in Ephesians 4:15-17. Countless Christians flood churches and never come to an understanding of the will of the Lord, not for the body of Christ as a whole or their own individual life. It is a true tragedy but a fact nonetheless. Graham Cooke said, "We are not here to be overwhelmed by life, by circumstances, or by the wickedness of people, or by what the enemy is trying to accomplish. We are here to be overwhelmed by who God is for us." In other words, Christ already overcame the world and death and, because He dwells within the believer, we are automatically equipped to express His completion of overcoming the world. The key is growing in maturity by learning how to properly put to use what God has given us.

It is the most natural thing to lash out when someone comes against us. We live in a world where we are more consumed with our "rights" rather than doing what is right for the greater good. It is a "tit for tat" way of life. We feel justified in our "I'll give you what you gave to me" attitude. The world will applaud your retaliation and encourage you to continue doing that. Modern psychology will insist you look out for number one if you want to have peace in this life but it is in direct contradiction to the inerrant Word of God. Luke 6:31 tells us to, "Treat others the same way you want them to treat you." To say it another way, "Don't do as it is done to you" because the cycle will never break – *never*.

I mentioned my mom in an earlier chapter and a snippet of what she endured (from *Extinguishing the Inferno of Anger*). As I look at her life and the lineage from which she hails, I see a tragic pattern of one generation after another doing the same old thing. But, thank God, she broke that pattern of violence, sexual abuse, perversion, lovelessness, bad parenting, and other negatives. As bad as what my grandmother did to my mom by punishing her for what my grandfather did to her, I can only imagine what had been done to my grandmother in her youth which would lead her to respond in such a manner.

Looking back, her mother, my great-grandmother, had six children. She was divorced and remarried a bootlegger. He was eventually arrested for bootlegging and she was left to take care of a tribe of children with no money. As a result, she became a prostitute. My best guess is that my grandmother and her siblings were abused by men who came to purchase sex. Looking back further, in my great-grandmother's younger years, her family had a boarding house. A man at least ten or twelve years older than Queen (my great-grandmother) moved into the boarding house. Her sisters were so enamored with him that they encouraged my great-grandmother to marry him since they were already married.

At the tender age of 16, she married this older man. As the story goes, he would go from bedroom to bedroom making the rounds of sex with each of them on an ongoing basis. O, the depravity! What must that have done to that young girl?

People are the way they are for a reason. Since her parents (my great-great-grands) didn't stop any of it and allowed her to marry this man. My observation is that they were no better. Each generation was full of bitterness, misinformation of right and wrong, anger, and, as far as I know, fury, rage, bitterness, unforgiveness, and malice. Who could stop it? Who was willing to overcome evil with the goodness of the Lord? My mom, that's who! She chose to raise her daughters adversely to her upbringing (if you can even call it that). She had no one to whom she could turn for comfort, aid, protection, balance, wisdom, knowledge or anything a grounded parent would offer.

My mom is a unique individual who, knowing little about the Bible or its instruction therein at that time, refused to perpetuate the filth and depravation of her early years. Not knowing how to "overcome evil with good", the instinctive nature of her Creator kicked in. Although she was grossly angry, bitter, unforgiving, and full of rage, she still somehow allowed good to overcome all the wickedness of the generations before her. She maintained a relationship with the woman who, basically speaking, threw her to the wolves. I honestly don't know how she did it, at least not in my natural thinking. However, I know that I know that Holy Spirit guided her into righteousness though she was unaware of His leading. Though she had never known love, she gave it to us the best she could. Though no one protected her, she protected us from my uncle. Though no wisdom was available to her, she mustered enough to give it to us. She truly overcame evil with good and I am a living testament to how that works and what that can produce. My deceased grandfather who molested her was a living testament to that and is in Paradise with the Lord today instead of hell.

Prayer:

Heavenly Father, hallowed be Thy name in all the Earth. I sincerely thank You that You have endued me with power from on high. In such power, I have the supernatural ability to overcome all evil with Your goodness. I demand of myself that I will not repay evil with evil, but I will render good to those who persecute me, who do evil against me. I will not avenge myself in accordance to Your direction. Just as Jesus was on the cross forgiving those who hung Him, I will say to my enemies, "I forgive you because you do not know what you do." Teach me Your ways, O Lord, that I may forever walk in the goodness of the Lord, our Savior. You rescue those in need; therefore, I will not worry about what the day brings or what my enemies forge against me. I trust in You and in You alone. I will concede to Your ways. Selah

Scripture References:

> Repay no one evil for evil, but give thought to do what is honorable in the sight of all. If possible, so far as it depends on you, live peaceably with all. Beloved, never avenge yourselves, but leave it to the wrath of God, for it is written, "Vengeance is mine, I will repay, says the Lord." To the contrary, "If your enemy is hungry, feed him; if he is thirsty, give him something to drink; for by so doing you will heap burning coals on his head." Do not be overcome by evil, but overcome evil with good (Romans 12:17-21).

> "But Jesus was saying, ;Father, forgive them; for they do not know what they are doing.' And they cast lots, dividing up His garments among themselves (Luke 23:34)."

"Whoever makes a practice of sinning is of the devil, for the devil has been sinning from the beginning. The reason the Son of God appeared was to destroy the works of the devil (I John 3:8)."

"The Lord is not slow to fulfill His promise as some count slowness, but is patient toward you, not wishing that any should perish, but that all should reach repentance (II Peter 3:9)."

Journaling

SIXTY-SIX

##

Commentary:

Parents must not be their children's friend until they are an adult. Our job as parents is to teach, train, and discipline, not to appease them by giving them whatever they want. One thing I learned early on is that discipline and punishment are two different things entirely. I never *punished* my daughters for wrongdoing. What I did was *discipline* them. I John 4 states that fear has to do with punishment, and those who fear are not perfected in love. Too many parents punish their children with good intentions, but stir nothing but fear within them. Children need to experience the discipline of a parent who loves them so entirely that they will take the time to correct and lead them into righteousness.

Punishment is a sign of fear and will breed torment and insecurity. Punishment makes a child feel as though they are a "bad person," whereas discipline indicates they are so loved they will not be allowed to continue down a destructive path. Many parents punish children with the words, "*You're so bad! Stop being bad!*" and commence enforcing some corporal punishment. This should not be because the child is left feeling that they are inherently evil. Additionally, they have no idea what they did wrong or why it was terrible. They only know their parents are disappointed, and they feel unworthy of love.

Conversely, parents who discipline their children look at their kids with so much love that they will do anything to aid them in gaining success. When they see their child doing something wrong, they stop them, correct them, explain why their actions are wrong, and express the consequences if they do not stop. *Discipline* is a sign of love that breeds faith and confidence. Discipline says to the child, "*I am so in love with you that I will not allow you to harm yourself.*" This is the way of God.

Even today, we live in the day of God's grace, not His punishment. When the Lord corrects His own, He does so with the heart of protecting us from ourselves and the evil one. As parents, we must all ask ourselves, "*Why did I punish him or her in the way I did? Was it out of my anger? Was it a result of my childhood fears or torment? What am I teaching my children? How am I training them in the way of the Lord? Are they experiencing my love or my wrath?*" These and other candid questions will help get us on the right track of discipline. Too many have misused the "*spare the rod, spoil the child*" verse to beat their children mercilessly. "The rod" referenced here is the rod of God's discipline, not necessarily a physical rod. Though I have, at times, spanked my daughters, it was not often. I have found that correcting them and backing up the correction with instruction was far more powerful than a stick or belt. Children must know they are loved if you expect them to heed your discipline.

The old, "*Because I said so,*" routine doesn't work. Children need to know why their actions were wrong, not just that they were wrong. Otherwise, they will continue through life, making the same mistakes since they don't know the "why" of their incorrect behavior. Parents must take the time required to teach their children right from wrong. It demands an awful lot of energy, and many parents aren't prepared to lend such time to their children. This is why so many young adults are rebellious, angry, and out of control. Punishment dictates that the child stands in fear of their parents and never again to do the wrong deed. The fear overrides any love the parent may have intended to extend. Discipline evokes thought in the child to reason good from evil. Badgering children into correctness is also bad because it will drive them to the very thing they should abstain.

Prayer:

Father, teach me Your ways. Discipline me so that I will be able to lovingly and adequately discipline my children. Show me Your strength, love, mercy, grace, and power so that I will be able to emulate You in the presence of my children. Help me, Lord, to raise my children in the nurture and admonition of the Lord so that, when they are old, they will not depart from Your Word. I pray for Your Holy Spirit to lead, guide and direct me in the edicts of the Kingdom of Heaven. Help me to obey You so that they will obey me until they learn to follow You. I pray to know the difference between punishment and discipline, teaching, and provoking. I pray for Your Spirit to guide me in all wisdom and knowledge so that I will not veer to the right or the left. Cause me to hunger and thirst for Your Word that I may have enough daily manna from Heaven to pour into my children. As a parent of children who are gifts from Heaven, thank You for allowing me such an honor as raising them in Your image. Selah.

Scripture References:

> "No discipline seems pleasant at the time, but painful. Later on, however, it produces a harvest of righteousness

and peace for those who have been trained by it (Hebrews 12:11)."

"Whoever spares the rod hates their children, but the one who loves their children is careful to discipline them (Proverbs 13:24)."

"Train your children in the way they should go and when they are old, they will not depart from it (Proverbs 22:6)."

"Discipline your children, and they will give you peace; they will bring you the delights you desire (Proverbs 29:17)."

"Do not be anxious about anything, but in every situation, by prayer and petition, with thanksgiving, present your requests to God. And the peace of God, which transcends all understanding, will guard your hearts and your minds in Christ Jesus (Philippians 4:6-7)."

"Fathers, do not provoke your children to anger, but bring them up in the discipline and instruction of the Lord (Ephesians 6:4)."

But as for you, continue in what you have learned and have become convinced of, because you know those from whom you learned it. and how from infancy you have known the Holy Scriptures, which are able to make you wise for salvation through faith in Christ Jesus. All Scripture I God-breathed and is useful for teaching, rebuking, correcting and training in righteousness…(II Timothy 3:14-16).

"There is no fear in love. But perfect love drives out fear, because fear has to do with punishment. The one who fears is not made perfect in love (I John 4:18)."

"My son, do not despise the Lord's discipline, and do not resent His rebuke, because the Lord disciplines those He loves, as a father the son he delights in (Proverbs 3:11-12:)."

Journaling

SIXTY-SEVEN

Patience

Prayer:

Father, I pray for patience, despite how many have said in heresy, "*Never pray for patience.*" I reject that falsehood of religiosity and fully embrace Your patience. Your patience has saved countless people; therefore, I learn from You. I choose to acknowledge that patience is my best friend in this life as it keeps me from making poor life-altering decisions. Help me to retain and maintain, in the forefront of my mind, that impatience breeds my enemies, much like Abraham with his illegitimate son, Ishmael. Keep me in Your grace, Father, so that I am not allowed to veer too far in any wrong direction. I choose Your wisdom, encouragement, and love, which includes Your admonishment when I begin to be impatient. Keep my spirit at peace with You no matter what is buzzing around me. In the anxieties of life, I purpose to be patient, calm, and self-disciplined. Selah

Scripture References:

"Whoever is patient has great understanding, but one who is quick-tempered displays folly (Proverbs 14:29)."

"Be completely humble and gentle; be patient, bearing with one another in love (Ephesians 4:2)."

"Be joyful in hope, patient in affliction, faithful in prayer (Romans 12:12)."

"Let us not become weary in doing good, for at the proper time we will reap a harvest if we do not give up (Galatians 6:9)."

"Better a patient person than a warrior, one with self-control than one who takes a city (Proverbs 16:32)."

"Therefore, as God's chosen people, holy and dearly loved, clothe yourselves with compassion, kindness, humility, gentleness and patience (Colossians 3:12)."

Journaling

SIXTY-EIGHT

Peace and Joy

Prayer:

Father, I come to You in the name of Jesus and thank You for the joy and peace, which can come only from Your hand in this alarming and chaotic situation. Stir faith within me so that, no matter what my natural eyes see, my ears hear, or my mind thinks, I will receive only that which comes from the Throne of Grace (Matthew 13:15-17). Thank You for giving me Holy Spirit to usher peace that passes all understanding, joy that comes only from the Lord (Romans 15:13), and discernment of how to handle this according to the Spirit and not according to fleshly emotions (Galatians 5:16). May the joy of the Lord be my strength and my utter dependency. Amen

Scripture References:

> "Be anxious for nothing, but in everything by prayer and supplication with thanksgiving let your requests be made known to God. And the peace of God, which surpasses

all comprehension, will guard your hearts and your minds in Christ Jesus (Philippians 4:7)."

"Now may the God of hope fill you with all joy and peace in believing, so that you will abound in hope by the power of the Holy Spirit (Romans 15:13)."

Blessed be the Lord, because He has heard the voice of my supplication. The Lord is my strength and my shield; my heart trusts in Him, and I am helped; therefore my heart exults, and with my song I shall thank Him. The Lord is their strength, and He is a saving defense to His anointed (Psalm 28:6-8).

Journaling

SIXTY-NINE

Pretense Removal

Prayer:

In the name of Jesus, I declare that I will no longer feign submission to You and Your Kingdom authority. Father, as I became very gifted in looking like a good Christian, I admit I was nothing more than religious. I do not want to hear on Judgment Day, *"Depart from Me, I never knew you, you worker of lawlessness."* Help me, Abba, transition from rigid religiosity into an authentic life of Christ. Show me how to love You and receive Your boundless love so that I will be supernaturally equipped to extend such love to those who are lost and hurting. Keep me from trying to look holy so that I may become holy as You are holy. Allow me access to Your Spirit and transform me by the renewing of my mind. I lay down all pretense and the façade of holiness that I may become all You have called and created me to be. I long to hear, *"Well done, My good and faithful servant."* Help me to walk in spiritual authenticity with You. Selah

Scripture References:

> Not everyone who says to Me, "Lord, Lord" will enter the Kingdom of Heaven, but the one who does the will of My Father who is in Heaven. On that day many will say to Me, "Lord, Lord, did we not prophesy in Your name, and cast out demons in Your name, and do many mighty works in Your name?" And then will I declare to them, "I never knew you; depart from Me, you workers of lawlessness (Matthew 7:21-23)."

Journaling

SEVENTY

Quickened Spirit

Prayer:

Heavenly Father, I thank You for enabling me to relinquish myself that I may become disciplined like You in every aspect of my life. Illuminate the eyes of my understanding so that I can see as You see, open my ears to hear as You hear, and let the mind that is in Christ be also in me. I bind away from myself, by the authority of Christ Jesus, a spirit of selfishness, worthlessness, emotionalism, independence, disobedience, and pride. I bind to myself selflessness, the worth of Christ Jesus, the Holy Spirit, and humility. I will begin today a walk worthy of the gospel of Christ. My mind, will, or emotions will no longer lead me. Alternately, the Holy Spirit in me will be my driving force. Quicken my spirit to life so that Your Spirit is fully able to commune with mine, allowing me to be self-disciplined in all my ways. I bind away from myself spirits of fear, death, lies, shame, and condemnation. I bind to myself truth, faith, life, and confidence in He who lives through me. I praise You, Father, that there is now no condemnation in Christ against me since I choose to live by the Spirit of the living God instead of my flesh. Thank You for Your life's breath and the Holy Spirit whom You freely offer. I receive You. I ignite the flame of Holy Spirit. Amen.

Scripture References:

"I am afflicted very much: quicken me, O Lord, according unto Thy Word (Psalm 119:107 (KJV))."

To know wisdom and instruction, to discern the sayings of understanding, to receive instruction in wise behavior, righteousness, justice and equity; to give prudence to the naïve, to the youth knowledge and discretion, a wise man will hear and increase in learning, and a man of understanding will acquire wise counsel, to understand a proverb and a figure, the words of the wise and their riddles. The fear of the Lord is the beginning of knowledge; fools despise wisdom and instruction. Hear, my son, your father's instruction and do not forsake your mother's teaching; indeed, they are a graceful wreath to your head and ornaments about your neck (Proverbs 1:2-9).

Journaling

SEVENTY-ONE

Racism

Commentary:

Racism is as commonplace as ever. Yes, we have evolved some—to God be the glory. No, we have not come far enough. Humans, namely Christians, still judge according to the outward appearance of mankind. I can understand why the world does it, but why do God's people? There's abounding racism in the world: black against white and white against black, black against brown and light brown against dark brown. There's racism among Hispanics, Africans, Americans, Europeans, Middle Easterners, and on and on the list goes. It is a heart problem. We cannot blame anyone but ourselves. It will not be until we as a united people turn toward God and relinquish our skewed, fleshly perspective of who we decide is sufficient or insufficient. God judges according to the heart, not the skin. We must become Kingdom-minded. Judging anyone according to their skin color, race, nationality, social status, or anything else is sin in God's sight.

Prayer:

O, gracious heavenly Lord, I repent on behalf of the body of Christ collectively. I repent for my family and myself for carrying any level of racism. I repent for fueling the fire of racism, either by being racist, making racist jokes, or being completely silent when I should speak against it. I pray for the hearts of people, including myself, to heal from false judgment against those who do not look like me. I pray for Your sovereign hand of balance to overtake the body of Christ as we have never seen before. I know You are not a prejudiced God because You created all mankind in Your image. In Your single vision, we are equal one with another. Help me to see others as equal to me. Keep my mind from wandering into enemy territory, causing me to think like the world, family, friends, or anyone who does not align themselves with You. Keep me from fear and stir faith within me. I pray for Your all-consuming fire to overtake me and burn me from the inside out. I pray this for Your holy bride and the nations. Bless our governing authorities to act in alliance with Your Spirit. Cleanse me and us from all unrighteousness. Teach me the ways of the Lord, O Holy One of Israel. Allow me to see with Your eyes and understand with Your mind. Allow me to be impartial and judge only according to the heart of God. Selah

Scripture References:

> "Therefore from now on we recognize no one according to the flesh; even though we have known Christ according to the flesh, yet now we know Him in this way no longer (II Corinthians 5:16)."

> "But the Lord said to Samuel, 'Do not look at his appearance or at the height of his stature, because I have

rejected him; for God sees not as man sees, for man looks at the outward appearance, but the Lord looks at the heart (I Samuel 16:7).'"

"For there is no partiality with God (Romans 2:11)."

"For he who does wrong will receive the consequences of the wrong which he has done, and that without partiality (Colossians 3:25)."

"For the Lord your God is the God of gods and the Lord of lords, the great, the mighty, and the awesome God who does not show partiality nor take a bribe (Deuteronomy 10:17)."

"Opening his mouth, Peter said, 'I most certainly understand now that God is not one to show partiality, but in every nation the man who fears Him and does what is right is welcome to Him (Acts 10:34-35)."

"For there is no distinction between Jew and Greek, for the same Lord is Lord of all, abounding in riches for all who call on Him (Romans 10:12)."

"If you address as Father the One who impartially judges according to each one's work, conduct yourselves in fear during the time of your stay on earth (I Peter 1:17)."

Journaling

SEVENTY-TWO

Release and Let Go

Prayer:

Father, I release myself to You totally and completely without reservation. I release to You all that bothers me, all that causes me distress, all the people whom I attempt to carry in my flesh, and all their problems and mistakes. I am now making a conscious choice to let go of all that is weighing me and keeping me from peace. Thank You, Father, that Your yoke is easy and Your burden is light. Remind me that, when my life's yoke is hard, and my burdens are heavy, I have strayed from Your perfect will. Refresh my memory morning by morning so that I can cast all my worries, anxieties, fears, frustrations, dilemmas, problems, children, grandchildren, family, friends, enemies, bosses, co-workers, employees, etc. upon You. You are the only one capable of carrying such a heavy load. Additionally, I purpose to let go of my past failures, wrongs, sins, rejections, abandonment, abuse, neglect, insecurities, and anything else which stands in my personal freedom in Christ. I release every encumbrance to You. Amen

Scripture References:

"Casting all your anxiety upon Him, because He cares for you (I Peter 5:7)."

Come to Me, all who are weary and heavy-laden, and I will give you rest. Take My yoke upon you and learn from Me, for I am gentle and humble in heart, and you will find rest for your souls. For My yoke is easy and My burden is light (Matthew 11:28-30).

Journaling

Repentance Scriptures and Commentary

"If we say that we have no sin, we are deceiving ourselves and the truth is not in us. If we confess our sins, He is faithful and righteous to forgive us our sins and to cleanse us from all unrighteousness (I John 1:8-9)."

"Let us behave properly as in the day, not in carousing and drunkenness, not in sexual promiscuity and sensuality, not in strife and jealousy. But put on the Lord Jesus Christ, and make no provision for the flesh in regard to its lusts (Romans 13:13-14)."

Definition of Repentance: summons to a personal, absolute, and ultimate unconditional surrender to God as Sovereign. Though it includes sorrow and regret, it is more than that. In repenting, one makes a complete change of direction (180 degrees) toward God.

Repentance is mandatory in our relationship with the Lord Jesus Christ. It is an act of humility, acknowledging that we, compared to the magnificence of Christ, are nothing. If we want to receive the cleansing of the Lord, repentance is not an option. There is, of course, our initial repentance when we are first introduced to Jesus and are receptive of the mercies of Christ—that's an awesome thing. Most people who refer to themselves as a "Christian" understand this foundation of repentance or, in other words, a turning away from one thing toward a better way. King David says in Psalm 51:4, "*Against You, You only, I have sinned and done what is evil in Your sight, so that You are justified when You speak and blameless when You judge.*"

Just as there is the war between God and Satan, there is a war between God and us. So long as we don't bother to acknowledge

God, we can, in a good earthly-conscience, do whatever we want, how, when, and where we want. However, on the day God finds us, and we stand face to face with His holiness, we would be diminished to nothing short of humiliation and contrition. I have quoted Job more times than I can count, so I won't be ashamed to quote him once more. Job, having been taken down to virtually nothing upon God prompting Satan to test him, Job pridefully defended himself, his character, and his honor. Eventually, after the young prophet Elihu chastised him, God entered, and spoke sternly to Job. God admonished his stance of defending himself and asked, "*Were you there when I laid the foundation of the Earth? Where were you when I...*" and continues to list the times where God moved mightily without Job's presence or assistance.

Job, in the end, trembling in the presence of One so great, said, "*I know that You can do all things and that no purpose of Yours can be thwarted. Who is this that hides counsel without knowledge? Therefore I have declared that which I did not understand, things too wonderful for me, which I did not know. Hear now, and I will speak; I will ask You and You instruct me. I have heard of You by the hearing of the ear; but now my eye sees You; therefore I retract, and I repent in dust and ashes* (Job 42:1-6).'"

When Job used the words "dust and ashes," he infers repentance though the word doesn't appear. Even though he had been a "perfect man,"—which means "pure of heart" not sinless— deeply hidden within him was mounding fear and rebellion, aka pride. Look at Job 29:11-14, 23-24, which reads, "*Whoever heard me spoke well of me, and those who saw me commended me, because I rescued the poor who cried for help, and the fatherless who had no one to assist him. The man who was dying blessed me; I made the widow's heart sing. I put on righteousness as my clothing; justice was my robe and my turban. They waited for me as for showers and drank in my words as the spring rain. When I smiled at them, they scarcely believed it; the light of my face was precious to them.*" In Job 32:1 we see, "*So these three men stopped answering Job, because he was righteous in his own eyes.*"

Job thought more highly of himself than he ought as he got caught up in his own greatness. In the middle of reading the very long book of Job, we see where Job grew weary and demanded the counsel of the Lord, but the Lord did not acknowledge him, at least not right away. Job felt sorry for himself, demanding that the Lord explain why He allowed such things to come upon one so righteous as himself. Job felt undeserving of God's silence while he lost nearly everything and suffered inexplicably. *"For he adds rebellion to his sin; he claps his hands among us and multiplies his words against God,"* Elihu said in Job 34:37. Please, read this for yourself in your private studies. Don't read the beginning and the end without the middle as many do. It's all very enlightening as to the full scope of why God allowed his trials.

My point? Job suffered longer than he should have because he lacked simple repentance. Pride stood in his way. What God was attempting to do—and was in the end successful—was to purge Job of his self-righteousness he didn't know he had. Job was such a "good and perfect man" that he missed the need for repentance. He felt as though God wasn't as good to him as he deserved; he thought way more highly of himself than he should have. This was Job's war with God. At the end of God's discipline, Job repented in recognition that, no matter how good of a person he was, outside of God, he was still just as sinful as the next, not because of blatant sin, but because of the Adamic nature with which he was born. In encountering the One True God, he said, *"Therefore I retract, and I repent in dust and ashes."*

Repentance is the road to God. Although Jesus was yet to come, repentance was still a requirement. Once Job relented and repented, God blessed him doubly and blessed his intercession for his fair-weathered friends. God honors and blesses the contrite of heart. Humility is the gateway to the Lord's heart. Repentance is ongoing as we all sin daily, blatantly, or unaware. We do this in our attitudes, words, and deeds. Even the best of the best fail and falter, present company included. Paul called himself the "chiefest of sinners," and I can relate. The things I want to do, sometimes, I do not do. The things I will to not do, I do anyway, nearly out of my control. Sin lives within the shell of the natural man. No matter how long we walk with the Lord and commune intimately with Him, we are sometimes drawn into sin because we walk in a shroud of death. Repentance must be our constant position.

"Do not be overcome by evil, but overcome evil with good," is found in Romans 12:21. This is quite a simple statement, yet full of power! In this one verse in Romans, we see that evil is running rampant; otherwise, God would not give us such a command. He understands that evil is the way of this Satan-driven world. The Earth and mankind were condemned because Adam allowed Satan to dethrone him from his position in the Lord. There are innumerable types of evil in the world which can, at a moment's notice, turn us from our peace toward anger and, in our anger, devastation is the outcome. So how do we overcome evil with good? How do we accomplish what is impossible for the natural man? For starters, repentance: it is the beginning to being equipped to overcome evil with good because we must first return to God before anything else good can spring from us. After repentance, let's look to II Timothy for more instruction so as to maintain a life of holiness.

For starters, II Timothy 2:22-26 tells us, *"Now flee from youthful lusts and pursue righteousness, faith, love, and peace, with those who call on the Lord from a pure heart. But refuse foolish and ignorant speculations, knowing that they produce quarrels. The Lord's bond-servant must not be quarrelsome, but be kind to all, able to teach, patient when wronged, with gentleness correcting those who are in opposition, if perhaps God may grant them repentance leading to the knowledge of the truth, and they may come to their senses and escape from the snare of the devil, having been held captive by him to do his will."* To simplify, here is a list of instructions:

1. Flee youthful lusts—sinful, incontrollable desires
2. Pursue righteousness—holiness
3. Pursue faith—in God
4. Pursue love—God's immeasurable, supernatural love
5. Pursue peace—contentment in all circumstances
6. Pursue godliness alongside those who call on the Lord with a pure heart
7. Reject foolish speculations—guesswork
8. Reject ignorant speculations—theorizing
9. Understand speculations produce quarrels
10. Do not be quarrelsome—argumentative, contentious
11. Be kind to all—everyone regardless of differing opinions, race, religion, background, etc.
12. Be able to teach—while in blatant sin, you are disqualified to teach—know the Word and live it
13. Be patient when wronged—don't allow your anger to cause you to lose your cool and snap
14. Correct those in opposition to you but do so in gentleness—do not harshly slam people who don't agree with you
15. Correct with the purpose of leading them to repentance—not to shame them
16. Correct with the purpose of leading people into the knowledge of truth—not to belittle or scorn them
17. Correct people with the purpose of directing them to come to their God senses—lead them into the mind of Christ
18. Correct people with the purpose of helping them escape the snare of the devil—not condemning making them feel they'll be forever evil
19. Correct people with the explicit purpose of setting them free from the chains of darkness and evil—not pushing them further into the grip of Satan through criticism

This is a pretty detailed list of what we are to do and, as I've mentioned numerous times, it cannot be done in the strength of our flesh. The greatest strength of our natural man is no match for the supernatural power of evil and perversion. This goes back to the fact that our true enemy is not our fellow man, but the devil and his legion of fallen angels—evil spirits, demons. Once we understand with whom is our fight, we will have a completely new outlook. With that new vantage, we will approach the worst with an altered sense of priority. No longer will our main objective be to retaliate against an oppressor but it will be to look beyond the veil.

The instruction, *"Therefore be careful how you walk, not as unwise men but as wise, making the most of your time, because the days are evil. So then do not be foolish, but understand what the will of the Lord is,"* are found in Ephesians 4:15-17. Countless Christians flood churches and never come to an understanding of the will of the Lord, not for the body of Christ as a whole or their own individual life. It is a true tragedy but a fact nonetheless. Graham Cooke said, *"We are not here to be overwhelmed by life, by circumstances, or by the wickedness of people, or by what the enemy is trying to accomplish. We are here to be overwhelmed by who God is for us."* In other words, Christ already overcame the world and death and, because He dwells within the believer, we are automatically equipped to express His completion of overcoming the world. The key is growing in maturity by learning how to properly put to use what God has given us.

Scripture References:

> "If My people who are called by My name will humble themselves and pray and seek My face and turn from their wicked ways, then I will hear from Heaven, and I will forgive their sin and will heal their land (II Chronicles 7:14)."

"If we confess our sins, He is faithful and just and will forgive our sins and purify us from all unrighteousness (I John 1:9)."

"Repent, then, and turn to God, so that your sins may be wiped out, that times of refreshing may come from the Lord (Acts 3:19)."

"Whoever conceals their sins does not prosper, but the one who confesses and renounces them finds mercy (Proverbs 28:13)."

"Produce fruit in keeping with repentance (Matthew 3:8)."

"The Lord is not slow in keeping His promise, as some understand slowness. Instead He is patient with you, not wanting anyone to perish, but everyone to come to repentance (II Peter 3:9)."

"From that time on, Jesus began to preach, 'Repent, for the Kingdom of Heaven has come near (Matthew 4:17)."

Journaling

SEVENTY-THREE

Repentance of Sin-Nature

Prayer:

Dear heavenly Father, I repent today of _____, which I have consciously allowed to remain in my life. I repent this day, Jesus, for my wicked disobedience and lack of reverent, respectful fear of You, Almighty God. I thank You that You will continue to give me the ability, strength, and courage to endure the rest of the plowing of the bad harvest I planted for myself. I repent of blaming You, O Precious Savior, for the repercussions of the iniquity of my hand. Lay Your righteous right hand of pure love upon me and show me how to die to my fleshly nature that I may become like You. Quicken my spirit to life so that You may be free to admonish me when I sin and to grant me the grace to recognize and repent quickly. Help me, Father, to love what You love, hate what You hate, do as You do, and go where You go. Bless You, Father. Teach me Your perfect ways that I may turn and minister to You. Show me how to be an excellent host for Holy Spirit. May it be done in my life as it is in Heaven. Whatever Your will for my life, I agree. I lay myself at the foot of the cross. Reveal to me Your holy Word that I may continue always to grow in maturity so that the world may see You in me and turn from their wicked ways. Pour into me the spirit of wisdom and revelation that I may know You better. Illuminate the eyes of my understanding that I may know the hope of my calling in Christ Jesus. I pray this all in the blessed name of Your Son Jesus. Amen

Scripture References:

"From that time on Jesus began to preach, "Repent, for the Kingdom of Heaven has come near (Matthew 4:17).""

"Produce fruit in keeping with repentance (Matthew 3:8).""

"I have not come to call the righteous, but sinners to repentance (Luke 5:32).""

Journaling

SEVENTY-FOUR

Repentance of Adultery

Prayer:

Father, I humble myself before You today in repentance of all unholy, adulterous activity, not excluding what I have entertained in my mind. I recognize that pornography is adultery as much as physically engaging in sex outside my marriage bed. I also acknowledge that forsaking any marriage vow is adultery, including putting my job or friends above my spouse. Father, I come before You repentant seeking to restore the error of my ways. Thank You for always giving grace in the face of my sinful state. May I never put anyone or anything above my spouse that I may always—for the man—love my wife as You love the church, and—for the woman—may I honor and respect my husband as the head of the household. May I always submit myself (man and woman) to my spouse in honor of You. Teach me the ways of righteousness. Show me the error of my ways that I may confess, repent, and be made whole, first with and in You and secondly with my spouse. Renew our marriage that we may honor You in all we say and do. May our marriage be the beautiful reflection of our marriage to Jesus. Amen.

Scripture References:

"You have heard that it was said, "You shall not commit adultery;" but I say unto you, that whosoever looks on a woman to lust after her has committed adultery in his heart (Matthew 5:27-28)."

"But He gives more grace. Wherefore He says, 'God resists the proud, but gives grace unto the humble (James 4:6, KJV).'"

Journaling

SEVENTY-FIVE

Repentance of Anxiety and Fear

Prayer:

Father, I come to you now in repentance of the anxiety and fear I have held these many years. I thank You that You are a forgiving, merciful, kind, and just God who does all You do for my good and the good of the Kingdom of Heaven. Great is Your faithfulness in all the Earth. Let the mind that is in Christ be also in me and, as a result, I purpose to pull down the thoughts and strongholds of the flesh and allow Your Spirit to guide my every move. Help me see through my trials all the way to the other side as do You. May the wisdom from above, which is first pure, then peaceable, gentle, and easy to be entreated, full of mercy and good fruits, without partiality and without hypocrisy rule in my heart all the days of my life. I surrender myself, spirit, soul and body, to You, O Sovereign King. I thank You, as it was with Job, the worst of times are set in motion to take me out of my comfort zone and into the throne of grace and the greatness You have prepared for me. Allow me to build and tear down according to Your will, and make my feet to stay or go wherever is pleasing to You. Father, I thank You for Your incredible loving-kindness in everyday life. I purpose to bless You, heavenly Father, with the words of my mouth, the work of my hands and the meditation of my heart. Let anxiety be far from me so that the peace of Christ rules in my heart. I replace anxiety with trust, and fear with faith. I command spirits of fear and anxiety to be loosed from their assignment over me. I release the Spirit of God to be my only spiritual force at work. Selah.

Scripture References:

"Anxiety in a man's heart weighs him down, but a good word makes him glad (Proverbs 12:25)."

"Cast all your anxiety on Him because He cares for you (I Peter 5:7)."

"Do not be anxious about anything, but in everything by prayer and supplication with thanksgiving let your requests be made known to God (Philippians 4:6-7)."

journaling

SEVENTY-SIX

Repentance of Idolatry

Prayer:

I repent immediately for ever making self an idol set before You. I surrender all to You and submit self that You are King and Lord over me always. May I forever seek first the Kingdom of God and Your righteousness above all else. I choose to abide in faith so that, when I walk obediently, all things that need to come to me, will. I cast out a demon of idolatry from my life. I surrender myself wholly to You. I repent of making other people, places, and things an idol above Your holiness. You are my God and I am Your people. Here I am Lord. Send me. Amen.

Scripture References:

> "Do not be idolaters, as some of them were; as it is written: "The people sat down to eat and drink and got up to indulge in revelry"…Therefore, my dear friends, flee from idolatry. (I Corinthians 10:7, 14)."

"Dear children, keep yourselves from idols (I John 5:21)."

"Put to death, therefore, whatever belongs to your earthly nature: sexual immorality, impurity, lust, evil desires and greed, which is idolatry (Colossians 3:5)."

Journaling

SEVENTY-SEVEN

Restoration of Health

Prayer:

Gracious heavenly Father, I thank You for promising to restore my health and heal my wounds. Many have called me an outcast, but You call me Your beloved. You have promised to restore the years the locust, cankerworm, caterpillar, and the palmerworm have eaten away. I fully expect restoration to come about in due season. I trust You, Lord, that it is counted as done though I have yet to see it manifested. I thank You, Yahweh, that You promised Your disciples—and I am one—have the power to resist going the way of wicked. I am equipped to go to the lost sheep preaching, 'The Kingdom of Heaven is at hand' while healing the sick, raising the dead, cleansing the lepers, and casting out demons. Freely I have received; freely, I will give to others (Matthew 10:5-8). I proclaim over myself, my household, my _____ that we are well, healed, and whole, in the name of Jesus. This begins with my inner-man—spirit—and then spreading to my outer man (Mark 5:34; Matthew 9:22; John 5:6). You bore my iniquities, and, by Your wounds, I am most surely healed (I Peter 2:24; Isaiah 53:5). Selah

Scripture References:

"For I will restore you to health and I will heal you of your wounds," declares the Lord, "because they have called you an outcast, saying: 'It is Zion; no one cares for her (Jeremiah 30:17).'"

"I will call those who were not My people, 'My people' and her who was not beloved, 'beloved' (Romans 9:25)."

"And I will restore to you the years that the locust has eaten, the cankerworm, and the caterpillar, and the palmerworm, My great army which I sent among you (Joel 2:25, AKJV)."

"Keep watching and praying that you may not enter into temptation; the spirit is willing, but the flesh is weak (Matthew 26:41)."

Journaling

SEVENTY-EIGHT

Restoration General

Prayer:

Father, I thank You that restoration belongs to me through the blood of Your Son, Jesus! I thank You that I am well, healed, healthy, and whole, inside and out! I patiently await the fullness of Your promise yet to manifest in my life. I come before You humbled, broken, and shattered. I ask that You reveal everything to me, both natural and supernatural, that needs to be addressed. Without You, I am nothing, and I have nothing. As I am dead, I seek Your face to breathe Your Holy Life into me. I prophesy to the breath of God from the north, south, east, and west that Your Spirit will breathe life into my old, dead bones. Show me the way from darkness into the marvelous Light that is You. O Lord, restore, refresh and renew me. Grant me supernatural ability to withstand the wiles of the enemy attempting to lead me astray. Amen

Scripture References:

"Brothers and sisters, if someone is caught in a sin, you who live by the Spirit should restore that person gently. But watch yourselves, or you also may be tempted (Galatians 6:1)."

"Come, let us return to the Lord. He has torn us to pieces but he will heal us; He has injured us but He will bind up our wounds (Hosea 6:1)."

"Then He said to me, 'Prophesy to the breath, prophesy, son of man, and say to the breath, "Thus says the Lord God, 'Come from the four winds, O breath, and breathe on these slain, that they come to life (Ezekiel 37:9).'"

Journaling

SEVENTY-NINE

Sacrifice of Obedience

Prayer:

Heavenly Father, I do not know how to sacrifice myself completely, but I want to. Please, show me how to give up all of me that I may be filled with all of You. I want Your desire to become my desire. I want Your will to become my will. Direct me how to be obedient to love what You love and hate what You hate. I do not want to make a move lest You lead and go before me. Give me the grace to accept what You reveal so that condemnation does not come upon me. I desire an authentic relationship with You, above all else. Teach me Your ways, O Lord. I choose to walk in love regardless of what the flesh feels. I choose You, above all else. I consign myself in all humility and obedience to Your commands. I defer to the Kingdom of Heaven, the Kingdom Constitution—Holy Bible—and all You desire in and through me. I am Yours. Selah

Scripture References:

"And walk in the way of love, just as Christ loved us and gave Himself up for us as a fragrant offering and sacrifice to God (Ephesians 5:2)."

"For whoever wants to save their life will lose it, but whoever loses their life for Me will save it (Proverbs 21:3)."

"But go and learn what this means: "I desire mercy, not sacrifice." For I have not come to call the righteous, but sinners (Matthew 9:13)."

"For even the Son of Man did not come to be served, but to serve, and to give His life as a ransom for many (Mark 10:45)."

Journaling

EIGHTY

Seeing God's Hand

Prayer:

I pray, O Father, to begin to see past the puppet (the devil) and see only You—the Master. You, heavenly Father, are the One by whom all is controlled. I confess there is nothing that does not originate from You. Light my path as I pass through the shadow of darkness. I bless You that, because of confidence in You, I will fear no evil, for evil has been overcome. Remind me daily that I have power and authority over this defeated foe as I walk according to the Spirit. Help me understand Your Word, Your will, and Your way so that I no longer stumble in the darkness. Make clear and straight paths for my feet. I thank You that Your understanding and knowledge are bound to me. Show me how to bless those who curse me, for all things are set in motion to bless me eventually. I pray that those around me will not be able to tell the difference between You and me. I desire to merge entirely with You to think, see, hear, and know as You. Selah

Scripture References:

"I form the light, and create the darkness: I make peace, and create evil: I the Lord do all these things. Drop down, ye Heavens, from above, and let the skies pour down righteousness,: let the Earth open, and let them bring forth salvation, and let righteousness spring up together; I the Lord have created it (Isaiah 45:6-8)."

"I have told you these things, so that in Me you may have peace. In this world, you will have trouble. But take heart! I have overcome the world (John 16:33)."

"Do not forsake wisdom, and she will protect you; love her, and she will watch over you. The beginning of wisdom is this: Get wisdom. Though it cost all you have, get understanding (Proverbs 4:6-7)."

Journaling

EIGHTY-ONE

Self-Control

Prayer:

Father, may I be self-controlled as was Jesus when He walked in human flesh. As I seek purity, reveal the weaknesses of my flesh to me that I will flee evil instead of deceiving myself into thinking that I have the strength I do not possess. Lead me into the path of righteousness that I will not cast my foot upon a stone and stumble and fall. I choose to crucify my fleshly man and receive the Holy Spirit to take His rightful position as the ruler of my heart. I repent of all impure activity in my past, and receive Your forgiveness. I choose to abstain from all impurity. Thank You, Jesus, for paving the way of holiness. I choose the path of self-control, to bridle my tongue and emotions, and yield myself to Your will. I bind from myself a spirit of lawlessness and anarchy and replace it with the spirit of obedience to the way of the Lord. Amen.

Scripture References:

"Better a patient person than a warrior, one with self-control than one who takes a city (Proverbs 16:32)."

"Like a city whose walls are broken through is a person who lacks self-control (Proverbs 25:28)."

"Rather, he must be hospitable, one who loves what is good, who is self-controlled, upright, holy and disciplined (Titus 1:8)."

"They will bear you up in their hands, that you do not strike your foot against a stone (Psalm 91:12)."

journaling

EIGHTY-TWO

Set Apart Unto God

Prayer:

O gracious Father, stir within me the desire to set myself apart wholly to You. Guide me into the paths of righteousness. Show me, O God, how to reverently fear Your holy name. I pray to have a clear vision from Heaven to recognize the difference between truth and a phantom so that I may not be lured away by fleshly deceit. Teach me how to seek first the Kingdom of Heaven and Your righteousness so that all other things I need here on Earth will be provided without having to ask. Thank You, Father, my Husband, and lover of my soul, for exposing everything that is a falsehood in my life. Continue to reveal every wicked and fruitless deed of darkness, attempting to lead me astray. I bind Your supernatural strength to myself to overcome the illusions of life. Amen.

Scripture References:

> "You have made known to me the ways of life; you will make me full of gladness with Your presence (Acts 2:28)."

"But seek first the Kingdom of God and His righteousness, and all these things will be added unto you (Matthew 6:33)."

"Let no one deceive you with empty words, for because of such things God's wrath comes on those who are disobedient (Ephesians 5:6)."

Journaling

Sexual Purity Scripture and Commentary

Because this topic is taught so little or, at the very least, insufficiently, I will take more time here to elaborate upon God's definition of sexual purity. I have listed numerous Scriptures on differing sects of sexual misconduct, discuss what the texts mean, and conclude with the problem's solution.

Sexual Immorality, aka Fornication:

> "You say, 'Food is for the stomach and the stomach for food, and God will destroy them both.' The body, however, is not meant for sexual immorality but for the Lord, and the Lord for the body….Flee from sexual immorality. All other sins a person commits are outside the body, but whoever sins sexually, sins against their own body (I Corinthians 6:13, 18)."

> "Marriage should be honored by all, and the marriage bed kept pure, for God will judge the adulterer and all the sexually immoral (Hebrews 13:)."

> "In the very same way, on the strength of their dreams these ungodly people pollute their own bodies, reject authority and heap abuse on celestial beings (Jude 1:8)."

> "But as for the cowardly, the faithless, the detestable, as for murderers, the sexually immoral, sorcerers, idolaters, and all liars, their portion will be in the lake that burns with fire and sulfur, which is the second death (Revelation 21:8)."

"Just as Sodom and Gomorrah and the surrounding cities, which likewise indulged in sexual immorality and pursued unnatural desire, serve as an example by undergoing a punishment of eternal fire (Jude 1:7)."

"Now the works of the flesh are evident: sexual immorality, impurity, sensuality (Galatians 5:19)."

"I (Apostle Paul) fear that when I come again my God may humble me before you, and I may have to mourn over many of those who sinned earlier and have not repented of the impurity, sexual immorality, and sensuality that they have practiced (II Corinthians 12:21)."

"For you may be sure of this, that everyone who is sexually immoral or impure, or who is covetous (that is, an idolater), has no inheritance in the Kingdom of Christ and God (Ephesians 5:5)."

According to "Got Questions," in the New Testament, the word most often translated "sexual immorality" is "porneia." This word translates as "whoredom," "fornication," and "idolatry." It means "a surrendering of sexual purity," and it is primarily used in premarital sexual relations. From this Greek word, we get the English word "pornography," stemming from the concept of "selling off." Sexual immorality is the "selling" of sexual purity and involves any type of sexual expression outside the boundaries of a biblically defined marital relationship (Matthew 19:4-5).

In other words, fornication is any sexual activity outside holy covenant between a wed man and woman. The Lord is very specific on this matter. Fornication or sexual immorality can be anything from homosexual sexual relations to heterosexual sexual relations between two people who are not married. Sexual impurity can be sexual intercourse, fondling private parts, or even allowing the mind to regularly indulge in sexual imaginations with another person who is not their spouse. Pornography is fornication just as much as if there were physical contact because all sexual sin begins in the mind. Masturbation within marriage—if both the husband and wife agree—is acceptable, but, otherwise, this is sexual misconduct as it generally comes from a place where there are fantasies about someone other than their spouse. Adultery is a no-brainer, which is sexual immorality. Sodomy, pedophilia, sex with a corpse, sex with an animal, rape, molestation, and anything of the like is sexual immorality and against God.

It is good and profitable to understand the parameters of sexual immorality, so that we not fall into unawares. My teen daughters just asked me the other night, *"What exactly is sexual impurity?"* On that note, we discussed this at length, and it led to writing all this. Furthermore, my friend's 85-year-old husband, who grew up Catholic, asked the same question. Raised in a Christian home, I knew not to have intercourse, but I had no concept of the "extras" that qualify as sexual immorality. I knew the Law, but I did not understand accountability, holiness, or that there are ramifications of sexual sin far beyond most Christians have grasped.

Now, at 52, I certainly understand all of that, and I purpose to train young and old so that they are not just "following Law." Merely being obedient because "God said so" can cause one to grow weary in doing what is right if they do not understand the "why" of it. The "why" is very important. It is imperative for a successful relationship with God. Before you start reading the Scriptures on specific sexual impurities listed below, I am compelled to explain this one paramount fact: *all sexual sin* is abhorrent to God. It is all sin against God as well as a sin against our bodies. Especially in America—but certainly around the globe, well-meaning Christians badger those participating in homosexuality as if it is the worst of all sexual sins, but that simply isn't so. Immorality, of any kind, keeps one from entering the Kingdom of God. The following texts will confirm this, and I didn't even list them all. This should prove that it all matters.

As a side note, idolatry stands side-by-side with sexual immorality. Why? Because all sin stems from pride. Pride will dictate that we can at any point and in any area of life, forgo God's will. This equates idolatry. It is placing our will and fleshly desires above the edicts of Heaven. Idolatry, simply stated, is worshiping something above the Lord. When we engage in any sin, it is idolatry because we are worshiping ourselves. That's the short of it. The extended version is that we want what we want, when we want it, and, by no means, should our love of God stand in our way of retrieving what we desire. Idolaters will not see the Kingdom of God any more than homosexuals, or anyone else fulfilling their sexual desires outside the marriage bed.

I had a group conversation on social media the other day, and the responses of "good Christians" were predictable. I had posted an article about a group of Christians who met with people at an LGTBQ parade. They had signs apologizing for the poor treatment of homosexuals within the church. I was clear that I do not support the act of homosexuality, but that the hatred they have experienced at the hands of Christians is unacceptable. One wrote, "*I will NEVER apologize for calling homosexuality sin! Disagreeing is not hatred.*" I responded that I am in no way condoning such activity, nor am I abstaining from calling it sin.

Furthermore, I agree that disagreeing is not hatred, yet there is blatant hatred coming from many within the church. Hatred is, indeed, hatred. When Christians stand around name-calling homosexuals with "queer" and "fag" and other derogatory words, when we are slandering them as though they are not people for whom our Christ died, that is hatred. I've witnessed it all my life. Slander is also a sin. Those who do it will not enter the Kingdom of God.

I commented that it is hypocritical to ban attending a gay wedding or serving them wedding accessories when, all the while, "good Christians" flock to heterosexual weddings where they know the couple has been engaging in sexual impurity. This is while they serve in their local churches as choir directors, missionaries, Sunday school teachers, and even pastors. *"Such a godly young couple,"* people say, yet it is a falsehood. Why do we slander one set of fornicators while celebrating another? It proves we don't understand sexual impurities or the ramifications of any of it. A heterosexual couple finally tying the knot does not undo fornication, it doesn't. It only compounds the problem because they are entering holy covenant with an unholy foundation. This can only lead to future marital issues because it wasn't based on the will of God. A man wrote, *"LGBTQ is worse than fornication in a heterosexual person because the former has the LGBTQ agenda to take over the world."*

Ummmm…seriously? Again, this points to a bigger, more significant breakdown in the body of Christ. The reason heterosexual sinners don't have parades is because we have already accepted their sin as sinless. We, the Church, have forsaken God in this area by accepting sexual impurity as, *"Not that bad, at least it's a man and a woman and not a same-gender couple."* God did not create mankind as heterosexual, but as holy. He is not consumed with whether or not one is tempted by one kind of sexual sin or another. Instead, we learn to overcome our temptations by surrendering to His will. We need to understand that each sexual sin has differing repercussions, but, at the heart, it is all against God. It is all idolatry. When we grasp the why of the rules, we will finally obey the Lord out of gratitude. Every commandment God has set before us is because He is in love with us.

Because of sexual immorality running amuck, we have created a godless and idolatrous society. It is entirely self-serving, all the while we excuse our poor conduct with, *"But I'm a good person."* It has led to innumerable abandoned, murdered, abused, neglected children from people who had sex with people, not their spouses. Some single mothers have multiple children with multiple fathers, and, because of it, she cannot afford them, and they don't have the male structure necessary for a well-rounded upbringing. Single moms are aborting—murdering—or abandoning their unborn because they cannot properly care for them. Men are raping, molesting, and altogether steeling young girls' childhoods and lives because they refuse to abide by the Law of God. Women cannot keep their legs closed because they possess zero self-control, or because they feel it's the only way to get a man. No one wants to wait. With all these neglected, abandoned, fatherless, motherless children, they grow up unbalanced and become a drain on society. They are unsteady in their minds, jobs, families, and community. Statistics prove that children raised in a married mother/father household are more secure in their identity and better able to focus on their education and future at large. All the AIDS and sexually transmitted diseases did not come from holy living but from disengaging from our Creator and living unto our fleshly desires. There are consequences to everything we do—some last a lifetime, and some into death for those who take too long to surrender.

There is no substitution for holiness, nothing. Living according to God's will, especially in the arena of sexual purity, is trustworthy and good. Learning to listen to the voice of Holy Spirit and purposing to set oneself aside unto God has nothing but benefits. Forsaking the ways of the world with all its lusts and idolatries making self our god equals nothing. God knew what He was doing when we gave us His Law and the reason for the Law—simply obeying without understating why will prove insufficient. God is in love with us.

I need now to address the "*I was born this way. God must want me to be homosexual.*" We are all born into sin because of the tainted, sinful bloodline of Adam. This is why Christ died for all, not some. The Christian argument to homosexuality has always been—or at least what I've always heard, *"God doesn't make junk"* or *"God didn't create homosexuality; therefore, no one can be born that way."* Well, that is quickly debunked because, just as anyone can have a birth defect physically, there can be birth defects spiritually. We call them generational curses. All of the sin-nature is a spiritual birth defect, and it came from Adam and Eve. For example, we are all born in pride. This is because the nature of the flesh is, in and of itself, prideful. We are all naturally born liars, as witnessed in even the youngest of babies. They learn quickly how to manipulate parents through crying when nothing is wrong. This is defective, as God is not a liar.

The list can go on and on about how imperfectly we all are born. It's only natural. Because of defective flesh, Christ had to die—for everyone. Christ didn't die to transform the homosexual into a heterosexual. He died for all liars, idolaters, murderers, slanderers, homosexuals, heterosexuals collectively that we may be transitioned out of death and into life. *All* are sinners. *All* need to be transformed by the renewing of our minds. Because of this, we who are authentically in Christ will quickly recognize that we are to reach the lost; the fornicators, slanderers, murderers, liars, and, yes, the outcast homosexual. We need to get back to seeing all sin as defiled, not just the ones we don't like or understand. We must cease singling out this one or that one as though "those people" are worse than the sinner you were before you were transformed. We cannot reach the lost—anyone) —if we are mocking them and treating them as the enemy. We are all God's enemies based on the fact that we are all born defective by nature. In #95, *Temptation*, I will discuss how anyone can overcome any temptation when they willingly yield to God's character and purpose for each of our lives.

Homosexuality:

> But we know that the Law is good, if one uses it lawfully, realizing the fact that law is not made for a righteous person, but for those who are lawless and rebellious, for the ungodly and sinners, for the unholy and profane, for those who kill their fathers or mothers, for murderers and immoral men and homosexuals and kidnappers and liars and perjurers, and whatever else is contrary to sound teaching, according to the glorious gospel of the blessed God, with which I have been entrusted (I Timothy 1:8-11).

> Because of this, God gave them over to shameful lusts. Even their women exchanged natural sexual relations for unnatural ones. In the same way the men also abandoned natural relations with women and were inflamed with lust for one another. Men committed shameful acts with other men, and received in themselves the due penalty for their error. Furthermore, just as they did not think it worthwhile to retain the knowledge of God, so God gave them over to a depraved mind, so that they do what ought not be to done (Romans 1:26-28).

> "A woman shall not wear mans' clothing, nor shall a man put on a woman's clothing; for whoever does these things is an abomination to the Lord your God (Deuteronomy 23:17)."

> "If there is a man who lies with a male as those who lie with a woman, both of them have committed a detestable act; they shall surely be put to death. Their bloodguiltiness is upon them (Leviticus 20:13)."

Adultery:

"But I say to you that everyone who looks at a woman with lust for her has already committed adultery with her in his heart (Matthew 5:28)."

"You shall not commit adultery (Exodus 20:14)."

"But a man who commits adultery has no sense; whoever does it destroys himself (Proverbs 6:32)."

The lips of another man's wife may be as sweet as honey and her kisses as smooth as olive oil, but when it is all over, she leaves you nothing but bitterness and pain. She will take you down to the world of the dead; the road she walks is the road to death. She does not stay on the road to life; but wanders off, and does not realize what is happening. Now listen to me, sons, and never forget what I am saying. Keep away from such a woman! Don't even go near her door! If you do, others will gain the respect that you once had and you will die young at the hands of merciless people. Yes, strangers will take your wealth and what you have worked for will belong to someone else. You will lie groaning on your deathbed, your flesh and muscles being eaten away, and you will say, "Why would I never learn? Why would I never let anyone correct me? I wouldn't listen to my teachers. I paid no attention to them. And suddenly I found myself publicly disgraced." Be faithful to your own wife and give your love to her alone. Children that you have by other women will do you no good. Your children should grow up to help you, not strangers. So be happy with your wife and find your joy with the woman you married – pretty and graceful as a deer. Let her charms keep you happy; let her surround you with her love. Son, why should you give your love to another woman? Why should you prefer the charms of another man's wife? The Lord sees everything you do. Wherever you go, He is watching. The sins of the wicked are a trap. They get caught in the net of their own sin. They die because they have no self-control. Their utter stupidity will send them to their graves (Proverbs 5:3-23).

"And I say to you: whoever divorces his wife, except for sexual immorality, and marries another, commits adultery (Matthew 19:9)."

"But since sexual immorality is occurring, each man should have sexual relations with his own wife, and each woman with her own husband (I Corinthians 7:2)."

Adultery is breaking holy covenant. It is not necessarily a sexual sin. For example, God divorced His people due to adultery against Him, yet there was no sexual sin. Some verses specify "sexual adultery" whereas others refer only to adultery. As did the Israelites with God, breaking covenant is adultery, which can be the breaking of any marital covenant vow. The adulterer has lost all his or her senses of wisdom and reason. Proverbs 5 is an excellent caution to people everywhere.

As for the issue of adultery when remarrying, I recommend my book *How to Get it Right: Being Single, Married, Divorced, and Everything in Between* or *Marriage Beyond Mediocrity*. I go into great detail about what this means. The point I'll make here is that 1. men used to toss their wives aside and marry another without a formal, legal decree of divorce, hence living in adultery. 2. as in everything, we must allow for God's grace and forgiveness. After studying this for years, I recognize God's forgiveness of any sin, including sexual sin. This is why we cannot be partial, where we extend grace, mercy, and forgiveness. God extended it to all who will repent and receive.

Sex with Father's Wife:

"It is actually reported that there is sexual immorality among you, and of a kind that even pagans do not tolerate: A man is sleeping with his father's wife (I Corinthians 5:1)."

"But I say to you that everyone who divorces his wife, except on the ground of sexual immorality among you, and of a kind that is not tolerated even among pagans, for a man has his father's wife (Matthew 5:32)."

I don't believe this needs any explanation. Men, do not commit immorality with your father's wife and, women, do not commit immorality with your mother's husband. Simple.

Source of Defilement:

And He said, "What comes out of a person is what defiles him. For from within, out of the heart of man, come evil thoughts, sexual immorality, theft, murder, adultery, coveting, wickedness, deceit, sensuality, envy, slander, pride, foolishness. All these evil things come from within, and they defile a person (Mark 7:20-23)."

"For out of the heart come evil thoughts, murder, adultery, sexual immorality, theft, false witness, slander (Matthew 15:19)."

This set of texts takes us back to the issue of the mind and keeping our thoughts pure and holy. Everyone who walks with God must take every thought captive. We must command ourselves to pull down every imagination, stronghold, and every high thing which exalts itself above the name of Jesus in our minds and cast them into the hand of God. We must demand of ourselves to be willing to punish our disobedience lest we find ourselves given over to a reprobate, defiled mind. Out of the mind comes every evil deed. Having a fleeting thought of evil does not make one condemned. Conversely, entertaining those wicked thoughts will corrupt us and turn us toward the very thing God hates.

Put to Death that Which Defiles:

> "Put to death therefore what is earthly in you: sexual immorality, impurity, passion, evil desire, and covetousness, which is idolatry (Colossians 3:5)."

Again, this confirms that one does not have to go from homosexual to heterosexual or from adulterer to non-adulterer. Instead, it is a matter of dying to that which is against God. It is dying to self, dying to sexual thoughts which do not pertain to our spouse. The death of something is a far cry from simply trying to stop being one thing to be another. Death ends sin. Spiritually, though our body lives, we choose to die to the nature of sinful Adam.

A Living Sacrifice:

> "I appeal to you therefore, brothers, by the mercies of God, to present your bodies as a living sacrifice, holy and acceptable to God, which is your spiritual worship. Do not be conformed to this world, but be transformed by

the renewal of your mind, that by testing you may discern what is the will of God, what is a good and acceptable and perfect (Romans 12:1-2)."

This leads us into being a living sacrifice. We are sacrificing ourselves, our selfish desires, to be a living, breathing, walking, talking physical manifestation of Christ.

Journaling

EIGHTY-THREE

Sexual Purity: Adultery and Fornication

Prayer:

Father, I confess I have committed adultery or fornication in my mind, heart, and physical body. As I am surrendering to You this day, I pray to keep my mind stayed on Your holiness. I accept that Your commands are for me and not against me; they are for my good and not for evil. I refuse to any longer jeopardize my relationship with You or my mental, emotional, physical or spiritual health. I repent and purpose to go and sin no more. I bind from myself a spirit of perversion and distortion and bind to myself the Spirit of purity and holiness. Amen

Journaling

EIGHTY-FOUR

Sexual Purity: Homosexuality

Prayer:

Father, I humbly come before the throne room of grace repentant of my sexual impurity with people of the same gender. I know that the temptation of any sin is not sin itself and that, in the temptation, you have previously made a way out. I look to You, gracious Savior, to ignite Your self-discipline in my body, mind, and spirit so that I will no longer sin against You or my body. Help me, Lord, to recognize the harm I do to myself and others when I participate in homosexual activity. I repent as dust and ash in faith that You will restore me. I command all spirits of condemnation, shame, fear, lies, and unworthiness to be loosed from their assignment over my life. I break a generational curse of perversion from my mom and dad's side of the family back to Adam and Eve. I sever it with the blood of Jesus and declare that it will afflict me no more. I thank You, Lord, that I do not have to live in shame because there is no shame for the redeemed. I am not a freak, just a person who needs redemption from the nature of Adam. Jesus, while in the wilderness, You were tempted on every side and resisted all temptations. Because You live in me and You are my life, I choose to allow Your obedience to the Father to become my obedience to the Father. I draw all my strength from You. Selah

Journaling

EIGHTY-FIVE

Sexual Purity: Masturbation

Prayer:

Father, I confess the sin of masturbation when I was committing adultery or fornication in my mind, or when I was using it to withhold sexual relations from my spouse. I repent of this sexual impurity and I receive Your forgiveness. Help me to abstain from all sexual sin and make me a vessel of honor in Your sight. I choose to cease sinning against You and my own body. Selah

Journaling

EIGHTY-SIX

Sexual Purity: Singlehood

Prayer:

Yeshua, I thank You for allowing me to learn from the mistakes of others so that I don't repeat bad behavior. May I be so consecrated unto You that I don't make a move, of any kind, especially in the arena of singleness or marriage, that would dishonor You or Your Kingdom in any capacity. Amen.

Scripture References:

> "Flee immortality. Every other sin that a man commits is outside the body, but the immoral man sins against his own body (I Corinthians 6:18)."

> Now the deeds of the flesh are evident, which are: immorality, impurity, sensuality, idolatry, sorcery, enmities, strife, jealousy, outbursts of anger, disputes, dissensions, factions, envying, drunkenness, carousing, and things like these, of which I forewarn you, just as I have forewarned you, that those who practice such things will not inherit the Kingdom of God (Galatians 5:19-21).

journaling

EIGHTY-SEVEN

Shield of Faith

Prayer:

In the name of Jesus Christ of Nazareth, I pray, O merciful Savior, that I will be fully equipped with the shield of faith. Remind me to never leave home without it. Grow me, O Lord, in faith so firmly planted in You that I will be sharp and keenly aware of the enemy's attack even before he attacks (Nehemiah 6). May I be sober, alert, and vigilant at all times and in every season of calm or distress. Break me, O God, so that You will be free to move through this earthen vessel anytime and in any way You desire. Instill in me, Father, the gift of faith so that I cannot be shaken or tossed about by any and every wind of doctrine. Give me heavenly vision, the single vision of God, to see everything You want me to see, hear, know, and understand in every dark spot I encounter along the journey of life. Bless You, O Lord of lords and King of kings, in all the Earth. Give me a teachable spirit so that I may learn the desires of Your heart. May I be worthy of being called a child of the King by allowing Your fruit to flourish through my unwavering faith. I thank You that, no matter the hardships I may face, the crouching dragon will not move me as You have given me authority over him, in Jesus' name. Amen

Scripture References:

"In addition to all, taking up the shield of faith with which you will be able to extinguish all the flaming arrows of the evil one (Ephesians 6:16)."

"Be sober, be vigilant; because your adversary the devil, as a roaring lion, walks about, seeking whom he may devour (I Peter 5:8)."

"For to one is given the word of wisdom through the Spirit, and to another the word of knowledge according to the same Spirit; to another faith by the same Spirit, and to another gifts of healing by the one Spirit...(I Corinthians 12:8-9)."

Journaling

EIGHTY-EIGHT

Sleep Disturbances

Commentary:

The following prayer is for anyone with sleep disorders, e.g., those who cannot sleep, cannot stay asleep, restless sleep, wake up irritable, angry or tired, sleep paralysis, etc. Lack of sleep or restless sleep can be spiritual, physical, mental, or emotional. I do not want to place a "one size fits all" on sleep issues, but I have written a scriptural prayer that can loosely apply to anyone. Notice Proverbs 3:24 and Matthew 8:24 below. I placed them together because, if Jesus could rest in the most treacherous of situations, so can anyone who is possessed by Jesus. Jesus trusted Himself, who is God. If we are hidden in Christ, we can have such abounding faith and peace in otherwise horrible situations. This applies to anything which can interrupt our sleep.

    Yes, there are physical conditions that can disrupt our sleep. For example, sleep paralysis is a known sleep inhibitor that causes hallucinations. This is because, as I have lightly studied, the conscious is awake while the body is still asleep. However, the spiritual side is the hallucinations. Seeing demons is not physical. It is spiritual, and there is a solution. If one has consigned him or herself to Christ, they have power over demons. If the person is walking under God's will (not that they are perfect), they have been given authority to use the power of God within them. With that, I defer to the earlier declaration of binding demons. Regardless of what's going on, God has granted sweet sleep to the humble, obedient servant of the Lord.

Prayer:

Father God, I come to You by Your grace and mercies, which are new every day. I thank You, in advance, that in peace I will lie down and sleep, for You alone, Lord, make me dwell in safety. I am a laborer of the Lord, Jesus Christ, and You have granted me sweet sleep. I will lie down and I will not be afraid; when I lie down, my sleep will be sweet. I come to You, YHWH, because I am weary and burdened. I know that You will give me rest. I take Your yoke upon me that I may learn from You, for I know You are gentle and humble in heart, and you will give me rest for my soul. You will not let my foot slip. I praise You that, You who watches over me, will not slumber. Father, because of Your goodness and infallible love for me, I dwell in the shelter of the Most High. I will rest in the shadow of the Almighty. I will say of You, "*He is my refuge and my fortress, my God, in whom I trust. Surely He will save me from the fowler's snare and from the deadly pestilence. You will cover me with Your feathers, and under Your wings I will find refuge. Your faithfulness will be my shield and rampart. I will not fear the terror of night, nor the arrow that flies by day. By Your Son's blood, I command every demonic spirit of hell who tries to steal my sleep and my peace to be bound, gagged, and loosed from their assignment over me. I release, Father, Your Holy Spirit to be the only Spirit in and through me.*" As I lie my head on my pillow, I thank You that rest will be uninterrupted and I will awaken afresh and rested. No demonic spirit nor any hallucination will be able to come upon me. I am safe and secure in Your presence. Amen.

Scripture References:

"When you lie down, you will not be afraid; when you lie down, your sleep will be sweet (Proverbs 3:24)."

"And, behold, there arose a great tempest in the sea, insomuch that the ship was covered with the waves: but He was asleep (Matthew 8:24)."

"In peace I will lie down and sleep, for You alone, Lord, make me dwell in safety (Psalm 4:8)."

"The sleep of a laborer is sweet, whether they eat little or much, but as for the rich, their abundance permits them no sleep (Ecclesiastes 5:12)."

"He will not let your foot slip - He who watches over you will not slumber (Psalm 121:3)."

Come to Me, all you who are weary and burdened, and I will give you rest. Take My yoke upon you and learn from me, for I am gentle and humble in heart, and you will find rest for your soul. For My yoke is easy and My burden is light (Matthew 11:28-30).

Whoever dwells in the shelter of the Most High will rest in the shadow of the Almighty. I will say of the Lord, "He is my refuge and my fortress, my God, in whom I trust." Surely He will save you from the fowler's snare and from the deadly pestilence. He will cover you with His feathers, and under His wings you will find refuge; His faithfulness will be your shield and rampart. You will not fear the terror of night, nor the arrow that flies by day (Psalm 91:1-5).

Journaling

EIGHTY-NINE

Slow to Speak

Prayer:

Father, I come before You in the name of Your holy Son, Jesus. Teach me Your ways, O Lord, that I will be slow to speak and quick to listen. Place a watch over my mouth that I may not sin against You. Stir discernment within me that I hear Your direction prior to making a wrong vow internally or externally. I bless You, O Lord, that You make every curse in my life a blessing through my love for You. I trust that, in time, all things work for good for those who love You. I vow my love for You so that I will walk a life of blessings in the Kingdom of God instead of curses set against the Kingdom of God. May the words of my mouth and the meditation of my heart be pleasing in Your sight. Amen.

Scripture References:

> "This you know, my beloved brethren. But everyone must be quick to hear, slow to speak and slow to anger (James 1:19)."

"Dear friends, do not believe every spirit, but test the spirits to see whether they are from God, because many false prophets have gone out into the world (I John 4:1)."

"Nevertheless, the Lord your God was not willing to listen to Balaam, but the Lord your God turned the curse into a blessing for you because the Lord your God loves you (Deuteronomy 23:5)."

Journaling

Sowing and Reaping Scripture and Commentary

"Do not be deceived, God is not mocked; for whatever a man sows, this he will also reap. For the one who sows to his own flesh will from the flesh reap corruption, but the one who sows to the Spirit will from the Spirit reap eternal life (Galatians 6:7-8)."

Personal Experience:

One day, I was sitting on the davenport with my daughter wishing my husband of several years did not have such a grueling work schedule. I hated he had to work six days a week, and many times twelve to fourteen hours a day. I had gotten off the phone with a friend of mine about a half-hour prior. We had been talking in general about people we know and how frustrating it is they cannot understand that what they sow now, they will reap in their future. I expressed my dismay that I can't get through to some people that the more they continue their path of sin, the harder it will be for them to become aligned in obedience to God.

Suddenly it occurred to me: "I am reaping what I sowed so long ago." Although it was not a shock, it was. I have paid a hefty price for my sinful past, yet this seemed to reveal a much deeper level of reaping. I know part of my husband's work hours is because God is working on *him*. However, I realized in an instant that, because *I* had spent so much intimate time with him years ago when he was not my husband and I was legally married to another—albeit we were separated—I am now harvesting that unfinished field of sin. The price for that stolen time is being paid current day. Everything has a price tag as nothing is free. It isn't God's punishment, just God's law in motion.

That was an unpleasant realization, yet it was without guilt or condemnation. I had long since repented, so that was not the issue. The issue was that I needed to understand this situation would not change until the harvest of bad seed was completed. Frankly, I don't know God's timing on this matter. I do know that, as I continue to sow good seed during the finishing of a bad harvest, the bad *will* end.

A family member is another part of my previously planted seed of sin. This person cannot get past the way they saw me live my life many years ago. This person is unrelenting in animosity toward me no matter how I live my life today. This has bothered me for years, but once I began to understand all this planting and reaping, peace and pure love began to take over. Although they will answer to God directly for their treatment against me, I am now better-equipped to love this person regardless. I understand that, though their attitude against me is unwarranted in the natural, in the spiritual, *I* planted poorly in my past; therefore, this is part of my reaping the harvest of bad seed.

Accountability:

With all this understanding of sowing and reaping, accountability belongs to me personally. With accountability, I can continue to walk in peace instead of constant anger and unforgiveness, regardless of someone else's bitterness. I can love them as *unto God* as opposed to *unto them*, which is impossible in the flesh. The only way to love the unlovely (those who hate and mistreat us) is to do it unto God. This way, God is responsible for rendering payment instead of the person. Though I wouldn't say I like their conduct against me, I can take responsibility in the situation and quickly be forgiving. Now the control over my own life belongs to me and not them. As I stated previously, *understanding* brings more exceptional ability and desire to do as God commands, which is to love our neighbor as ourselves and bless those who curse us.

My reason for sharing this is to help us wake up and stop sinning as soon as possible. Not because I am condemning anyone, but because I want the best for people's lives, as does Yeshua. He set the law of sowing and reaping in motion, and it cannot be changed. This is why He can't just swoop in making all our problems go away the moment we confess and repent. It is in no way a lack of love or power on His part. In fact, because of God's immeasurable love, He repeatedly tells us in His Word to stop our sinful ways, confess, and repent so that He may make us whole as soon as possible.

Please know that making us whole is instantaneous in His sight. The wholeness is His Son's infilling of those who receive; only Christ is the perfection of wholeness. Unfortunately, there is still a mess we have made for ourselves that requires time to clean in the natural. The more we extend our sinning in full consciousness, the larger our negative harvest will become, and the longer it will take plowing through it. Repenting is totally for our benefit. When we grasp a mental image of the intensity of the measure of planting sin into the Earth, I pray we will not hesitate to stop abruptly.

Look at Elijah. He is the greatest prophet ever. When he sinned by rising in pride in front of Jezebel by concocting an elaborate performance of God's power, he not only turned and ran for his life begging God to kill him, but his presence on Earth was shortened. God instructed Elijah to train Elisha to take over his duties. Forever blessed by God and highly exalted, yes, yet he still had to deal with the consequences of his actions. There is always a price to pay for sin, though forgiven.

Ultimately, God is still blessing Elijah today, yet he missed out on much of what God had for him here on Earth. Likewise, we will miss out on what God has for and through us in this life due to blatant disobedience regardless of what excuse we may present. As a son of God, we will be blessed in Heaven, but why would we purpose to miss out on what the Lord has for us here? It doesn't make sense when we put it in such light.

Look at Apostle Paul. Everyone uses him to cop out when tribulations come their way. They say that Paul was the greatest of the apostles, yet he suffered the most. He had a thorn in his side and asked God three times to remove it. That thorn, many times, was people who tormented and mocked him in his ministry. His "thorn" kept him humble, but that is not the context in this discussion.

Paul suffered much during his ministry. This is not solely because of the good seed he sowed along the way, but the bad. God did not remove the repercussions of his past wickedness the moment the anointing rained upon him. Paul, though forgiven and greatly anointed, never stopped reaping the massive field of evil. Of course, he was still blessed and favored because of the good seed he sowed post-transformation, but he could not wholly escape the seed he spent years planting. Let's look at the next couple passages:

> "For I am the least of the apostles, and not fit to be called an apostle, because I persecuted the church of God. But by the grace of God I am what I am, and His grace toward me did not prove vain; but I labored even more than all of them, yet not I, but the grace of God with me (I Corinthians 15:9-10)."

> "As to zeal, a persecutor of the church; as to the righteousness which is in the Law, found blameless (Philippians 3:6, 13)."

This is not to discourage us, but to encourage us to halt the road of wickedness we are traveling. Turn and be entirely separated unto God. The longer we go in rebellion, the longer the harvest of unpleasantness. If we are a person of the Law as was Paul, we will be judged by the same Law. No one can fulfill the Law except Christ, and He has done so. The Law will always condemn; faith through grace brings life. Saul, aka Paul before regeneration, said he was blameless in the Law. He abided the law to a tee, yet had no faith in Christ.

Accountability is for everyone, bar none. God's forgiveness wipes away our past in so much as we are a new creation. Nevertheless, while living on this Earth, we will reap a harvest based on what we plant, no exceptions. Many seem to have the *in the sweet by and by* mentality. So many of God's own are looking only at the result, yet miss the here and now. Multitudes make their hell on Earth because of disobedience and then question God as if *He* has wronged them. He is the Almighty, Supreme, Sovereign, Righteous, Holy, Majestic God. We need to respectfully reverence Him as such and stop blaming Him for the things of which we don't approve. He is the Perfect One. Checking ourselves will usher clarity as to what went wrong.

And yes, forgiveness is ever-present, but the Word is crystal clear: if we come into knowledge and return to sinfulness, there is no more sacrifice. What then? Our hands doom us. There is nothing more God can sacrifice to pay for blatant disobedience. Let's look at this from a different angle. Say we are someone who lived a sold-out life to Christ. We sowed good seed in Christ Jesus. Later, we turned from Him and went back to our vomit, per se. While we are currently planting bad seeds, we will continue to reap a good harvest until that harvest is depleted. It would be like living on borrowed time, much like Satan is doing today. He seems to get away with much, yet he is still doomed to eternal fire.

How it Works:

> "Now this I say, he who sows sparingly will also reap sparingly, and he who sows bountifully will also reap bountifully (II Corinthians 9:6)."

We can look at this verse and see several things. Of course, the obvious is that whatever good in Christ we sow, however much we sow, we will reap its harvest. Galatians, chapter six, is clear. This takes us back to *relinquishing* the flesh instead of attempting to *deal* with the flesh. Whatever we sow into the flesh, even if it is seemingly *good works for Christ*, we will reap only fleshly harvests which are corrupt.

I see it a lot in ministries where a person begins well desiring God, but ends up doing his or her own thing because they attain a level of stardom. They work through their flesh and, eventually, their ministry fails. I have heard of ministers, supposedly strong in the Lord, who commit suicide, theft, adultery, and fornications, both heterosexual and homosexual. This is a significant devastation to the Kingdom of God, and that is precisely what Satan wants. If he can convince people they are holy when they barely genuinely know Yahweh. They fall because of a lack of intimacy. Their feeble attempts at keeping the Law for the sake of the Law buried them under that same Law.

Every human is created in the image of God. Every human represents God—either for the positive or negative. E.g., if a person murders someone and the family of the victim is unsaved, they generally question what kind of god would allow such a tragedy. If there was a chance of the family coming into the Kingdom of God, it was minimized. Also, if a minister has a large following and the followers' lives are impacted for Christ by that person, they trust that minister. Let's say that minister strays from God and sins openly. The majority of his or her followers fall away because the one whom they trusted was a liar. Most likely, that minister taught truth but did not know how to walk in it according to God's love. Ultimately, they became a worse example for Christ than if they had never made a public testimony for Christ.

To sow good seed is to be led of, by, and through the power of Holy Spirit, not Law. Nothing to which we place our hands is good unless God is doing the doing through them. Allow Yeshua to move and direct every morsel of your person. Allow Him to give us the seed to sow and direction to the proper field so that our harvest will always be a blessing and not a curse, an asset and not a liability.

Change the Seed:

If we have sown good seed but shifted somewhere along the line and are currently sowing bad seed, don't think the good harvest will last. No harvest lasts forever. God's Law of sowing and reaping will either be to our advantage or disadvantage; it depends on our actions.

If we are seeking the Lord with all our heart, soul, mind, and strength, and we are still reaping a bad harvest, the fact remains that all harvests must end. The only ones that can last forever are the ones we continue to plant repeatedly. Even with Paul, his suffering ended when he transitioned from Earth to Heaven. He suffered long for the Lord because he suffered God's people so much and for so long.

If we stop planting corn and start planting beans, we will soon switch from a corn crop to beans. If we continue to plant corn, we will always get corn. The *type* of corn can't even change unless we change from yellow corn to white corn. There will be a time of overlap where we harvest both wheat and tares; the good and the bad. Endure. God will bless perseverance and endurance.

We change the harvest when we change the seeds we plant, it's that simple. We and our choices of righteousness or unrighteousness determine our lives of blessings or curses. Choose to stop sowing into the flesh and start sowing into the Spirit of God. Pray the grace of Almighty God will bless so that we may humbly finish whatever we started while currently planting seed from the Kingdom of God. For example, I used to be unforgiving, not so much on the surface for all to see, but only God could see in my heart. As the Lord changed my perspective, I eventually repented, relented, and became forgiving as God Himself. As I mentioned before, there are those few who refuse to forgive my past, yet I choose to forgive those who will not forgive me.

My first marriage was one of significant abuse and lies formed against me. In my despair, I married an upright man but on the rebound. I, within two years of marriage, left him, got back together with him, and left him again, both times right around Christmas. For good reason, neither he nor his family had anything good to think or say about me. Many years passed. The Lord completely transformed me into a new creation, and I eventually remarried.

One day I received a phone call from my mother-in-law from my second marriage. She lived many states away. She was here visiting and said she wanted to see *family and friends*. I couldn't have been more surprised that I fit either of those categories, but I agreed to go and see her. We visited for about two and a half hours, and it was a beautiful reunion. She had forgiven me without measure. I had the rare opportunity to apologize for my past poor behavior toward her son. She said she recognized that I had been a mess, and she understood. She went so far as to say she believes that, after everything was said and done, I am supposed to be married to my current husband. What an intense blessing from God to give me that relief of guilt and anguish.

My point is, as I began over many years to sow good seeds of unconditional forgiveness and love toward those who are not so toward me, the Lord rendered payment, per se, to me when I least expected it and in a form I could not have imagined. It far exceeded any payment from those who still hate me. When we sow righteousness but don't see immediate results in the natural, God's payment of our steadfastness in well-doing is exceedingly superior to that which we as mere men could grant. This harvest was most sweet to my tongue and satisfying for my belly.

I am a firm believer in not living in guilt and shame. Notwithstanding, this released me into a deeper level of freedom from guilt and shame. When the Lord says to "not grow weary in well-doing," be confident there is payoff yet to come. God is the Promise Keeper, and He *will* fulfill every promise He made. He will not fail us. Stay the course of planting righteousness and purity when those around us mock and ridicule even when it seems futile.

Journaling

NINETY

Sowing and Reaping: Finishing a Bad Harvest

Prayer:

Show me the error of my ways, that I may clearly see how I came into the life I am currently living. Give me the grace to accept what You reveal to my spirit, that I not allow condemnation to enter. Show me, Jesus, how to finish this bad harvest with all humility. Show me, gracious Lord, how to sow seed from Heaven so that the harvest will come up supernatural instead of natural. Make it clear to me what is of the flesh and what is of the Spirit. I praise You, Father, that I will begin to see, hear, and think just as You. Place Your mind in me that I never again be deceived by the world and its lusts. I declare victory now over the rest of my life that all crooked paths are being made straight. I praise You that everything Satan means against me for evil is being turned around for good because I love You. Bless Your holy name. Selah.

Journaling

NINETY-ONE

Sowing Good Seed

Prayer:

Most gracious, holy God, I surrender everything to You this moment. I desire to bear holy seed so that the harvest is large for the Kingdom of God. I want, more than all the treasures of the Earth, to be led by Holy Spirit so that I am no longer bound by Law. I recognize that I reap everything I sow (Galatians 6:7-9); therefore, in this knowledge, please sow Your heavenly seed through this earthen vessel. My longing is to please You in everything I say and do. I pray to not stay too long when You've guided me to move. Instruct me in Your ways so that I may move when you move, remain where You remain and do all according to Your perfect will. We know that the slave who knew his master's will and did not get ready or act in accord with his will, will receive many lashes (Luke 12:47). Allow me to bear good seed into the Earth and thereby sparing me from Your lashes. Amen

Scripture Reference:

Do not be deceived, God is not mocked; for whatever a man sows, this he will also reap. For the one who sows to his own flesh will from the flesh reap corruption, but the one who sows to the Spirit will from the Spirit reap eternal life. Let us not lose heart in doing good, for in due time we will reap if we do not grow weary (Galatians 6:7-9).

Jesus presented another parable to them, saying, "The Kingdom of Heaven may be compared to a man who sowed good seed in his field. But while his men were sleeping, his enemy came and sowed weeds [resembling wheat] among the wheat, and went away. So when the plants sprouted and formed grain, the weeds appeared also. The servants of the owner came to him and said, 'Sir, did you not sow good seed in your field? Then how does it have weeds in it?' He replied to them, 'An enemy has done this.' The servants asked him, 'Then do you want us to go and pull them out?' But he said, 'No; because as you pull out the weeds, you may uproot the wheat with them. Let them grow together until the harvest; and at harvest time I will tell the reapers, "First gather the weeds and tie them in bundles to be burned; but gather the wheat into my barn (Matthew 13:24-30).'"

Journaling

NINETY-TWO

Spirit and Truth

Commentary:

In this flesh, a mere mortal cannot contain the knowledge of Almighty God. To *know* God is to be *in relationship* with God on the deepest level. To be in a genuine relationship with Yeshua is to rid ourselves of ourselves. Since God and sin cannot coexist, He cannot be in relationship with anyone but Himself. The Lord is both Spirit and Truth. Outside Christ's resurrection power, we have no truth, and our spirit is cocooned within our soul. Only God is sinless. This is why mankind had to die. Through death—spiritually speaking, we become positioned to receive the Spirit of God through the blood of Jesus. In this, we receive the truth. We must recognize that God doesn't commune with our flesh, but with Himself merged with our spirit. This is the "spirit-to-Spirit" connection covered in earlier commentary. True worshipers are connected with the Lord in both spirit and truth—the death, burial, and resurrection of Jesus. Outside spirit and truth, worship is false and baseless. Religion should be an outward manifestation of what has already transpired inwardly.

Prayer:

Show me, Father, how to worship You in spirit and truth. Teach me how to be transformed in my inner-man so that my worship will be an outward display of inward transformation. May I forever allow You to be You through me. I choose to allow the Sword of the Spirit to sever my soul from my spirit. In so doing, grant me the privilege of being led of, by, and through the power of the Spirit of Christ and Heaven's truth. I love you, O God. Amen.

Scripture References:

"God is spirit, and those who worship Him must worship in spirit and truth (John 4:24)."

"For we are the true circumcision, who worship in the Spirit of God and glory in Christ Jesus and put no confidence in the flesh (Philippians 3:3)."

"…that though they are judged in the flesh as men, they may live in the spirit according to the will of God (I Peter 4:6)."

"And I will give you a new heart, and a new spirit I will put within you. And I will remove the heart of stone from your flesh and give you a heart of flesh (Ezekiel 36:26)."

Journaling

NINETY-THREE

Splitting Soul from Spirit

Commentary (from *The War*, chapter 5):

What's the Difference Between Soul and Spirit?

> "And the Lord God formed man of the dust of the ground, and breathed into his nostrils the breath of life; and man became a living soul (Genesis 2:7, KJV)."

Mankind is comprised of spirit, soul, and body. Genesis 2:7 expresses all three:

1. **Body**: "Dust of the ground"
2. **A living soul**: the person as well as the mind, will, and emotions
3. **Spirit**: "breath—neshamah—of life" given directly from God

Basically speaking, the soul of man is who you are. You do not possess a soul; you are a soul. Additionally, the "soul" is the mind, will, and emotions of a person, which includes, as my friend

Sandy Renner says, imaginations and memories. The latter two are a part of the mind.

Here's how my favorite author, Watchman Nee, breaks it down simply:

> **Soul** – that which relates us to ourselves and gives us self-consciousness; the meeting place or union of the flesh and the spirit; the lowest connection of man with the sensible and animal; our mind, will, and emotions
>
> **Spirit** – that which makes us conscious of God and relates us to God; the highest that links man with the Divine
>
> **Body** – that which causes us to be world-conscious

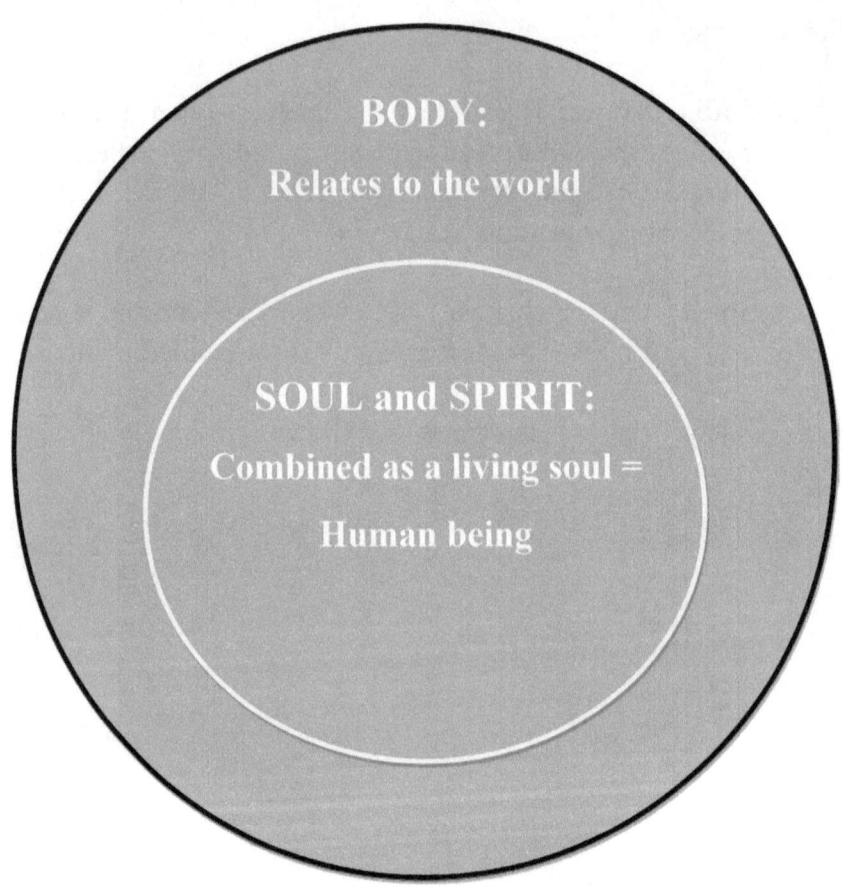

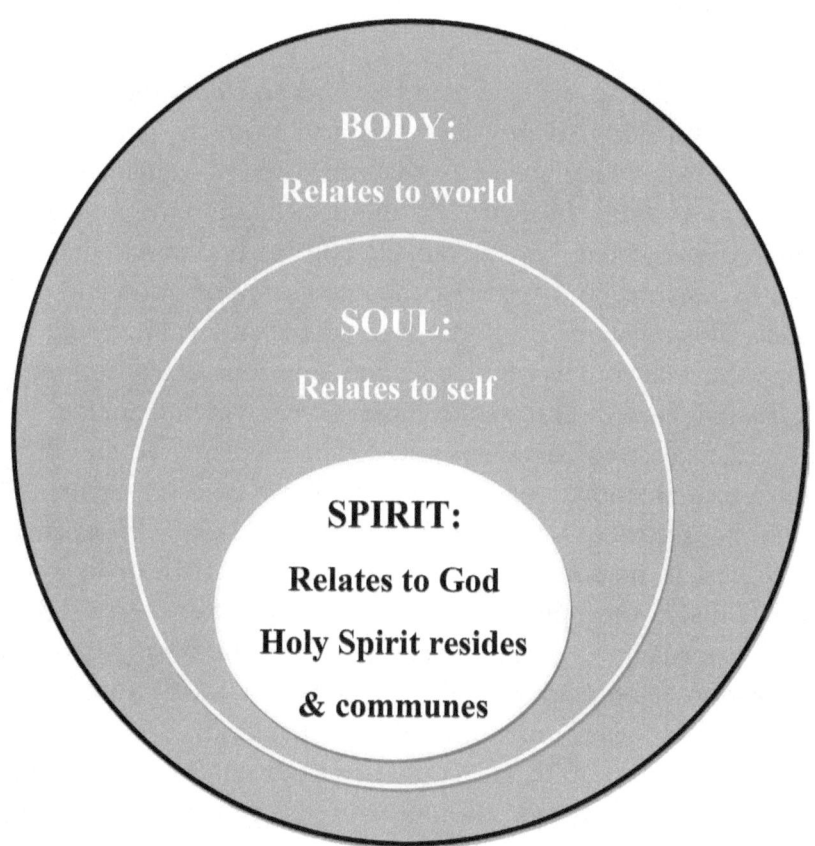

"For the word of God is living and active and sharper than any two-edged sword, and piercing as far as the division of soul and spirit, of both joints and marrow, and able to judge the thoughts and intentions of the heart (Hebrews 4:12)."

At the fall of man, the soul and body became corrupted. In the Garden of Eden, Adam ruled the Earth from the garden with soul-power—natural power. At that time, Adam—a living soul—was flawless, pure. Likewise, his mind, will, and emotions were pure. After the fall, he was tainted both in body and soul. He became ashamed and aware of the knowledge of good and evil, hence allowing him to choose one or the other. He could no longer be trusted. His mind, will, and emotions could no longer be trusted. God did not remove soul-power, yet humankind was no longer allowed to tap into it. From then on, we are all to utilize only the power of Holy Spirit lest we go astray again and again. Soul-power was natural because God designed it as such. Since he had no sin, he was not required to repent or to invite into Himself the Spirit of God. It was sufficient for God to move externally of Adam. Since the fall, soul-power is in direct opposition to Spirit-power, aka the power of the Spirit of God moving internally through the spirit of mankind.

Our soul and spirit are conjoined at birth. The soul is the one in control, not the spirit. It wills what it wills, it is overly emotional, and the mind wanders to and fro. This is dangerous territory and causes all sorts of dilemmas for folks. The soul, in this manner, tells the body it is or is not OK to sin. The spirit—the deepest part of man which connects and communes with Holy Spirit—is shut up within the soul and must be freed. Post-Christ's resurrection, we are to receive the Spirit of God through His Son. For this to happen, we are to take up the Sword of the

Spirit and allow it to divide soul from spirit, which liberates us so that we may commune with our holy God.

Once this occurs, our spirit becomes cleansed from all unrighteousness. Hence, the "spirit" of man is the place where we can relate to a holy God. It is His life's breath within us. This is how we become regenerated; this is transitioning from death unto life. God is a spirit. Our spirit connects with God's Spirit, and they are united as one when we surrender to Him. Our spirit becomes purified. Once united as one, the spirit can then dictate obedience to God to the soul, and the soul then leads the body into holiness. Our spirit is where the presence of the Lord resides. When the spirit and soul were joined, man became a living soul. The characteristic of the angels is spirit, and that of the lower animals, such as beasts, is flesh. We humans have both spirit and body, but our characteristic is neither spirit nor body, but soul. We are a living soul; hence the Bible calls man "soul" (Genesis 46:27; Acts 2:41).

At physical birth, the spirit is shrouded within the soul, which is encapsulated by the body. Anyone who has been in the church any length of time has heard that we are to be "in the world and not of the world." How many people truly know what it means or how to live it? This separation, which I have been expressing, is a condition that can come only through the Spirit of God, His holy Sword, the Word of God. It is powerful and quick enough to divide soul from spirit, joint from marrow, and is a discerner of the thoughts and intentions of the heart. The division of soul and spirit is the quickening of the spirit. Or rather, it is the "awakening" of the spirit that had been hidden and made dormant by the soul. It is that moment when the spirit—the "real" us—is excited, reactivated, revived, revitalized, and becomes able to be led by Holy Spirit versus the mind, will, and emotions, and the draw of the fleshly man.

The division of soul and spirit is entirely supernatural. It comes through faith by trusting the Lord over the lusts of this world and the ruler therein. It comes through saying, "I have come to the end of myself. I have no means by which I can accomplish God's will." We cannot will it to happen, think hard enough to enact it, or cause it to occur through emotionalism. We cannot work hard enough or do enough good deeds so as to incite such an occurrence. Too many believers attempt to be "good enough" to please God, but only that word I keep writing—surrender—will suffice. At the beginning of our lives, we are at war with God, hence the indictment of God's wrath from which we need rescue. We are born enemies to the Almighty, thanks to Adam, Eve, and Lucifer. We enter the world, albeit cute as a button, at war with God because we are automatically by nature in alignment with Satan. This is not because we have yet carried out a sin, but because of the Adamic nature.

The soul and spirit are naturally connected, and, as we grow, we are automatically led around by our wandering mind, strong will, and out of control emotions— a dangerous estate, to be sure. The soul wills certain things. The mind ponders certain things. The emotions, mercy, the emotions, they definitely flip-flop to and fro and are perpetually topsy-turvy! Until, that is, the spirit is released so as to begin dictating self-discipline and self-control through Holy Spirit. Until the soul and spirit are divided, nice people, even Christian folks, still can't get a grip on restraint in the department of fleshly lusts and temptations. The lack of self-control is the epitome of a "carnal Christian."

Thankfully, once soul and spirit are separated through consignment to the Lord, God's Spirit can begin a good work in us because we have shifted from the natural to the supernatural. God's Spirit can reign supreme in our lives, causing the flesh and soul to comply with the Spirit instead of whatever turns our fancy from one moment to the next. We must accept that the world will hate us. By "the world," I mean mother, father, sister, brother, and others who are supposed to love and accept us. Remember the Scripture Luke 14:26? The world will never comprehend why Christ's disciples don't look, act, or think like they. It becomes off-putting for them. It causes those around us who are not yielded to Christ to become uncomfortable in our presence, even when we say nothing. All too often, those uncomfortable people are those claiming Christianity. This must not move us. We need to be so confident in our separation from our natural man and the soulish-rule that we are God-pleasers instead of people-pleasers.

This condition is very difficult for people who hate to be hated or, at the very least, disliked. Having our identity wrapped utterly in Christ and not in our family, friends, or even who we "used to be" is serious business. It will cause those we love to hate us and we must love God more than we love their love and acceptance. Supernatural events of any kind will cause anger and wrath to be stirred in those who don't comprehend that which is supernatural of God. "I have given them Your word; and the world has hated them, because they are not of the world, even as I am not of the world. I do not ask You to take them out of the world, but to keep them from the evil one. They are not of the world, even as I am not of the world," states Jesus in John 17:14-16. When we are educated in the ways of God, His commands, His warnings, and heavenly edicts of the Kingdom constitution, we are better able to stand our ground all the while extending kindness in the face of hatred.

I John 2:15-17 says, "Do not love the world nor the things in the world. If anyone loves the world, the love of the Father is not in him. For all that is in the world, the lust of the flesh and the lust of the eyes and the boastful pride of life, is not from the Father, but is from the world. The world is passing away, and also its lusts; but the one who does the will of God lives forever." In reading this, I recognize that the phrase "things of the world" includes people as much as items. It's people with a worldly view or worse, a religious perspective, which muddies for us the spiritual waters. Remember, religion is worldly as Christ came against the religious who stood on pomp and circumstance instead of the holiness of the Lord. Discovering the meaning of "the world" is a staunch reality check, to be sure, but necessary for a successful walk of being "in" but not "of" the world.

When a person accepts Christ as Savior and Lord, this does not automatically cause the splitting of soul from spirit, though for some, it does. Receiving Christ is only part of the equation, much like a baby being born. Newborns are not mature and cannot walk, talk, or anything else. As a person must come to a place where they choose maturity over childish behavior, so must a person of God choose holiness over carnality, the spirit over the flesh. Division of soul and spirit happens only when a person says emphatically to themselves, "No more of me attempting to help God do anything. I have nothing to offer the Kingdom of God outside the person of Holy Spirit expressing His completed work through me. I need to get out of God's way. His least is far superior to my best."

With this mindset finally activated, splitting of soul and spirit can take place. Keep in mind, though, that most people take a very long time to get to this place, if ever. Frankly, most never do. Too many well-meaning Christians spend their lives striving to do the right things in their own power and ability. Their will wants to assist God with this or that, and, with the will in the way, the soul continues to guide their ship of life. Life in Christ, in this manner, is tedious, strenuous, and maddening. Regardless, a rare few do arrive once they are at the very end of their resources and choose to let God fulfill His purpose.

One can pray something such as, "Father, I recognize and accept that I can produce nothing of eternal value through the use of my intellect, emotions, will, talents, gifts, money, social connections, stress, anxiety, power, agility, or anything else of natural man. There is nothing I can contribute to the Kingdom of God outside total surrender. I willingly relinquish myself to You in spirit, soul, and body. I choose to take up the Sword of the Spirit which is the Word of God and sever my soul from my spirit so that only the Spirit of God communing with my spirit will lead the way through life. I insist that Your Spirit command my soul so that the soul will rightfully direct the actions of the fleshly man. I purpose to align myself with Your purpose no matter how much the flesh longs for things of this Earth. I will no longer allow soulish desire to drive this ship. I will daily surrender to You, Your will, plan, and purpose for this life created by You. It is truly no longer I who live but Christ who lives in me. Thank You for giving Your life so that I can have Your life in my mortal shell."

The difficulty in this is that most refuse to want this, much less do it. Because the soul is so strong, it is hard to recognize what it's doing or how destructive it is to be ruled by the soul. The mind, will, and emotions are the driving force behind most people, including Christians. We have excellent intentions but, ultimately, things go awry, and we cannot help but wonder why God didn't protect us from ourselves or certain situations. This is why countless people in charismatic churches love to be "slain in the Spirit" and experience emotional "moves of God" in service, yet when they return home, they still have no idea what to do with the Word. They can't quite figure out how to engage with Holy Spirit outside of emotion. I say this, not from opinion, but from knowing too many who are just like this. I have been in the charismatic community a very long time. Likewise, those who are in less charismatic churches are reserved because they, as a whole, dislike emotional displays of God. They err on the side of too much caution led by the mind. They reason that all that emotional stuff is ungodly as they desire to be reserved, poised, and in control of the situation. This, too, is problematic because they refuse to let go and let God take the reins. In both scenarios of the emotional, charismatic settings, and the unemotional mind and will-driven settings, the will of individuals and collective groups is really at the helm. The will for each says, "I want to worship God this way," whichever way they choose. Neither, very often, are led by the Spirit because the soul is in the way and calling the shots. All the while, the Spirit is nowhere to be found in action. Many are filled with the Spirit, but few are led by the Spirit. There is a big difference.

Case in point, the charismatic folks will themselves to run, jump, speak in tongues, fall out, etc. Though any of these can be a genuine move of the Spirit, primarily because these are people who believe this is how true worship should look, they manufacture "moves of the Spirit." They fake tongues, falling out, and being slain in the Spirit because they don't want someone to think they're not as spiritual as the next person. In like fashion, those in the quieter, more reserved churches, someone may begin to experience a move of Holy Spirit but, because they know the rules of the denomination, they sit quietly saying and doing nothing according to the Spirit. This is the soul, predominantly the will, in action, and it quenches the Spirit of God. This causes damage in many ways. For example, if one is faking a Holy Spirit experience, they will probably altogether miss an actual move of the Spirit. If one refuses to move with the Spirit, they too will stop hearing because they tune Him out. It hurts the individuals as well as onlookers who are leaning on the elders to show them the way.

If this can happen in well-meaning Christians within a church setting, imagine the intense damage the unbridled soul can have while living in the world regarding relationships with people, be it romantic, sexual, friends, enemies, employees, employers, families, spouses, and everyone else. Just look around at all the adultery and various forms of sin stemming up the line to the clergy. The unwanted children being murdered, abandoned, or neglected because the parents don't want to hurt their Christian reputation. The evidence of soul-led Christianity is everywhere we turn. The spirit must, of necessity, be purposely split from the soul so that the Spirit of God can rule through our spirit. It is imperative for willing battles.

Prayer:

In the name of Jesus, I take God's authority given to me through Jesus and divide my soul from my spirit with the Sword of the Spirit, which is the Word of God. I pray, Father, that the only life in me is Your Holy Spirit communing with my spirit. I pray to no longer be led by my emotions, but through Holy Spirit. Teach me daily how to walk in a manner worthy of the gospel of Christ Jesus. Teach me Your ways. Consume me with Your Word so that You have the freedom to work with Yourself in me. Reveal truth to me so that I can authentically worship You in spirit and truth all the days of my life. Quicken my spirit to life. I love You. Selah

Scripture References:

"The Lord be with your spirit (II Timothy 4:22)."

"That which is born of the flesh is flesh, and that which is born of the Spirit is spirit (John 3:6)."

"God is spirit, and those who worship Him must worship in spirit and truth (John 4:24)."

"I pray that out of His glorious riches He may strengthen you with power through His Spirit in your inner being, so that Christ may dwell in your hearts through faith… (Ephesians 3:16-17)."

"Now the Lord is that Spirit: and where the Spirit of the Lord is, there is liberty (II Corinthians 3:17, KJV)."

"What? Do you not know that your body is the temple of the Holy Spirit which is in you, which you have of God, and you are not your own? For you are bought with a price: therefore glorify God in your body, and in your spirit, which are God's (I Corinthians 6:19-20)."

"The first man Adam became a living soul. The last Adam became a life-giving spirit. Howbeit that is not first which is spiritual, but that which is natural; then that which is spiritual. (I Corinthians 15:45-46)."

"Now may the God of peace Himself sanctify you entirely; and may your spirit and soul and body be preserved complete, without blame at the coming of our Lord Jesus Christ (I Thessalonians 5:23)."

"For the word of God is living and active and sharper than any two-edged sword, and piercing as far as the division of soul and spirit, of both joints and marrow, and able to judge the thoughts and intentions of the heart (Hebrews 4:12)."

"Take up the…Sword of the Spirit, which is the word of God (Ephesians 6:17)."

"For the one who sows to his own flesh will from the flesh reap corruption, but the one who sows to the Spirit will from the Spirit reap eternal life (Galatians 6:8)."

"If you were of the world, the world would love its own; but because you are not of the world, but I chose you out of the world, because of this the world hates you (John 15:19)."

"And do not be conformed to this world, but be transformed by the renewing of your mind, so that you may prove what the will of God is, that which is good and acceptable and perfect (Romans 12:2)."

Journaling

NINETY-FOUR

Storms of Life

Prayer:

Thank You for seeing me through the storms of life by teaching me humility, faith, tenderness of heart, rest, peace, and obedience. Show me how to lean and depend entirely upon You. I desire to be purer than I have ever been. I want to rest during the storms of life, just as did Jesus on the boat during the storm. Take me to the next mantle in You, O God of Heaven and Earth. Teach me Your sovereign ways that I may become the very life of Christ to manifest His holiness. Reveal to me how to be as dust and ashes. May there be no life-breath in me except the breath of Elohim, the Creator, powerful and mighty Lord of lords. Shake out of me whatever is not planted by Your righteous hand. Expose the darkness within me so that I can adequately address it with Your truth and light. Purify me from the inside out. Let no stone be left unturned. Shake out of me ungodliness, defilement, and unrest, as that is what storms do. Blow the wind of change into my atmosphere, Lord. I am ready to receive the newness of Your Spirit. Amen

Scripture References:

"Trust in the Lord with all your heart and lean not on your own understanding; in all your ways submit to Him, and He will make your paths straight (Proverbs 3:5-6)."

"For in Him all the fullness of the Deity dwells in bodily form (Colossians 2:9)."

"For You have been a defense for the helpless, a defense for the needy in his distress, a refuge from the storm, a shade from the heat; for the breath of the ruthless is like a rain storm against a wall. Like heat in drought, You subdue the uproar of aliens; like heat by the shadow of a cloud, the song of the ruthless is silenced (Isaiah 25:4-5)."

Journaling

NINETY-FIVE

Submission

Prayer:

Yahweh, I earnestly pray to understand submission to You that I may turn and walk in submission with my fellow man. I seek guidance from Holy Spirit to recognize curses stemming back to the Garden. I desire to properly apply the blood of Jesus to become free. Continuously reveal in my spirit my new origin from Heaven that I may die daily to the nature of the old man. I thank You that, as I die to that which was crucified at Calvary, I am open to receive deeper levels of knowledge, insight, and revelation. I bless You, Lord, that You willingly share Your Kingdom with such a lowly creature as I. Thank You! I release myself to You totally and completely without reservation. Make me mindful that I am an heir to the Promise through Your Spirit and not through external actions of my flesh. I thank You, Jesus, that, by Your stripes, I am healed, and by Your wounds, I have been transferred from death unto light. I bless You, Almighty, that You did not leave me abandoned, but adopted me as a rightful heir to the Kingdom of God. Amen.

Scripture References:

"Submit yourselves, then, to God. Resist the devil, and he will flee from you (James 4:7)."

"You shall not bow down to them or worship them; for I, the Lord your God, am a jealous God, punishing the children for the sin of the parents to the third and fourth generation of those who hate Me (Deuteronomy 5:9)."

"For if you are living according to the flesh, you must die; but if by the Spirit you are putting to death the deeds of the body, you will live (Romans 8:13)."

Journaling

NINETY-SIX

Surgery

Prayer:

I plea the blood of Jesus over my conscience, unconscious, and subconscious mind so that nothing can enter me that is not of You. I take full authority over my mind and place it in Your righteous right hand. I thank You that no dream, vision, spirit, or thought come to me from any demonic force, but let only that which is from God come to me. Let me remember and understand that You have given me supernatural ability to discern what is revealed and to walk in obedience. I pray for Your Holy Spirit to go ahead of me to spiritually sterilize every instrument, medication, and hand that touches my body so that no harm can come near my dwelling place. Anoint the doctors, nurses, and staff with wisdom from above. Allow everything hidden to be revealed and let nothing go unnoticed. I thank You that I will wake up from anesthesia with no complications of any kind. I bless You, Lord, that the pain will be minimal post-op, in the name of Jesus. Amen

Scripture References:

"We are destroying speculations and every lofty thing raised up against the knowledge of God, and we are taking every thought captive to the obedience of Christ (II Corinthians 10:5)."

"Every person is to be in subjection to the governing authorities. For there is no authority except from God, and those which exist are established by God (Romans 13:1)."

"But examine everything carefully; hold fast to that which is good; abstain from every form of evil (I Thessalonians 5:21-22)."

"For Christ also died for sins once for all, the just for the unjust, so that He might bring us to God, having been put to death in the flesh, but made alive in the spirit (II Peter 3:18)."

Journaling

NINETY-SEVEN

Teach Me Your Ways

Prayer:

Father, teach me Your ways to such a degree that I will not only know how to overcome the false identities of the world but also strongly desire to take the measures I must to become who You have called and created me to be. Teach me in my spirit-man to know only the identity of the Savior. I rebuke every negative, hurtful, false words spoken out against me in the name of Jesus, and I replace them with Christ's attributes. I am fearfully and wonderfully made by Your holy hand with a destiny here on Earth. I have a sound mind, pure heart, and a steadfast spirit, and I *will* walk with You all the days of my life. Thank You, Jesus. Selah

Scripture References:

> "Teach me Your way, O Lord; I will walk in Your truth; unite my heart to fear Your name (Psalm 86:11)."

"For I know the plans I have for you," declares the Lord, "plans to prosper you and not to harm you, plans to give you hope and a future (Jeremiah 29:11)."

"No weapon that is formed against you will prosper; and every tongue that accuses you in judgment you will condemn. This is the heritage of the servants of the Lord, and their vindication is from Me," declares the Lord (Isaiah 54:17)."

journaling

NINETY-EIGHT

Temptation

Commentary (from *The War, chapter 16*):

> "Therefore, since we have a great high priest who has passed through the heavens, Jesus the Son of God, let us hold fast our confession. For we do not have a high priest who cannot sympathize with our weaknesses, but One who has been tempted in all things as we are, yet without sin. Therefore let us draw near with confidence to the throne of grace, so that we may receive mercy and find grace to help in time of need (Hebrews 4:15)."

> "Keep watching and praying that you may not enter into temptation; the spirit is willing, but the flesh is weak (Matthew 26:41)."

We're back to the subject of the soul, specifically the *will*. As previously discussed, we cannot will ourselves to resist temptation. We cannot be strong, brave, or educated enough for our will to have such power outside the will of the Spirit directing our path. We read that we have a high priest, Jesus, who passed through the heavens. But, for Jesus to have done this, He was first born a human in the lineage of King David. He was tempted on every level, as we are tempted today, and was sustained in the face of such temptation through having complete focus on God. Because of this unchanging truth, I Corinthians 10:13 confidently states, "*No temptation has overtaken you but such as is common to man; and God is faithful, who will not allow you to be tempted beyond what you are able, but with the temptation will provide the way of escape also, so that you will be able to endure it.*" Jesus, who is our life, overcomes each of our temptations for us. On our behalf, when given over to Him, His power is greater than the power of the temptation.

The Godhead understood the plight of man. Before the foundation of the world, God knew what would have to transpire due to the impending transgression of one man, Adam. We are perishable, vulnerable, weak in our natural estate. God can readily sympathize with our natural man because He placed Himself within the confines of natural man so that He may save us from His wrath, hell, death, and this perverse generation. God is that powerful, that righteous, and that merciful. What we truly need to grasp is the fact that God is in love with us. He doesn't merely love us as one would love ice cream or an inanimate object. God is our Father, and He *loves* us as His children. Moreover, He is our Husband, our Kinsman Redeemer, and, as such, He is *in love* with us now and forever. Due to this immeasurable, abounding, endless love, He is merciful in our dilemma of temptations.

God tells us that pride comes before the fall, not because He wants us to feel ashamed, but because His love will not allow Him to leave us ignorant. What we do with that information is up to us. The responsibility to obedience to His commands lies solely on our shoulders. If we allow ourselves to be led into temptation, we cannot rightly cite, "*I didn't have the power to resist,*" at least not those who have invited Christ into themselves. His Word is ever available to all, at least in countries with freedom of religion. We cannot blame the pastors, parents, teachers, friends, or strangers who did not correctly teach us. Ultimately, no one is responsible for our obedience to the Word except us.

When my first husband abandoned me, I blamed everyone and their dog for not enlightening me prior to marriage as to his true nature. My temptation was to retain bitterness, resentment, hatred, etc. because my predicament was everyone else's fault. I had a High Priest who could sympathize with my plight, even that of marrying a man I ought not and harboring unforgiveness and unrighteous judgment after his departure. I had to educate myself in the ways of the Lord by studying God's Word and seeking His face of my own volition aside from traditional religion and denominations. Only then did I discover that I was responsible, at least in part, for my situation. Once I became well acquainted with such an extraordinary God, I was able to humble myself, repent, forgive, and learn to listen and adhere to the instruction of Holy Spirit. God does not drive temptations, but, by God, we learn how to surrender to the One who has already overcome every temptation known to man.

The world of flesh, in which we have a temporary residence, will always be tempted, if not by an old thing, by new things which come along every day. When we finally accomplish overcoming one temptation, there will be an unlimited array of new temptations that will present themselves in subtle ways so as to catch us off guard. There is no "one and done" scenario where we have somehow arrived in perfect holiness, and there are no more lessons to learn. Apostle Paul said it this way in Philippians 3:12, "*Not that I have already obtained it or have already become perfect, but I press on so that I may lay hold of that for which also I was laid hold of by Christ.*"

Every day we face new challenges, and every day God grants new mercies. His grace is sufficient in any scenario presented. There is no temptation, I repeat, no temptation of any kind which is uncommon to man or that Jesus did not already face and conquer in His humanness. "*No temptation has overtaken you but such as is common to man; and God is faithful, who will not allow you to be tempted beyond what you are able, but with the temptation will provide the way of escape also, so that you will be able to endure it,*" promises I Corinthians 10:13. This is a *promise*, not a *maybe* or *possibility*. Through the power of which we read in a previous chapter, we can overcome *if* we choose to do so. The choice is always ours, and therein lies the perpetual battle. We can only win once we have surrendered our flesh to God. The battle belongs to the Lord.

Prayer:

Father, I genuinely desire to lay aside every earthly encumbrance of the fleshly, natural man. I purpose to fan the flame of Your Holy Spirit so that I will be supernaturally equipped to resist, just as did Jesus in the wilderness. I know that no temptation has overtaken me but such as is common to man; and You are faithful, who will not allow me to be tempted beyond what I am able, but with the temptation, You have provided the way of escape also, so that I will be able to endure it. I choose to flee from idolatry. Lead me not into temptation but deliver me from all evil. I give You all praise, honor, and glory for Your great name's sake. I recognize that I can only overcome evil and the lures of Satan by the blood of the Lamb, who was slain for my transgressions. Give me Your daily bread of life so that I will be sustained in all areas of life. Cause me to love You more than I love life itself. I choose to rebuke the enemy and take up the cause of Christ. I purpose to die daily to everything that is not of the Kingdom of Heaven. I choose to pull down every imagination, stronghold, and every high thing that exalts itself above the name of Jesus in my mind and cast it at Your feet. I willingly punish all disobedience until my obedience is made complete. I thank You that no temptation has befallen me except that which is common to man and there is a door of escape. Selah

Scripture References:

> "No temptation has overtaken you but such as is common to man; and God is faithful, who will not allow you to be tempted beyond what you are able, but with the temptation will provide the way of escape also, so that you will be able to endure it. Therefore, my beloved, flee from idolatry (I Corinthians 10:13-14)."

Do not love the world nor the things in the world. If anyone loves the world, the love of the Father is not in him. For all that is in the world, the lust of the flesh and the lust of the eyes and the boastful pride of life, is not from the Father, but is from the world. The world is passing away, and also its lusts; but the one who does the will of God lives forever (I John 2:15-17).

But now I come to You; and these things I speak in the world so that they may have My joy made full in themselves. I have given them Your word; and the world has hated them, because they are not of the world, even as I am not of the world. I do not ask You to take them out of the world, but to keep them from the evil one. They are not of the world, even as I am not of the world. Sanctify them in the truth; Your word is truth. As You have sent Me into the world, I also have sent them into the world. For their sakes I sanctify Myself, that they themselves also may be sanctified in truth (John 17:13-19).

"For this reason, I remind you to fan into flame the gift of God, which is in you through the laying on of my hands (II Timothy 1:6)."

Pray, then, in this way: Our Father, who art in Heaven, hallowed beThy name. Your Kingdom come, Your will be done, on Earth as it is in Heaven. Give us this day our daily bread. And forgive us our debts, as we also have forgiven our debtors. And do not lead us into temptation, but deliver us from evil. For Yours is the Kingdom and the power and the glory forever. Amen (Matthew 6:9-13).

Journaling

NINETY-NINE

Thankfulness

Prayer:

In the name of Jesus, I first want to pour praises upon the Most Holy God for loving me, the unlovable, forgiving me, the unforgivable; giving mercy where I have been merciless, and granting grace when I deserve hell and death. As You have poured Your love into me, direct my path that I may know how to give unprecedented love to those around me. May Your supernatural expression permeate every place I step my feet. Change my heart, Lord, that Your heart will beat so vigorously through my body that only Your heart will touch those I contact. I choose to lay aside all bitterness, malice, revenge, hatred, and all other lusts of the natural man so that I am positioned to honor You with my spirit, soul, and body. I give thanks in all circumstances; for this is God's will for me in Christ Jesus. I do it all in the name of the Lord Jesus, giving thanks to God the Father through Christ. Above all else, I will guard my heart, for everything I do flows from it. Amen

Scripture References:

"Give thanks in all circumstances; for this is God's will for you in Christ Jesus (I Thessalonians 5:18)."

"And whatever you do, whether in word or deed, do it all in the name of the Lord Jesus, giving thanks to God the Father through Him (Colossians 3:17)."

"Above all else, guard your heart, for everything you do flows from it (Proverbs 4:23)."

"Create in me a pure heart, O God, and renew a steadfast spirit within me (Psalm 51:10)."

"Let all bitterness and wrath and anger and clamor and slander be put away from you, along with all malice (Ephesians 4:31)."

Journaling

ONE-HUNDRED

Transformation

Prayer:

I seek Your face, Almighty God, that You may descend upon me and transform me as Christ Himself was transformed on the mountaintop. I will not be conformed to this world but transformed by the renewing of my mind so that I may prove what the will of God is, that which is good, acceptable, and perfect. Make me aware of how much I have been forgiven. Show me, Jesus, how to die to my flesh that I may operate completely selflessly in all things. I lay myself on the altar before You and I ask that You reveal to me Your pure love. Teach me how to be unashamed of how You made me, fearfully and wonderfully. Show me how not to be prideful of how I look or what I possess on the outside, for I am saved by Your grace like all those before and after me. Teach me how to be a gracious host for your Holy Spirit within. Remind me daily how to walk a walk of heavenly love, not the superficial love that isn't worth more than wood, hay, or stubble. Convey to me, O gracious Lord, how to not only forgive those who have sinned against me, but to repent of my judgment against them, that I may be forgiven. I pray, O

Sovereign Lord, that You, man, and demons will testify that I am a child of the King. Amen and amen. Selah.

Scripture References:

"And do not be conformed to this world, but be transformed by the renewing of your mind, so that you may prove what the will of God is, that which is good and acceptable and perfect (Romans 12:2)."

"For this reason I say to you, her sins, which are many, have been forgiven, for she loved much; but to whom little is forgiven, he loves little (Luke 7:47)."

This is My commandment, that you love one another as I have loved you. Greater love has no one than this, that someone lay down his life for his friends. You are My friends if you do what I command you (John 15:12-14).

"For all that is in the world, the lust of the flesh and the lust of the eyes and the boastful pride of life, is not from the Father, but is from the world (I John 2:16)."

Journaling

ONE-HUNDRED-ONE

Trauma

Prayer:

Father, I take the authority given to me through Jesus' blood and sever every ounce of trauma inflicted upon me by any source. I take up the Sword of the Spirit, which is sharper than any two-edged sword and cut all ties to events, people, places, and things that have traumatized and paralyzed me. I apply the blood of Jesus to myself and receive the peace which passes all understanding. I replace all evil deeds of darkness with the light of Christ as You, who are light, pierce through the deepest, darkest recesses of my person. Thank you, Lord and Savior, for comforting and rescuing me from all that Satan meant to kill me. You will cover me with Your pinions, and under Your wings, I will find refuge; Your faithfulness is a shield and buckler to me. I will not fear the terror of the night, nor the arrow that flies by day, nor the pestilence that stalks in darkness, nor the destruction that wastes at noonday. Because I listen to You, I will dwell securely and will be at ease, without dread of disaster. Selah

Scripture References:

> He will cover you with His pinions, and under His wings you will find refuge; His faithfulness is a shield and buckler. You will not fear the terror of the night, nor the arrow that flies by day, nor the pestilence that stalks in darkness, nor the destruction that wastes at noonday (Psalm 91:4-6).

> "But whoever listens to Me will dwell securely and will be at ease, without dread of disaster (Proverbs 1:33)."

> "But He was pierced for our transgressions; He was crushed for our iniquities; upon Him was the chastisement that brought us peace, and with His wounds we are healed (Isaiah 53:5)."

Journaling

ONE-HUNDRED-TWO

Unbelief

Prayer:

O, Lord my God, I do believe—help me with my unbelief! I choose faith. I long for faith. I stand firmly in faith in the One True God! I thank You for conditioning me for allowing trials and struggles to sharpen and refine me in the faith. There is nothing and no one more important than You. There is no one greater, higher, more just, more forgiving, more magnificent than You. Grow me, stretch me, purify me, Yeshua, so that I never walk away from faith, but grow ever stronger that I may say courageously and emphatically, "You are my God, and I am Your people. Nothing can pluck me from Your hand." Amen and amen.

Scripture References:

> Jesus said to him, "If you can believe, all things are possible to him who believes." Immediately the father of the child cried out and said with tears, "Lord, I believe; help my unbelief!" When Jesus saw that the people came

running together, He rebuked the unclean spirit, saying to it, "Deaf and dumb spirit, I command you, come out of him and enter him no more (Mark 9:23-25, NKJV)!"

Journaling

ONE-HUNDRED-THREE
Understanding Personal Application

Prayer:

Father, I pray to understand what You want me to apply to my life. I desire to know what You know and understand what You understand. I thank You for helping me move out of the normal thinking of the traditions of man and step into a new dimension of revelation. May I walk in freedom and holiness as You have designed for Your people. Reveal to me how to apply Your Word to everyday life. Help me to know what is for me and what isn't. Remind me that every assignment isn't mine, even though it may be good. Let my 'yes' be 'yes' and my 'no' be 'no.' Amen.

Scripture References:

> "To whom God willed to make known what is the riches of the glory of this mystery among the Gentiles, which is Christ in you, the hope of glory (Colossians 1:27)."

"For who has known the mind of the Lord, to instruct Him?" But we have the mind of Christ (I Corinthians 2:16)."

"Now the Lord is the Spirit, and where the Spirit of the Lord is, there is freedom (II Corinthians 3:17)."

Journaling

ONE-HUNDRED-FOUR

Understanding the Mysteries of Christ

Prayer:

In the name of the Lamb of God, Jesus the Christ, I pray to understand the mystery of Christ, which in other generations was not made known to the sons of men, as it has now been revealed to His holy apostles and prophets in the Spirit. As a Gentile, I am a fellow heir and fellow member of the body of Christ, and fellow partaker of the promise in Christ Jesus through the gospel. Allow me to understand the unfathomable riches of Christ; to bring to light what is the daily activity of the mystery which has for generations been hidden in God. I pray the manifold wisdom of God might now be made known to me for my good and the good of those around me. Show me how to execute the eternal purpose which You carried out in Christ Jesus our Lord, in whom I have boldness and confident access through faith in Him. I ask You to make it apparent to me how not to lose heart in my tribulations, for they are Your glory. For this reason I bow my knees before You, Father, from whom every family in Heaven and on Earth derives its name, that You would grant me, according to the riches of Your glory, to be strengthened with power through Your Spirit in my inner man, so that Christ may dwell in my heart through faith; and that I, being rooted and grounded in love, may be able to comprehend with all the saints what is the breadth and length and height and depth, and to know the love of Christ which surpasses knowledge, that I may be filled up to all the fullness of God. Now to Him who is able to do far more abundantly beyond all that I ask or think, according to the power that works within me, to Him be the glory in my daily life, in the body of Christ, and in Christ Jesus to all generations forever and ever (Ephesians 3). Amen.

Scripture References:

Ephesians 3 (all)

Journaling

ONE-HUNDRED-FIVE

Unity

Prayer:

In the name of Jesus, show me how to get past this foolish pride that causes all sorts of division in my home, job, church, and other places of life. Remind me that, at the Tower of Babel, the unity of people nearly caused them to reach Heaven to make a name for themselves. Remind me that unity is power, and division is powerlessness (Mark 3:24). Nothing, Father, is impossible for those who unite as one (Genesis 11:5-6). I choose to keep my mind on things above and not things below so that I do not allow pride to cause me to stumble and fall. May I always lay aside petty foolishness for the greater good. I unify with Your plan and purpose. I will operate in Heaven's wisdom to see past the earthly and into the Kingdom of God. A three-strand cord is hard to break. Amen

Scripture References:

"I appeal to you, brother and sisters, in the name of our Lord Jesus Christ, that all of you agree with one another in what you say and that there be no division among you, but that you be perfectly united in mind and thought (I Corinthians 1:10)."

So Christ Himself gave the apostles, the prophets, the evangelists, pastors and teachers, to equip His people for works of service, so that the body of Christ may be built up until we all reach unity in the faith and in the knowledge of the Son of God and become mature, attaining to the whole measure of the fullness of Christ (Ephesians 4:11-13).

"Bear with each other and forgive one another if any of you has a grievance against someone. Forgive as the Lord forgave you. And over all these virtues put on love, which binds them all together in perfect unity (Colossians 3:13-14)."

"I in them and You in Me, that they may be perfected in unity, so that the world may know that You sent Me, and loved them, even as You have loved Me (John 17:23)."

journaling

ONE-HUNDRED-SIX
Victory Over Darkness

Commentary:

For we who are in Christ, we are to face battles and obstacles *from* victory, not *to* victory. We do not need to see ourselves as trying to attain victory because we are already positioned in it. We are already victorious in Christ Jesus whether we feel or see it or not. Christ completed victory at His resurrection. For everyone who surrenders their life unto the Lord, they receive the victorious, overcoming, supernatural life of the Christ. What is in Christ may not yet be manifested in your life, but it is already complete in the Lord. Our future is already God's past. In this, we must stand before our giants of life with a victorious mindset instead of waiting for God to swoop in and make us victorious.

Prayer:

Father, I come boldly and humbly before the Throne Room of Grace. I thank You for the blood of Jesus, for Your everlasting mercy, grace, and love that I do not deserve. I bless You, O Lord. I surrender myself to You and purpose to resign myself to You every day hereafter. I am nothing outside You, but You have made me everything inside You (Romans 8:17). In Jesus' name, I claim victory over every black hole of life because my life is Jesus, and He has overcome every imaginable temptation and crisis. It is no longer I who live, but Christ who lives in and through this mortal body (Galatians 2:20). I thank You, most gracious Yeshua that no weapon formed against me shall prosper, and no words spoken against me will prevail (Isaiah 54:17). Though a host will surround me to destroy me, I will fear no evil (Psalm 27). I will not fear what man or circumstances can do to my body, but only will I fear the One who can kill the soul and body (Matthew 10:28). I stand in awe of You today (Psalm 33:8), King of kings, knowing in full confidence that everything Satan throws at me for evil will be turned for good because I love you with all my heart, soul, mind, and strength (Romans 8:28). I am confident in the face of every enemy, tangible and intangible, as I know it is a sign of destruction for them and salvation to me (Philippians 1:28). Thank You, most holy One of Israel. Selah.

Scripture References:

"But the loving-kindness of the Lord is from everlasting to everlasting on those who fear Him, and His righteousness to children's children (Psalm 103:17)."

"For all have sinned and fall short of the glory of God (Romans 3:23)."

"But thanks be to God, who gives us the victory through our Lord Jesus Christ (I Corinthians 15:57)."

Journaling

ONE-HUNDRED-SEVEN

Victory Over Your Enemy:

Prayer:

I thank You, exquisite Savior, that You have conquered sin and death and every work of the enemy. I am grateful that You contend with those who contend with Your people (Isaiah 49:25). There is no God like You and I and my children are protected from the arm of the enemy (Isaiah 49:25). Father, as I stand boldly and confidently before my oppressors, it is a sign of victory for me and a sign of defeat for them (Philippians 1:28). You promise that my enemy, though they rise against me, cannot prevail against me because You are building Your Kingdom through me. I will not look to the right or to the left (Proverbs 4:27), but only at You. You promise to pity the weak and needy and save them from death (Psalm 72:13) and that is me. Amen

Scripture References:

Oh, death, where is your victory? O death, where is your sting? The sting of death is sin, and the power of sin is the law; but thanks be to God, who gives us the victory through our Lord Jesus Christ (I Corinthians 15:55-57).

"He said, 'O Lord, the God of Israel, there is no God like You in Heaven above or on Earth beneath, keeping covenant and showing loving-kindness to Your servants who walk before You with all their heart (I Kings 8:23).'"

"I also say to you that you are Peter, and upon this rock I will build My church; and the gates of Hades will not overpower it (Matthew 16:18)."

Journaling

ONE-HUNDRED-EIGHT

Washed with the Water

Prayer:

Wash me with the water that ran from Your side, allow Your Spirit to move into my now purified body, and seal me with Your holy, pure blood. I thank You, Father, that I am, without question, a child of the King. Show me how to be perfected and to rest in You. I allow You to move through me instead of me "doing" work in the flesh. Show me how to die daily to my flesh so that You are never quenched. Allow me, O God, to be as a poured out drink offering and a sweet aromatic fragrance to Your nostrils as I am burned in sacrifice to You, my righteous Husband. Allow me to be a part of Your bride without spot or wrinkle. I love You, Jesus. May I ever grow more deeply in love with You with the passing of time. I dedicate my life to You, yielded and consecrated before You. Help me to touch nothing unclean. Wash my evil heart with the water of Your holy Word. Amen

Scripture References:

"So that He might sanctify her, having cleansed her by the washing of water with the Word (Ephesians 5:26:)."

"Instead, one of the soldiers pierced Jesus' side with a spear, bringing a sudden flow of blood and water (John 19:34)."

Come to Me, all you who are weary and burdened, and I will give you rest. Take My yoke upon you and learn from Me, for I am gentle and humble in heart, and you will find rest for your souls. For My yoke is easy and My burden is light (Matthew 11:28-30).

"Therefore, come out from their midst and be separate," says the Lord. "And do not touch what is unclean; and I will welcome you (II Corinthians 6:17)."

"And when the Lord smelled the pleasing aroma, the Lord said in His heart, 'I will never again curse the ground because of man, for the intention of man's heart is evil from his youth. Neither will I ever again strike down every living creature as I have done (Genesis 8;21).'"

"For we are the aroma of Christ to God among those who are being saved and among those who are perishing (II Corinthians 2:15)."

"But even if I am being poured out as a drink offering upon the sacrifice and service of your faith, I rejoice and share my joy with you all (Philippians 2:17)."

Journaling

ONE-HUNDRED-NINE

Prayer:

O, most gracious heavenly Father, bestow me Thy wisdom. Give me the spirit of wisdom and revelation that I may know the hope of my calling in Christ Jesus. Pour into me Your holiness, purity, humility, and reverent fear. I confess that, without You, I am nothing. When I abide by the Living Vine, I am everything with, in, and through You. My hope rests in You, not in myself. My confidence in change lies in Your perfect Son, Jesus Christ. Please separate my spirit from my soul that I may fully commune with Holy Spirit. Show me how to be like You in all my ways. Bridle my tongue from sin and iniquity. Tame my tongue as only You can. Put a watch over my mouth that I not sin against You. I praise You that, as I seek Your wisdom, she will be my sister, and understanding will be my intimate friend for the rest of my life. Deal with me ever so severely if I sin against You. Do not let me fall. Chastise me through Your loving-kindness. Teach me self-discipline and how to say 'no' to the flesh. I declare and decree my everlasting love for You as You have already proclaimed over me. Selah

Scripture References:

"That the God of our Lord Jesus Christ, the Father of glory, may give to you a spirit of wisdom and of revelation in the knowledge of Him (Ephesians 1:17)."

"Therefore, since we have these promises, dear friends, let us purify ourselves from everything that contaminates body and spirit, perfecting holiness out of reverence for God (II Corinthians 7:1)." [1]

"For whoever would love life and see good days must keep their tongue from evil and their lips from deceitful speech (I Peter 3:10)."

"And see if there be any hurtful way in me, and lead me in the everlasting way (Psalm 139:24)."
"For those whom the Lord loves He disciplines, and He scourges every son whom He receives (Hebrews 12:6)."

Journaling

ONE-HUNDRED-TEN
Words of My Mouth

Commentary:

We began this book with understanding the *"Word of God's Power."* Words are vital to our existence. We must all become aware of the words we speak; of the power they possess to speak life or death. Death and life are in the power of the tongue and by the tongues nations are built strong or destroyed. Through the tongues, families, cities, and countries are built or destroyed. The tongue is divisive and full of evil. Only a tongue tamed by the Spirit of the Living God will bring life. James 3 (below) is clear about the power of the tongue. We must stop speaking curses over ourselves and others. I don't mean, necessarily, that we are saying, "I curse so-and-so." No, our words in everyday life bring about curses. "I hate you," "You're nothing, worthless, no good," and so much more. Even though we may apologize later, the words are dangling in the atmosphere of a person's mind and heart. We must be mindful. Those in leadership must particularly be mindful of the words they speak. They must not be hasty, but quick to listen and slow to speak so that we're teaching others to do the same. We all need to speak life.

Prayer:

Father, I pray for You to put a watch over my mouth. Let me speak as the oracles of God with words that are seasoned with salt and full of grace. Allow me to be prepared in season and out of season with an answer for every question; to speak with the tongue of the learned with a word in season for those who are weary. Make me ever aware that life and death are in the power of the tongue so that I do not speak death into myself or others. May no unwholesome speech leave my lips. Allow Your Word to ever flow from Holy Spirit within me through my mouth. Make my lips a ready writer (Psalm 45:1). Allow the words of my mouth and the meditation of me heart to be pleasing in Your sight (Psalm 91:14). Keep my tongue from speaking evil and my lips from telling lies (Psalm 34:13). Set a guard over my mouth, Lord; keep watch over the door of my lips (Proverbs 10:19). I recognize that the mouth of the godly person gives wise advice, but the tongue that deceives will be cut off (Proverbs 10:31). Let words of wisdom drip from my lips because they have many benefits (Proverbs 12:14). Remind me that a gentle answer turns away wrath, but a harsh word stirs anger (Proverbs 15:1). Let my tongue be gentle because it is a tree of life (Proverbs 15:4). Selah

Scripture References:

> "Death and life are in the power of the tongue; and they that love it shall eat the fruit thereof (Proverbs 18:21)."

> (If you claim to be religious but don't control your tongue, you are fooling yourself, and your religion is worthless (James 1:26)."

Let not many of you become teachers, my brethren, knowing that as such we will incur a stricter judgment. For we all stumble in many ways. If anyone does not stumble in what he says, he is a perfect man, able to bridle the whole body as well. Now if we put bits into the horses' mouths so that they will obey us, we direct their entire body as well. Look at the ships also, though they are so great and are driven by strong winds, are still directed by a very small rudder wherever the inclination of the pilot desires. So also the tongue is a small part of the body, and yet it boasts of great things. See how great a forest is set aflame by such a small fire! And the tongue is a fire, they very world of iniquity; the tongue is set among our members as that which defiles the entire body, and sets on fire the course of our life, and is set on fire by hell. For every species of beasts and birds, of reptiles and creatures of the sea, is tamed by the human race. But no one can tame the tongue; it is a restless evil and full of deadly poison. With it we bless our Lord and Father, and with it we curse men, who have been made in the likeness of God; from the same mouth come both blessing and cursing. My brethren, these things ought not to be this way. Does a fountain send out from the same opening both fresh and bitter water? Can a fig tree, my brethren, produce olives, or a vine produce figs? Nor can salt water produce fresh (James 3:1-12).

"The Lord God has given me the tongue of the learned, that I should know how to speak a word in season to him that is weary: He wakes me morning by morning, He awakens my ear to listen as a disciple (Psalm 141:3-4, KJV)."

"Set a guard, O Lord, over my mouth; keep watch over the door of my lips (Psalm 141:3)."

"Whoever speaks, is to do so as one who is speaking the utterances of God; whoever serves is to do so as one who is serving by the strength which God supplies; so that in all things God may be glorified through Jesus Christ, to whom belongs the glory and dominion forever and ever. Amen (I Peter 4:11)."

"Let your speech always be with grace, as though seasoned with salt, so that you will know how you should respond to each person (Colossians 4:6)."

"Preach the word; be ready in season and out of season; reprove, rebuke, exhort, with great patience and instruction (II Timothy 4:2)."

"He who restrains his words has knowledge, and he who has a cool spirit is a man of understanding (Proverbs 17:27)."

"Watch your tongue and keep your mouth shut, and you will stay out of trouble (Proverbs 21:23)."

"Like cold water to a weary soul is good news from a distant land (Proverbs 25:25)."

"You see a man who is hasty in his words? There is more hope for a fool than for him (Proverbs 29:20)."

"When she speaks, her words are wise, and she gives instructions with kindness (Proverbs 31:26)."

"But I tell you that every careless word that people speak, they shall give an account for it in the day of judgment. The words you say will either acquit you or condem you (Matthew 12:36-37)."

"It's not what goes into your mouth that defiles you; you are defiled by the words that come out of your mouth... but the things that proceed out of the mouth come from the heart, and those defile the man (Matthew 15:11, 18)."

"For assuredly, I say to you, whoever says to this mountain, 'Be removed and be cast into the sea,' and does not doubt in his heart, but believes that those things he says will be done, he will have whatever he says (Mark 11:23)."

"For with the heart one believes unto righteousness, and with the mouth confession is made unto salvation (Romans 10:10)."

"Do not let any unwholesome talk come out of your mouths, but only what is helpful for building others up according to their needs, that it may benefit those who listen (Ephesians 4:29)."

"If you want to enjoy life and see many happy days, keep your tongue from speaking evil and your lips from telling lies. When you take control of your words, you take back your life! As long as your words are in line with the word of God, Satan can't touch you. As you practice, don't be discouraged if you miss it now and then. Just repent for anything wrong you've said and get right back on track. You will have what you say (I Peter 3:10, NLT)."

Journaling

Introduction to Christ

If you have come across this book, and it happens you have never been properly introduced to God, this closing is a brief overview of how to come into the Kingdom of God through Christ.

Believe:

> "He then brought them out and asked, 'Sir, what must I do to be saved?' They replied, *'Believe in the Lord Jesus*, and you will be saved (Acts 16:29).'"

> "For John came to you to show you the way of righteousness, and you did not believe him, but the tax collectors and the prostitutes did. And even after you saw this, you did not repent and believe him (Matthew 21:32)."

"For all have sinned and fall short of the glory of God" is found in Romans 3:23. You must believe you dwell in a sinful nature derived from Adam and The Fall of all mankind. Secondly, you must believe that Jesus is Lord, that He gave His life for sinful mankind—you—and accept such a supernatural gift. It is simultaneously the easiest and hardest decision of anyone's life.

In response to such a belief in the Savior, you can take hold of this Scripture: "whosoever shall call on the name of the Lord shall be saved (Acts 2:21)." You are "whosoever." Call out to Him – He's waiting.

Repentance Requirement:

> "This is what is written: The Messiah will suffer and rise from the dead on the third day, and *repentance for the forgiveness of sins* will be preached in His name to all nations…(Luke 24:46-47)."

> "Jesus answered them, 'It is not the healthy who need a doctor, but the sick. I have not come to call the righteous, but *sinners to repentance* (Luke 5:31-32)."

Repentance is a turning away—turning your back—from the direction you're going. It is not for God; it's for you. It's an act of absolute humility—also a requirement for the presence of God to rest upon you. Repentance ushers God's grace through such humility.

Baptism to Eternal Life:

> "For *you have died* and your life is hidden with Christ in God (Colossians 3:3)."

> "I baptize you with water, but He will *baptize you with the Holy Spirit* (Mark 1:8)."

> "He who has believed and has been *baptized shall be saved*; but he who has disbelieved shall be condemned (Mark 16:16)."

> "Therefore we have been *buried with Him through baptism into death*, so that as Christ was raised from the dead through the glory of the Father, so we too might walk in newness of life (Romans 6:4)."

> "For all of you who were baptized into Christ have clothed yourselves with Christ (Galatians 3:27)."

This takes belief a step further. Baptism here, contrary to the modern-day church, *precedes* salvation not *succeeds*. This is not physical baptism but spiritual. We are to surrender ourselves unto death in the spiritual sense to be able to receive a spiritual new life; hence the Scripture, "I have been crucified in Christ; therefore it's no longer I who live but Christ who lives in me (Galatians 2:20)."

Baptism, metaphorically speaking, is the equivalent of crucifixion, aka death to self. We are "buried in His death." When we come to Christ, we must see ourselves as dead so that we can receive His life. Just praying a "sinner's prayer"—which isn't scriptural—is not the same as surrender; surrender is death.

Think about it like this. When one drowns, it's because they can no longer breathe underwater; if they could, they'd save their life. When they finally recognize they have no power to rescue themselves, they literally surrender their lives unto the watery death. When we take on Christ's baptism—water of the Word, we must visualize ourselves as "going under"; we are drowning our natural man because we have no power to save ourselves. In the spirit-realm, we baptize into death all that came from the bloodline of Adam. In this death condition, we are now available to take His new life; we are regenerated by a new bloodline from Jesus who is of Heaven. We take a brand new origin. We are no longer "of the Earth" but are "of Heaven." This is how we become "strangers in the land of Earth."

With this new origin, we are to think from the vantage of our homeland, the Kingdom of God. This level of surrender causes a person to stop giving in to the temptations of the natural man. This brings us back to understanding we have but one nature while renting space in that of another nature. You are not your flesh or any of its feelings, desires, or temptations. When tempted with sexual sin such as homosexuality, adultery, pornography, pedophilia or fornication in any form, the flesh wants what it wants, no doubt. However, the surrendered spirit—the real you—within a human shell desires to please the One who gave him new and eternal life. In this condition, he will say 'no' emphatically because he comprehends that life in the flesh is nothing short of despair, anguish, suffering, and destruction.

Drowning in Christ causes the newness and you cannot have newness without first going through such drowning. Many in the modern-day church preach 'accept Christ and then be baptized with water immersion.' However, Scriptures would indicate the opposite. We are to believe in the Father and Son unto salvation, be baptized into His Spirit, then water baptism may follow; however, the man on the Cross received the Kingdom of Heaven through faith yet was never water baptized. Unfortunately, we often misrepresent the purpose of baptism as if it's merely by water.

Grace and Repentance:

"Produce fruit in keeping with repentance (Matthew 3:8)."

"Three times I pleaded with the Lord to take it away from me. But He said to me, 'My grace is sufficient for you, for my power is made perfect in weakness.' Therefore I will all the more gladly boast about my weaknesses, so that Christ's power may rest on me (II Corinthians 12:8-9,)."

"For it is by grace you have been saved, through faith – and this is not from yourselves, it is the gift of God, not by works, so that no one can boast (Ephesians 2:8-9)."

Definition of Grace:

1. the free and unmerited favor of God, as manifested in the salvation of sinners and the bestowal of blessings
2. God giving you what you do not deserve (Heaven vs. hell; life vs. death; peace vs. chaos)
3. the catalyst for an otherwise impossible transformation from the old man of Adam to the new man in Christ

Definition of Repentance:

1. to turn from sin and dedicate oneself to the amendment of one's life
2. to feel regret or contrition *leading* to change one's mind
3. to cause to feel regret or contrition
4. to feel sorrow, regret, or contrition

Anyone who teaches grace outside repentance and surrender is a false prophet. Surrender and repentance are a requirement to receive the grace of God. Yes, we live in the Day of Grace, so it is extended to all mankind on a general level, but in respect to walking in personal grace regularly comes through a heart rent before a Holy God. In this condition of perpetual repentance of the sin-nature as a whole, His grace is surely sufficient for you and whatever situational crisis you may face.

When I write "perpetual repentance," I mean, simply stated, walking perpetually in an attitude of cosigning all the lusts of the flesh unto God. It's as the Scripture directs, "being ready to punish all disobedience until personal obedience is achieved." An attitude of repentance does *not* mean to self-abase, that is sin (Colossians 2:18, 23). Insulting, belittling, and beating oneself is self-abasement — that is not repentance. Repentance insists that you apologize to God for your action(s), you go and sin no more, and continue unashamedly going about the Father's business. In true repentance, you are neither ashamed nor boastful in yourself because self is dead to the world and its lusts.

Fruit of the Spirit of God can produce only from a place of humility, which leads to repentance, which leads to grace.

Faith:

> "Now faith is confidence in what we hope for and assurance about what we do not see. This is what the ancients were commended for (Hebrews 11:1-2)."

> "Without faith it is impossible to please God (Hebrews 11:6)."

> "Therefore, since we have been justified by faith, we have peace with God through our Lord Jesus Christ, through whom we have gained access by faith into this grace in which we now stand. And we boast in the hope of the glory of God (Romans 5:1-2)."

Faith is an extension of belief but stronger than belief alone. Even the demons believe and shudder (James 2:19). Faith says, "I not only believe You exist, but I place all my hope in You," unlike the demons. Faith moves the immovable, touches the untouchable, and makes the impossible possible.

Forgiveness:

> "Therefore, my friends, I want you to know that through Jesus, the forgiveness of sins is proclaimed to you. Through Him, everyone who believes is set free from every sin, a justification you were not able to obtain under the law of Moses (Acts 13:38-39)."

Forgiveness has been extended by God through Jesus to all mankind, whether or not any of us receive it. It was granted to all mankind at the Cross and resurrection of Christ. To receive it, all you must do is repent and it's yours. From there, the rest will come with great ease!

Repent to God. Accept His forgiveness. Forgive yourself. Forgive others. Let go of the shame, guilt, remorse, and condemnation; let go of the lies, fear, doubt anxiety as they lead you further and further into darkness.

A New Master!

> "For sin shall no longer be your master, because you are not under the law, but under grace (Romans 6:14)."

> "If the Son sets you free, you will be free indeed (John 8:36)."

> "But now that you have been *set free from sin* and have become *slaves of God*, the benefit you reap leads to holiness, and the result is eternal life (Romans 6:22)."

> "It is for freedom that Christ has set us free. Stand firm, then, and do not let yourselves be burdened again by a yoke of slavery (Galatians 5:1)."

"'I have the right to do anything,' you say – but not everything is beneficial. 'I have the right to do anything' – but I will not be mastered by anything (I Corinthians 6:12)."

"In him and through faith in him we may approach God with freedom and confidence (Ephesians 3:12)."

"You, my brothers and sisters, were called to be free. But do not use your freedom to indulge the flesh; rather, serve one another humbly in love. For the entire law is fulfilled in keeping this one command: 'Love your neighbor as yourself (Galatians 5:13-14).'"

"Once you were alienated from God and were enemies in your minds because of your evil behavior. But now He has reconciled you by Christ's physical body through death to present you holy in His sight, without blemish and free from accusation – if you continue in your faith, established and firm, and do not move from the hope held out in the gospel. This is the gospel that you heard and that has been proclaimed to every creature under Heaven, and of which I, Paul, have become a servant (Colossians 1:21-23)."

There is no greater gift from God than freedom! There is no greater pleasure or fulfillment in life than serving such a master because this master is like no other. He is Father, Husband, Comforter, Healer, Redeemer, Forgiver – this is a master I can follow through eternity!

By surrendering to such a magnificent, loving God, you will begin to see that jumping from a ledge to "end my problems" will no longer appear feasible; its facade will no longer have the power to overtake you. In Christ, there is no greater place of peace, regardless of the storm, which stems from the liberty found only in knowing and consigning your life to Yahweh. That proverbial ledge will be revealed for what it is – of Satan.

Whatever mess you've concocted, whatever trial besets you, no matter what is happening or for whatever reason, when you submit unto death the nature of the flesh, God commands Himself to take what Satan means against you for evil and turn it for good. I've quoted this Scripture a million times over, yet I will continue to do so because many folks still don't get it. In Christ, there is no dilemma, only benefits from His Kingdom solution. Every horrible, disastrous, despicable situation is a platform God utilizes to catapult His people onto higher ground.

For more detailed information on this matter, I suggest reading the Bible beginning with the gospels to follow the life of Christ, the One who overcame death and the grave and every temptation known to man. He overcame the flesh while living in it. Once He is allowed to take over your life, you too will be able to do as He because His completed work will begin to manifest through you. Additionally, I have written numerous books elaborating on the subjects of knowing your identity in Christ, who you are in the Kingdom of God, how to draw closer to the heart of God, and much more.

If you learn nothing else from this, know that God is in love with you and always will be. He formed you in your mother's womb. He allowed your life to be spared thus far. There is life beyond this crisis. There is joy beyond this sorrow. There is acceptance beyond your rejections. There is gain after your loss. There is life outside death. Be encouraged and of good cheer, for Christ is in love with you today!

Author Catalog

What was God Thinking?
Looking for God, 3 volumes
Discovering the Person of Holy Spirit, 4 volumes
How to Get it Right: Being Single, Married, Divorced, and Everything in Between
Thy Kingdom Come: Kingdom vs. Religion
Holiness or Heresy: The Modern-Day Church
Navigating the Fiery Black Holes of Life: A Book of Faith
Talking Yourself off the Ledge: Encouragement at a Glance
Walking the Path of Freedom
When All My Strength has Failed
Wielding the Sword of the Spirit
Learning to Digest the Truth
Marriage Beyond Mediocrity
Wise as a Serpent, Innocent as a Dove
Philadelphia: A Kingdom Call to Brotherly Love
Casting
Extinguishing the Inferno of Anger
The War: The Flesh vs. The Spirit
Wrecked by My Ex: Finding Peace Amid the Rubble
Out of Obscurity

www.ingramcontent.com/pod-product-compliance
Lightning Source LLC
Chambersburg PA
CBHW031748220426
43662CB00007B/320